The Adventures of ABFoe

Jeremy
This makes
it even
more real.
Patrick.

The Adventures of ABPoe

Vol. One

Patrick Ovington

Copyright © 2017 by Patrick Ovington.

Library of Congress Control Number:		2015919892
ISBN:	Hardcover	978-1-5144-3094-1
	Softcover	978-1-5144-3093-4
	eBook	978-1-5144-3092-7

All rights reserved. No part of this book may be reproduced or transmitted in any form or by any means, electronic or mechanical, including photocopying, recording, or by any information storage and retrieval system, without permission in writing from the copyright owner.

Any people depicted in stock imagery provided by Thinkstock are models, and such images are being used for illustrative purposes only.
Certain stock imagery © Thinkstock.

Print information available on the last page.

Rev. date: 01/20/2017

To order additional copies of this book, contact:
Xlibris
1-888-795-4274
www.Xlibris.com
Orders@Xlibris.com
713899

CONTENTS

Hello. Allow myself to welcome you. ix
"What is grace?" xi
The Restoration xv

PART ONE

BRIEFLY TO BE ALONE.
THE VACANCY OF BRUISING IS NOT TOO DEEP.
TOLD TO DO THIS, BUT PASSION REGAINED.

Chapter One 3
Chapter Two 18
Chapter Three 46
Chapter Four: These are from the archives 52

PART TWO

A COMPARITIVE ANALYSIS OF THE PROPOSED BUDGET ESTIMATE FOR SUNDANCE UNIT NO 6

Prologue 63
Chapter One: A Less Experienced Speaker 65
Chapter Two: What can it be now? 74
Chapter Three: Already? 84
Chapter Four: The End of Reality 91
Chapter Five: This So-Called Sinister Grim 99
Chapter Six: Sitting in the Sun's Purge with Salt 107
Chapter Seven: Sleeping in the Moon's Luxury with Pepper 110

PART THREE

FOR A BUMPY RIDE IS SURE TO FOLLOW

Article One 124
Part One 186

PART FOUR

IMPOSITION CAN DISRUPT THE PAST

Autobiography 291
Synopsis 293

This is dedicated to all the souls I have known and lost,

AB Poe

HELLO. ALLOW MYSELF TO WELCOME YOU.

YOU SEEM TO be startled and nervous, have a seat, put your feet up, and make yourself more vulnerable. May I take your coat? Your hat? Your shoes? Let us have a drink together shall we, and what is your preference? That is better is it not? Just relax. Let all your worries out, release all those crinkles, and rest within strident ease. Let those concerns in your head loosen, and please my leaned inspection by putting down your guard and setting free your shield. Watch this waking moment.

It swims and swims to run upstream, but lacks a note for currency. The moment swims and swims without affixing mourning. It swims and swims and swims forever with no destination for the distance. It just swims sustained by gills of certainty. Perhaps it is like what our mothers told us, "Be careful what you wish for."

Let me get you another drink to allow for further conversation. Bring back these strips of irony to clasp these bonds within us. Let me tell you a tale before boredom induces another thought sincerely stressed to wish you everything is fine. How are you? Do you feel better? Here is hoping good things should happen, good cheer, and more importantly good health even better than before. To recover in advance, this comes, and you are well to feeling good so hasten recovery in a most effective way.

The blankets are wrappings that just grow richer with each year to those who hold them dear. Let the joy we are all sharing be loved by one and all. May hours be somewhat less to bear by knowing others sympathize and truly care, deep and true, all the happiness lies ahead for you! Many more years to share this special time. Pleasant wishes from me to you for the rest of the year. Best wishes it is understood so get well, and stay that way irrevocably. A simple, little phrase, but when it comes to you, it means the same, old wish that you have heard before, along with many more, but every time that it is said may it bring elation by simply coming true. Hold what is the happiest as options hurry passed. Grow in turn more than the last because the longer the turn the greater the treasure in a manner to fill this life with pleasure. The perfect life may be the future that life can hold for you.

ABPoe

"WHAT IS GRACE?"

CLIPPINGS OF REMEMBRANCE grow from an infantile placement, emerge into adult consequence, and implore an unfathomable procession of progression. Humans appropriate the mass, absolving past, present, and future with the concentric concept of the self. Although what is consumed, created, and consecrated spans beyond the singular meaning of life, the extension of the interior and exterior self define grace.

Wounds heal, slowly itching, and scathing memory the preoccupied, subsiding balance seeks refuge in burial. The remains equate the worn age of life and form, tabulating the contest of scarred feet, blistered hands, and weeping heads. The premature comfort of quickened compassion strikes the derelict memories with concentrated righteousness. The sequential bliss stretching eternity, but the brevity of joy does shroud the light with shadows. Flamboyant uncertainty and menial bounty construct conception out of working life. The proposition of choice, the declaration of independence, and the undisputed resolve of reason that within the amalgamated love, grief, and destiny manufacture experience.

The filtered optimism of opportunity and the possibility to believe something else is the complicated department of truth. The questions pondered in the tactile, aesthetic value of provision and posterity awaken alert and alive with the problematic argument that instills the truth with lies. Every person in the universal truth is ingrained in a personal trap that cannot entangle the universal whole because physical evidence counteracts the effect of truth. Superiority, reason, even the consideration of the truth reproduces objective feelings and thoughts that resemble antithetical activity. The exposition of life, love, and understanding are minimized by the balance of body, mind, spirit, and of course perspective. Every person contains perspective within the restoration of the truth. The world of non-physical enterprise does discover the essence behind it all.

Grace is enthralled in routine, submerged in personality, and coexists to provoke an ascent of growth. It incites individual truth, but also protests against it via the use of examples. It retorts when spoken to, and the explanation insists it is best to not mistake progress for the appraisal of worth. This postulation proves something amidst the transparent tides of mood and mission. The bewildering dilemma of life remains sin and salvation. Safety consults monoliths of security, and the landscapes of syndication dance steps across the sky. The confused dots wobble, pulse a circular dance to praise this friendly assembly. Silence upholds the grave in clamps of scrap. The social view is to garnish faces with belief in the awareness of this overcast resolution. The loss of ideal, the collected fear and atrophy abiding in broadcasts of subterranean, subconscious standards sensing the solution not by responsibility, but because the future contains what we receive, reprieve, and resent. Our fate in one word, "Grace."

Dew on the table makes the paper stick like glue. A firm surface with a glistened, gliding stance, and the dysfunction comes with the application. Horny? Do you want my baby? Sexual intercourse is inherent in our creation, and its fundamental basis is unavoidable. The display of such an open ideal has allowed for endless depravity. Orgies, homosexuality, and the divergent subcultures created by men and women to increase pleasure do prey on increased numbers. Marriage has declined, child birth has increased, and sexually transmitted diseases as well as physical trauma develop with the inscription of sex. It is a powerful drug, an emotional attachment, and divergence from mundane existence, but precedence over order, decency, and enlightenment is not more rewarding. Man is on his way, cross stepping the stay, "In order to succumb to death one has to live a life."

The story never changes, and the lyrics stay in tune. No more Mr. Nice Fellow, here comes Mrs. Bright Mellow! Step forward through the motion, and no longer by the notion of slight reprieve in calm belief for sweet relief; the remedy does come. The maker comes quicker with the vexing light that flickers endless, paraphrased nonsense. Gum boots for the wicked. Boredom on a sloppy habit. Nothing ever changes, but it does evolve, erects itself as an implemented method, and breaks away the directory. It means energy flushes a wind of coherent voice, and it dictates pervasive prose in the indoctrinated meaning of life. The dissuaded guide of love and happiness bends a fierce storm that lacerates the world. The ship is torn apart, and the deck mates shriek in anguished blindness. The waters cloud everything with whispers of deep decay, and the stinging salt destroys the air in the absolving, murky light. The boat does sink in swift distortion, and Poseidon's gurgling grasp awaits the swollen remains of oblique blackness. Down and down into the truth. The swallowed whole of awakening. Breath. The stillness of shamed caresses, lips aback the ear, and hands upon the back. Wanton misdirection, endless synopsis for the ordinary blame, and conscripted nonsense in the daily routine. Guilt and awareness, truth and consequence, belief and faith; all are equal formations of discourse to deliver the ritual, and the dance therein is one's own. Each contain a different step to the connation of the mass, and conformity is idealized discovery. Words and only words, but discussion brings us beyond their meaning. Their proportions manipulate the mass to implicate the order, but transcendence through a literati means distraction, abstraction, and malleable words. The mangled prose to disclaim the end, and postulate abiding time. Massive strokes of change, and the unending dichotomy of self and choice. The peripheral view of aim, and the discontent, discerned state of being. Compassion, coincidence, and circumstance afloat on a sea of limitless options. Images maim the sounds, smell taints the taste, and touch falsifies the sight of this colorized management of persuasion.

What does this mean? These opulent words on a crazed spree of contained nothingness, and the messages convey more than assurance, redemption, and waiting. The mass with hope is harmoniously at home. The beliefs of history are mourned in the wakened change of tomorrow, and the discernment congeals the mass with the state because all things are as they appear and not as they are seen. Perception riddles the course, personality alters the affect, and problematic continuation allows for progression with or without a realization for right or wrong, true or false, wonder or woe.

Memories of the path, messages in the clearing, and measurement of the mass. The words inform the motive, and personal logic illuminates the faded assimilation of usage. We are as we are, and we do design this sense of worldly creation, but how we articulate it is us naturally, and does not reside with knowledge of awareness. One is unlike the next in this worldly notion of unravelling time, but we attribute this contrived movement of progress to a presented result. Life remains the beginning, and the directed self believes in tomorrow, the world, and the wonder.

ABPoe   070404840p

THE RESTORATION

THE WISE TRUTH from logs are moments adding such refinery that the pressure brings them out, and losing track the rails collide. The lost become the found in a remedy mixed by grinding souls. The resource reacts quickly and the figments evolve into life. Choice reasons action, meaning instills the truth, and we all play our part in this world of restoration.

Masquerading, dirty, and disheveled secrets run the width of a soul lying dormant hoping not to come out from the dark. Lies, silence, and common disinterest fondling the dark with imperfection. The reverence in resolution revolving the world's decay as tomorrow praises the silence. Promises ask the web of sweet conviction to break the rows of resolve and question these points of kindness. We devolve further still to catch the fire burning our well.

Ignorance regrets the walking ire. Cold steps waking quips of messy mission. Action catapults a thousand dreams, wisdom sees it justly, and discarding the truth the secrets swirl in the cycle of life. Unknowns, indecision, and fraud are false morals of design and defeat, but the actions themselves live in repeat. Nonetheless these things are not mentioned in this light of day. They tremble in fear of ownership, and walk with every man, but there is no intended bias due to the truth forming the truth. Here, however, the average, simple man does not last long.

Women within this realm beseech the smoke. For whatever the reason they bridle time with theory in order to manipulate their secrets. They want the truth, recognize it, but deny themselves to evoke a trial of hardship. Women weave deeper gloom than the average man, but they all cringe in the shadows as they saunter to the light. We all weaken and lose, may well win to choose, or wilt within the defiled force of life's majestic atonement.

Here forgiveness cannot be found. Persecution is restless in a tainted heart, and the consequence does not dwindle lightly. Men and women within this realm are forged to play the cycle of life with slow tears, crumpled time, and forgotten dreaming. The faint hearted apathy enrolls the mind with these secrets. The created smog of certainty and the debris of sanity are in the mangled past of discontent love. Laid open, scorned, and ravaged life becomes relentless, staggered personality, and time entails the sense therein. What is done becomes the objective as growth due to age retires. Death answers the actions with the balance of opportunity granting life the riddle of recognition. Framed and hung, the essence of breath fills the lungs. Eternity passes, takes it in, puts it out, and watches the conclusion code the person.

Where the ruins practise bleak observation there is the presence of mimicked individuals. The secrets contort in order to pass the future here. When the future is consequence the choice to hide within the lies rides the truth with daylight, and the singular meaning of time behind closed doors and drawn windows radiates solemnly. The provoked sensations of continued exploitation, and the abhorrent, little people prove their schemes amidst the twilight of doubt and certainty. We recede to the darkness, and the diverse landscape enters an everlasting alley. The moon hangs low in a dream of captivity with danger tuned to ignorance, and discomfort stitching imagination in an ordeal of spectacular horror. The puddles that cast the moon's reflection are the scolded eyes of recollection.

Death weevils eating nature's composition as days go by with the inconsistent duty of life strayed from reason. Sobriety seldom stays the night, but the welcomed wishing in the well supports the self. Debased and fawning, the head is held high in the domain of resistance. The shifted purpose of wanton experience is understood frankly.

The wise do believe the willing truth and light regardless of stature. Up, down, and all around the proof remains the same. We merely need to know what to do with the moment standing now. Freedom runs the race off course, and wins by the sheer logic in the direction of duty. It calls the self the world in order to display the sense of wonder we disbelieve. The steps of living trial, doubt, and fear burden the balance of blessing, but the questionable acceptance of this persuasion proves instability and deceit. The torturous rendition of being alive accepts what is given, chances what one can, and paces an ordinary cage for sleazy beasts like us.

Condemned by freedom, choice approaches decline, and the ebb of flowing circumstance gives answered law the preference of desire according to its just desserts. This relies on those of us here. Those of us lingering on the furtive edge of peace, time, and reason. The disdained ordeal, trivial meaning, and reproach of activity fold into the response of decay. Death holds our bearing like a granule of sand that sifts through thought to present the fabricated details that provide sulking hope, but death's random features have brought us here as the straight and narrow hold tomorrow. Preparing the waking light, and watching the interest and bias result from the gnarled snare, we trap worldwide mercy, spreading whim, discovered sin, and these wasted days. More discouraged endearment exhaled in the decrepit mind. Here we are in the web of intention, and stuck in the plans of continuance we remain here.

Dark clouds entice the sky with depth no mortal eye can see, and the enthralled mist succeeds the clouds of Heaven with what there is in this moment. Rain contemplates the air as the space furls cold shade. Light illuminates the object, but study flails without sight. The slipping view of a moistened medium spurring the memory to take over. Wait it out. The smudged strain of experience qualms the malevolent sky with shudders of residual pleasure. The choice ascertains the stormy miles of raging sea. The inhale of a vacuous urge dispelling time in the repelled demonstration, reverence of doubt, and motion of passive feet. The discourse nods with full awareness, and expands with the sullen clouds because victory is the enrichment as loss falls clear of any meaning. Frozen nothing, persistent want, labored thought, and mourning meadows weep silky tears. The lush scraps of time, and there is no luck in hearts when endowed with problematic answers. Wisdom and freedom are man's reprisal, however harsh things exist within our nature. Cultivation tells of the wicked and the sublime bliss of time and repetition. The cutting tie of passionate experience articulated like the rouse of a rooster. Tree parts curling on the ground, dissembled, dismembered wood looking like squatted frogs. Crows calling capture in their habitation of the world. Whispers twinkling in solitude on a single branch, and the introspection grins a passing wink at consciousness.

It has been said that society contains a lack of morals. Physical experience would agree with this, however, what we lose by looking away, not getting involved, or praising what is right far surpasses action itself. Not only do limitations occur, but they increase with the shrinking action. The proposition of right and wrong is based on experience, upbringing, and belief. Our vast population cannot equate a moral majority without the general application consistent with singular reality. At birth we are immersed in a lie. A fundamental flaw for physical temperaments to tap away the untruth. Constructed of ideal, popularized by culture, and substantiated with justice, we have the world through cause and effect. Innate nature via our personal characteristics. The person involves the whole benign hole, and the concrete of sense and discourse effect the construct. The sense dissembles the sequence of possibility with the foreclosure of chance and choice. Any limitation results from the personal equation of the total truth and is a slight potential of accurate nature. Removal warrants distance the success of participating response. The common reaches the ground, and appreciates the horizon. The driving resonance from every action activates the original question of prospect, and saturating corrosion, promising growth, and furthering the distance we close the difference. Boredom turns into the next fluctuating life, eats a doughnut, and forgets the truth of being. Choice is circumstance, and the eternal suffering of grandiose thinking verifies idiosyncratic acceptance. Boredom needs to stir the acceptance so nuance can reason response, and the claustrophobic detail can agree with purpose. Undo purpose and recognizable defeat swallows the underlay of tomorrow. The unremitting sonorous depravity in the soul is the silence of a golden apple that grows in raging improvement. We do indeed lose with every ounce of aspect distilled in false, contagious definition. Every pedigree can stipulate illegal retorts of sanctioned acceptance. The world continues in isolation with forgotten remarks. Ignorance creates the difference and corrosion strokes the world of growth with denial. Tomorrow does not tally the equality of today.

Pen snags paper, and conscious deliberation closes tight. We are damned with the deliberate direction and condemned with the aspiration of collapse. Today we stand, tomorrow we fall, and what preconceived notions we have of both accurately and swiftly tilt the plain. No matter what the plan, we lose, no matter what the concentration on swollen definition, we lose. The diction of rising tempers are the accustomed privilege of free will. Dark delusion occupies the realm of dislocation. Plans do not work, but nausea surely spills interest into the slick control of a salivating, crazed dog. We linger to our means with warbled views of dissonance. Discontent joy weighing commitment with a watch for repair. The intoxicated perspective reigns the limits of warranty, and success as an impromptu language covers the pleas of insanity with meaning. We wail our wear to compose the world.

Taking too much, and giving too little un-argued time. The tactile sense directed by curiosity, and the mental framework of all the passed being circumvented by an idea for tomorrow. Tomorrow is not today! Not knowing what to say does not rectify the mistake. The one who suffers the most is not worth the hassle. Bandaged wounds continue to heal, and the search for inherent wisdom seeps within them. Banter excuses the outpost. The digression of tomorrow to balance today. Do we see passed the weathered antiquity or do we subside forgotten and broken? The soul never tells, but meagrely welcomes the disposition of progress. Antagonistic prose strains the view, forgives the art of artifact, and encourages the current display of representation.

We consume our death with gratitude and wealth. Salt and peppered occurrence overriding the ideal for intent. Fear, unscathed security, and the paroxysms of faith devoid of following. We see the light, but turn away to wait for darkness. The bequeathed state of tomorrow flourished in the blossom of disquieting finesse. Enjoy yourself! We do lose no matter how refined the laughter, and we do lose no matter the wash of the wear. The loving impression of representation, and this life of denial recline in slumber, but the awareness stifles the fabled rest. Tomorrow is not today, and without knowing how many see this act of synonyms plunging into derivation. The exclamation is in the decline, the expression in the sublime, and the cure is in the sense. We seek our derivation, that point that brought us here, and the irreverent display that contorts the missed citation. The ascent of representation, and the doodled eyes bewildered by request foreseeing the conclusion loose from insight. It distorts the age of reason by uniting a degree of resentment and conformity. Mix well or stand out. Definition cries an answer of groans to sear the bellowing allocation. We define the means, accentuate the parallels, and reason with decline.

The parallels remain, tomorrow discusses progression, and the slaughter of decline is repressed by forgotten ritual. Incorporate what we dislocate, and the remembrance dissects the speaking soul. The sense of ordeal diminishes the goal, adds to the addiction, and prose becomes perversion. The indecent frottage of shifting position in the peril of the self's preservation. Sitting in a mirrored ball the truth basks in reflection. The pre-used words have to state the originality layered in description, and crashing across the damaged tide, the trials of living create the world from the acceptance of encouraged fault. The decline, and a slumber of pleasantry will expose more thought than havoc. It will receive a pass for a second suggestion. Pure speculation defines the whole as it is made of many ones. Any belief of singular view is committed to the fall of morality. The choice of creation and condemnation we have made with a simple schematic. Every choice, breath, and thought creates or abolishes another choice. Being one option eliminates the other, and experience disdains the proud winds of change as life unravels definition. The intention is clear, morals are dilapidated because interests change, time evolves, and consequence is outdated. The mass requires survival, and this calls for action and not preservation through that action. The blame does not fall on us. One and all convict life, and the operation of duty remains a natural movement through the stages of ceremony. Suffering momentum with what preparation we have tried like a candle morals will fade with time. The persecution and preparation represent the praise for the self, and the convoluted theory of personality will mean a panorama of diluted and distorted meaning. The choice dictates the consequence, and thus every experience is singular. Morals coincide to extend from the individual being. If society lacks morals then the individual does also. If society's morality declines further then the individual's standpoint does also.

  The opposition of truth is existence. The perception and rationale of these things appease, regroup, and apply for justice. The dichotomy of morality wavers, and as it has been said is based on the allocated individual. The passion of presence, the trend of discovery, and the persistence of the trapped self in secure features favour the feverish consistency of a training soul. Partial truths spoken in order to ambush an incredible promise. Love, happiness, and beauty possessing the tranquil things beyond us. Deeper into eternity, recruiting enjoyment, passed remembrance is best avoided. We know the difference, can discourage the effect, and fear the reaper in a dance of fragile steps. Weakness affects the whole with the spurned aspects of independence that trollop with the world. Repetition erases originality, but dusk closes in, and stands on the shoulders of mountains. It is nature's reminder of fetal growth in the superior glance of organic strength, and the fragrant fruit of sunshine, rain, and wind. Fire scorns creation, but soothes the exposure. Death reasons a simple attachment to physical experience, and the conception of loss thrives on the wings of rapid change. Sing in the pity of growth, and the digestion of folly will enlighten the grasp of truth. The lies we tell ourselves without agreement can become the truth, but why? We are waiting for something, but is it the same thing?

Time draws no conclusion, but irate noise. The continual, boisterous indifference of a cathartic spectrum of decision. The uprooted privilege under the current of proposed being in the inconsistent descent of life. The perpetual, unchanging doubt in the conviction of our lives. Nothing is proven to define our waking hours, but this constant state of unknowing. All we have presents our morality, and this delivers our individual meaning. This is all the consistency we can congruently consume, but with so much being said, how can it be identified clearly?

Words endless words. Face upon face, hand upon hand, and world upon world forever dancing on a fiber of stupefaction. A non-greasy chain that unravels instead of getting caught, and a stacked continuance gains the loss already paid. The lines develop a stutter and build the universe in interrupted splendor as we develop the feed for tomorrow. God sits high, and watches over, but this time and generation pronounce the point of principle. God does laugh at our flailing attempts. Regardless a pin point does have focus, and it is at this point where we begin.

ABPoe

A brief inventory completely sold. Left at seven thirty something. Walked into seven eleven cold and miserable. Asked the Mary working for a cab, and she said, "Which one?"

United. Two jolts, and a payment. Waiting outside, smoking, someone asks for a cigarette, people get gas, and nothing brilliant is said in the expression of a beautiful day. The cab comes, and says goodbye. The driver, a mean looking woman talks of the weather.

"It is supposed to get better. Rain on Sunday."

Later. At the bus depot a man waits for the technology to print a ticket. A receipt to consume three minutes. The turn progresses, and the short waif wearing glasses glares with perfume and magic saying, "Now I can help you."

"One to the city."

"Now is that this side or that?"

The void in the head has to think.

"Departure point or arrival?"

"Departure is fine, but can I get a return ticket here or is it better to do it there?"

"There because my machine does not access that area."

"Is it too old?"

She does not hear because the machine erupts with clamour. "Thank you."

"Thanks."

Having the receipt, marking the numbers, and walking away outside. An old, wood staircase made to construct two steps holds a platform at the top. Smoking more, cold hands check the time, and constitute the wait. The driver exits the building, looks for luggage, and people begin to get on the bus. No one, but tickets, entering and waiting to leave with four passengers and the driver. Sleep with snow laden roads seen previously. Briefly people transfer at the first, major stopping point. Sleepy drool, waking, and sleeping again. The terminal enters the view, and we are here. Leaving the bus, smoking once more to return to a tollbooth and the lady there, "It is a ten thirty sailing."

Checking the time it was quarter to ten, "One please."

Smoking again with the snow shading the water, and the mountains soaking in vibrant stature. Winter wraps the terminal with silvery vengeance. Waiting the line begins to accumulate. The distance is still ahead, but showing my ticket the departure is almost behind.

The water stretched for three days, and upon land work had to be done. Columnists scattered to tread new footsteps. The green bounty spreading higher than the chapel, and emancipated within the snow brilliant, blinding light. Vast beyond the sea that had brought us here, and spy glasses look at the difference with awe and accentuation. Danger left the sentiment with the steps from the boat, and the people frolic in the snow and swaying trees. We extend over history with new, found absurdity.

The confusion raps on the marshy, thickened scope to reveal the innards of a vile thing. A mess of stringy mass suspended in the cloudy heights of the sea. A mass of sturdy levels amazing in the reef. The lines of flesh are abstract versions of life in a flowing fjord of gushing liquid. The ooze is not so dirty, and it is a design that is understood. The staggering views of our response are in the very core of this primitive mud slide. Physics have extended logic beyond the sense, and without the academics, warmly sheathed in its most wriggling exposition, our concentration was breaking. The fundamental quake of too much or too little too late. The contest of unending time raises the potential only to the depth of tomorrow. Lingo and slogans, jargon that has been deciphered to the world, and there is no adding to the cliché.

PART ONE

BRIEFLY TO BE ALONE.
THE VACANCY OF BRUISING IS NOT
TOO DEEP. TOLD TO DO THIS,
BUT PASSION REGAINED.

"Poised posterior postulating postwar. Photocopied personality pastured posthumously pacified, peculiar, personal pessimist. Paid postscript prescribed. Poise posture positively! Pandas perceiving paradox point programmed phantasmagoria, preach particular positions, pasteurizing progress. Passed past participles plead process. Paranoid perks plant pause. Pandora poked present paroxysm poignantly picking public performance. Piss perfectly, passionate Patrick."

102411252p

CHAPTER ONE

WE HAVE ONE person, and physical characteristics are not specific other than male and under forty. Clothes are nondescriptive, no slogans, no visible brands, but also not noticeably second hand. His name is minimal, and due to reclusive behavior it is only said twice, and not right away. We begin with candlelight, maybe seven or so scattered more for shadows than light, and we see our character lying on a bed with his head hanging toward the floor. He stares up at the ceiling. He is deep in thought, and although he does not speak we hear his voice.

"Another queer theme in the piece of the pie. One more day in the life of a homo. To burn brightly with earnest flare, and be extinguished with the stigma of a preference. Judgment comes so quickly even though extremes are inherently habitual. Vague terms due to a broad band of specimens. People perverse themselves for pleasure, comfort, and self-ideology. They hold on and hope no one cares more or less than themselves. Hiding, hoping figures that bathe in shadows to hold the light. The universe really is vast and incredible. That we live, breathe, and create our destiny with every turn is remarkable. Trying to cheat by breaking the rules is one of God's intentions."

He continues to think, "Leviticus 20:13 states, the penalty for homosexual acts is death to both parties. They have brought it about themselves."

"Death to the buggers! Yet life resides before death, and although choices have been made can the consequence really be so vindictive? Do I die upon sex or does death find me when it is ready? Really can this even be substantiated? Shoplifters are prosecuted to the full extent of the law when caught, but I still have to find a corpse after sex. Sex and punishment amazingly remain separate. Homosexuality is a choice, and no longer a distortion of the mind. We are allowed the freedom to be gay, and so the only condemnation comes from those people that believe literally the transcendental history and not the living facts. Homosexuals do not die having sex, and the AIDS argument is levied by health and circumstance, not just sexuality alone, and so we are to die, and we shall, but as people and not homosexuals. We may be gay, but with concession comes the act, and if we are to both die, we shall, but not with ejaculation. Seamen creates, and if it is lost in the circle to contribute nothing then cannot the sanctity of acceptance be enough? Love, warmth, and compassion should measure more than whether or not my wife builds my breakfast or my lover. Tenderness should be revelled in and not persecuted. Choice should be freely welcomed and not disapproved of."

The monologue is witnessed by spectators of all sorts, and the result endures as one of speculation. The fifty-fifty chance remains, and unfortunately not one of us can disprove it. Freedom remains stigmatized, should people too?

Nine am.

The doors open, the lights raise, and we are open for business. Today we have leftovers here from last night, left by someone who got here too late. Two bins of stuff, but he is on time today. The boss pushes in a wire cart from Fourth Avenue and complains his back is sore with a sniveling wheeze. He allows the stuff to be sorted and is paid. So long and thank you.

Another day and the receipt tallies two hundred and thirty four aluminum cans for Charlie who is eighty or so. He was wearing sunglasses, a straw hat, green pants, and carried his wielded cane. Prodding and poking a small box a younger gentleman carries in more restlessly not knowing what to do. He is approached to set him on track. The cans are counted with a loose remainder and a quick, good job.

"I am by myself."

"Bye," here is twelve dollars and seven cents. A girl enters with a bag.

"What is in the bag?"

"Stuff."

That is specific, but we can figure it out as we go.

"I just cannot handle this today."

"O.k."

Random, constant occurrences persist here. Car honks, dead mice, wasps in August, and freezing water in winter. Rain through a leaky roof, snow through a missing pane of window, and endless, un-flattened cardboard.

"What time do you open?"

People do work here, but the customers are more important. For example, the lady who is always sorry or the unsorted bag of crap guy. Any given Saturday has the same routine as garbage cans find their positions. Palettes are arranged, and we stand around discussing such a great day.

"Good morning."

"Brisk this morning."

Beat no ball point, but the spine instead. There is no explanation for reality as reality is truly explained by our interplay with it. Just be today with roots to replenish the isolation and irreverence with the catharsis of time reflecting turmoil and denial, but the unknowing, exalted reality is thinned by breathing, active tissue. The decline of time and the restraint of the soul, but twitching.

"I am proud to write."

Roots. Warmth and expansion within the thievery of privacy and the corporate sale of existence. A penniless surmise with the sunglasses on, but where is the brink once it is gone? Direction redeems classification with clarification, but the stagnant thoroughfare buying strategy determine warm decomposition. The facets of ordained nature disguise the couth imposter.

Redial to determine if there are any victims. Time is peril, and second guessed advances by the instinctive, impartial mirage of being coaxes sweaty palms and greased discipline. The promise is gilded exposure of the modern mass, and its demise has each of the children we bear with their children. Choice and free will dissolve with the interaction of fluid lines and unclear usage. Who can stand all this heat?

"Not me."

P.C only had one song, and now it is over.

Nervous and preoccupied, but with a life all our own. It is father's birthday, one of many, but the first to be recognized by us. He has aged since we met him, but no one pays attention all the time. Seasons flow, ebb in and out like a tide caressing the shore, and baking a cake to write out the perplexity of being here and now. Any selfish reminiscing and obsessive compulsions ride in stride the ticking clock as the only fear remains bad breath. Desire clicks like mute cymbals concise with a steady hand. The sense of purpose avoids conclusion like a fearful decision denying objection or even acknowledgement.

The time remains ours as the words stir definition and the actions abuse the condition. Sadness and disbelief skip stones across the myriad of time, and unconsciously we implore ignorance. Saying futile advances all the while spreading defeat. This time runs out, life draws a thinner straw, and comprehension craves removal. The bloated memories of the past declare the truth in cautionary tales of legends and fables long since forgotten. The cliché points of personal regard and finite application trying responsibility, but the best is beaten by terms of comfort. Fear and anger aimed and fixed as denial and doubt loosely transfix the opposition boasting openly, "You could do better?"

"Why?"

Content in the despairing array of pyrotechnics the mass continues amused and forlorn. Perched anew with a fragmented insight of loss dazed in the explicit usage of time. Frozen in the headlights as it were, basking in the illumination, and trapped by the truth of ordeal.

"But what does it mean?"

Cruel confusion coursing correspondence. Sloppy words coruscating the triumph with guilt and the possibilities of tried circumstance displaying the open future. Ashamed we do accept it.

"But what does it mean?"

Left to our own devices, penniless and drunk, isolated and tortured by the deliberate memories of sabotage, and wishing for a brighter future.

"But what does it mean?"

The emotional refuge is the rise and decline of time. The over used influence that breaks the point of no return with the questionable design of now. Trepidation, lust, admission, and continuance.

"Don't run over me."

The air is cooling, but the body blends the temperature with words. Do not be afraid for it is only us. Just be now whatever it is. The effects are the same bizarre and torrid trash. Full of food and feces, built on strength and weakness, the fair is in town, but who is laughing up a good time? The pressure does not matter, but the wear carries the whole toward the infinite light at the end of decay. The composition requires the total meaning, and not simply one part or another, but all to transpose the now. Any underlying message resides in the self. Yes this self, right now, and all the right, and all the wrong encompasses nothing more than labelled decision. Now not then is the self itself.

Now.

Courteous sentiment is watered down by alcohol and company. The lights are low and the promiscuous details permit visions of shamed existence. The smell of coffee permeates the illusion with reality. The misused intention plummets into the unknown although societal convention quickly solicits polite understanding. Today, now, here, hovering openly above the abyss and captivating an audience is how.

"How?"

"Now."

Pretentious dialogue of sighted abundance and the unknown acceptance of a stranger. We are all strangers in a surreal land, but awaken a deeper stretch of Immaculate Conception and deliver us together, one and all, forever. The pretension returns, but it is our own. Today, now, and forever animates the woodcuts with choice and its consequence. The fervent awakening of substance and pattern within the concrete enclosure of classic weather. Passing steps, repetitive vice, and the voice of a victim straining the agriculture. Temptation again sweeps the weeping heartache into inexperience, but the full throttled response glorifies exposure with vindictive deception. The illicit affair of the breathing, damaged repair of living, reverberated despair. The joyous, ridiculous spots of worn tenacity and depravity. Acceptance may deny the usage, but behavior consecrates meaning today, now, forever. Alone, inhibited, and tumultuous description weaving inception with today, now, and forever. The jitters take hold because the time is not quite right and curiosity hinders progress with its blind, courteous demeanor. Today, now, and forever. Stand up and chase the appropriate demand.

"Why?"

"What does it matter?"

Seen or unseen articulate bodies compose the wealth of obedience to convey a safer bet. The wager however returns undeclared, yet the rules of the game have not changed. The additions accumulate even further silence as steadfast, building blocks erect observation. The ghastly preservation of idling worth yawns technical ignorance as we all think we are alone, inhibited, and tumultuous.

"Is judgment so righteous?"

Biased and blamed, but crying for freedom. Comfort may deny the margin, but expansion brings forth the meeting of minds. Youth and age contort to the meaning of their intention, but where is the ditch in this mental, small town?

"Today is the day!"

Now and forever.

The shadows find dawn to recollect their posture and retreat. Hiding from the now, forever, we postulate further explanation to ourselves. There is no gain or failing beyond progress. The lessons cry out oblivion with retrospective devices knowing more. Freedom strings together the bittersweet if only someone would notice.

"Disprove now, always, and forever."

The fruit bears its name only through interaction with it. The slow spelled incompetence of now argues suspension with belief and rattled attention.

"I may be wrong, but tomorrow tells the truth."

Maybe the words and actions are incorrect, but who knows any better? Self-pity brings no weight, but neither does aggressive sympathy. Weakness is merely tomorrow sporting more than victory. We shall die even if we cannot spell it correctly. Subsidence gave us power, but is that wrong? More or less who knows? Who learns? Tired and empty tomorrow wails.

"Are we ignorant and young enough to stagger and sleep?"

Are we to believe wrong doing deserves belief or the ignorance therein? Weakness and age compose more than we know, but still we are disproved. Fleeting passions and pensive observations impose more, but dissolving on the brink of the truth they disappear. Wasted by words and death we should be drunk to decline the knowledge based on such a feeble attempt at purity. Laughing and living, urine and feces, and foul, indiscriminate confidence tries harder. Forever missed, but who concedes concern? Life is too short. The parameters of "I" define us, and the closer we may look, the more we may see that we have missed. The soup of the day. The heat from the food on the plate is a character witness looking away to listen somewhere else. The dislocation does present a problem here in modern culture. The disregarding whole for the self. The dynamic community is condemned, and the fabrication we design condemns us too. Fractured with reality and a bleeding pen, scattered reason tears us apart, and any proactive decision leads the way away.

Too high with tight nerves. Fast then slow breathing surfaces, and acting normal becomes labored. Slow down, breathe, breathe, deeper, succumb to loss already and propose less forceful facts. The mission of sweaty herds is for eyes to breathe, force focus to breathe because even the air flow sweats. No one knows you are high until you are high. The last word is a worldly projectile of city lights and heartburn. Time spreads instead of inserting a word because the internal restriction deserving credit for hand spelled tones is lost. Miss spelled, my sweet, focus and breathe.

Repeat! Repeat! The nerves stream silence with such a pen it spooks the solitary. Tobacco stained roofs jerk to compact the silence, but safety was thrown out by the reckless reserve of the self. A purer transparency is safety on the side of the self. The spark of nerves ruthlessly repeat like gum or tar or spit gluing together the silence passing us by. Brown, chicken breath fingering toes with obtrusive behavior. The defeat is the sweat and breathe of nature. In and out the dirty senses emit being a partnership with power, prestige, and air dried drama.

"How many simple people fill a bus?"

One too many not to say full.

We die with extensive nature at the back of the bus. Do not be unaware, and turn both sides of the option into practice and closure. An air tight awareness rests in death exhuming life in the unknown. Do we realize the effort of nature is lost and handicapped? Even wearing glasses to see, the light floats by as the dark swallows it faithfully. Policing rats down empty alleys in a gloomy paced fiction seems an exhausting fate if being good is fighting hate. The steps trace fear and courage, and it is us who must step up.

Come close and laugh in disbelief as life is so temporarily abandoned. The reasons have no audience because fortune and nature have handed in time without sadness. The bonds are broken with a fine tooth comb. Breathe, relax, point and press change with some more sweat as death and self calmly live. Up north with an assault on who knows best the smokers inhale an exit.

"Praise be, eat more!"

Reading and writing with a twisting pain and even the nausea spots the overload. Big bugs if not the small ones snap back, spit up, and still cannot read or write. The silence spasms without explanation. A blank, drugged yawn crossed at an intersection without an intended direction, and the physical attention holds so much they collided. Broken to violence the precognition becomes the law, and reticence again yanks at yearning Mother Nature. It is gone again like rates of privilege and privacy. The composition of silence is truth on the page that I cannot write. Practical speech sounds out the word, but no one is speaking. A pen and the being holding it remains an ape. Is that the term best describing the truth? Be good, be now, and swallow!

"Punch the pregnant bitch! Right now! Tie her down and beat her up to forget."

Life has a sandwich for those with bread, and those with meat, and those with tomato, and those with lettuce. Lettuce? Not having a spotlight has become the fear for most.

A tonal poem also known as do not trip over my feet. The sound escalates as the bugs' trip on my back and the police come with paranoia. Really? Stagger with breath and live to swoon with ecstasy. Follow through with the police and guard the system. Have I truly found a bug? Question everything because it is not just me. This is now for all. Do not delay because the eye watches everything in a harvest of depletion. Taking one and all the base poetry declines us both, but a torrid affair of romance strokes any heir. Passion or person with or without bugs has solace in the lessons ringing through the buzz. Atmosphere aside, the muscles flex with the world's call for home fitted pleasure. The eyes they are a watching. The numbers are receding, but a granted response beckons one from all.

A rest from the pitfall comes as a fern in a massive, sunlit fixation that mimics the sight. The pleasure does seek the meek, and shall thus follow us always, but the lights on the path bicker and scavenge. Cross merit and stream more burden with chance, but stop on a lesson and a lesson will stick. The sandwich of perspective is lined with time and the self. The engorged feast relies on air, flesh, and the awareness to eat like a slovenly dog in heat, dry humping the air with a congruent beat. The whimsy of perception denies nothing, but the awareness therein discerns a problem. The antiquated foresight of action and decline predict the outcome here. The eyes they watch and the truth outlives the naked flesh forced upon them. Breath and life are foreign products the mass carries, and with a look of the eyes, a flexed tongue speaks, and science renders the patterns into a quilt of warm innocence. Progress is deployed by the relevant mass in expressions and whimpers and words. They are misspelled perhaps, but the action bears its consequence forthwith with able taste. The future is a problem not of itself, but with us the traffic flows. The skin discolors, the mind pacifies, and the recumbent visions of now retain growth. An eccentric pedigree pulls the voyage further as active duty calls the morbid flesh to collect the resilient coils of decay and apathy. The neurotic terms of pride dictate the source of any breakthrough, but the trap is refused. Propose the stains and have a spirit capture the victim in abandoned passion, nullified by reason, and being more seethe with seizure. Pushing the threshold further we brazenly climb the hill, and descend the fates with fruitful steps of refusal. The basket of harmony overflows when preying eyes do see, but the notice of embodied wisdom waves ahead at the worldwide here to be full out and free.

The configuration profits admission with the truth as walking feet hold passage. The eyes peer forever, but like an ambulance in the wind the sight is gone before the sound. Warbling heads perceive its grasp asunder. The ink without the knowhow is a period for a question. The formation and the delay of ownership. A strain revoking pavement with its permanent demeanor. The steps get cold in progress as desire brings a deal to a stale throat. The liquid turns as the solids bewilder sounding motion. Direction quantifies the reason, closes in, and shuts us down to rest amidst the grime. Effort surges choice and the focused strain of desire with a resourced meaning. The stains. Smears like angry words piercing the skin. Bragging feet spreading the disease of the unknown as the mathematical figures are indeed afraid of each other. Kin shuddering in the light with a fear for a change in weather. The hum it buzzes, and stirs alive the echoes it thrives on with effort and nature. Trampled and blue on the horizon of desperation things settle into tepid degrees of allusion.

"What do I want?"

"Other than the others?"

Truth, sex, fulfillment. Long term partners only maintain the sex if even that. Walk away with regret, and deserve more. Think clearly and stop the blame; change. Truly this is over, and what meaning is singular? Speculation at best, but can one do better?

Stand behind tomorrow today. No spite, malice, or anger can possibly grace the turning way of receptive growth. Time is irrelevant, the self is inflated, but growth cannot happen with force. The seclusion would reveal greater works of social disease. Uncertain that it matters, but confident what happened was short of nothing more than unspecified, arrogant judgment cannot make decisions for the knowledge of growth.

Minimal math.

Digest or congest? One over one equals two over two. One over two parents equals four parents over two. One over one no matter what two is remains one. Love what we have because we have it. Thank you junk, and Happy New Year!

Time plus death equals passion. The resource is reason. The definitive source is the two toot salute! Fracture now and become tomorrow. The translation is dysfunction at a dance, repeating dance, but falling teased, booze tempted pretense can spill over.

This man is terrified of being hurt or made a fool of. He needs to be loved. His whole being cries out for affection, even though you may never guess it. The usual, deep family anxieties or disappointments in childhood are what make him wary. Masking feelings with iron self-control. Soft, gentle, and more than a little bewildered by his own emotional impotence. Try as he may, he just cannot express his feelings adequately. Try a little tenderness. Understand he's very self-conscious in company, but has a very strong sexual appetite. He may be a heavy drinker, but alcohol helps to relieve his self's doubt. He is slow and he is steady, but he is a pretty sure bet.

Overwhelmed with the lack of knowledge concerning the acceptance of change. Disconnected from the purpose of a group dynamic even though it is understood. Generally concerned about the upcoming journey.

"The cliff!"

"Try to avoid smoking during our fresh air break."

The determination of dislocation has dissolved the self's withdrawn function. One out of eight can translate. Reach without reaching. Smile when frowning. Do more productive activities. Physical shape is only an asset, but the diet needs work. The preservatives will kill you.

Seduction tears out a page and pinches the square. Beat the sleep, but rest and sparkle either with a drink in the morning or into the night, see you soon.

Sorry is the first word that comes into mind. Lost for good without going back. Fault is a vicious tongue, but also suave sees both sides. Fair is best, and criticism is selfish. Meaning is letting go, but this may not improve happiness. The past still strangles the future with our allowance. The expectations break the rules every time. There is enough death or denial saved for later on the bridge of Hell, but can I do it? There is peace and comfort, tried and failed, but no future gives into the loss. I fail too. Life hurts, but it will let go for given safety. Be well and love. Remain the love of my life, and I will learn to treat you better.

Proverbs.

Hiccups on the last day, consequence and turmoil within the sweat of a moment. Hot, damp, hard, and even dark within the territorial waters. The being is distorted by mass and experience expounding momentary gain. The rain on the cinder block and the blueprints at our fingertips travel. Yes we have made it, but wrought, iron fencing basks around the cool, autumn evening. The rain and bitters slightly guise the pleasures of scattered, literal crumbs assembling discipline. Luck or chance run out of hand, but the peripheral view presents discarded moments of lamenting memory in order to prepare the encountered difference. You do the math.

Supply and demand in the encore of oblivion calls the mass of catalyst a furrowed brow, and an awareness of this now. What small part we play resides in the observation of reason and the citation of comment, albeit watered down inclination for a sorry soul. One stop and we exchange, one more and we discuss the ramifications, but one more still acquaints us with the possibility of sideswiping the first. Appointed time does disagree with our conversation, but our subtle interim stands firm. The disagreement stands alone allowing terminal degrees to squash solitary pastures with immense regurgitation.

The sweat dies down as a calm returns with boredom upon boredom. This new tenacity amidst the neighbourly scholars looks at perplexity.

"Who would want to live here?"

Exasperated and vacant we joyfully move in, and if the great goal is indifference then we have won. Dirty and scorned with weary disbelief we do journey forward. The importance of vague injustice leaves a fragmented whole for the significant unknown. A clasped resistance chatters jaws like chewing gum. The muscles flex although absconded by use, and the designated closure again straps the bell with signature. A premature burial in the cold, autumn air as reason stokes pride like the waves of the ocean. Silent pictures displaying the hard of hearing in an amplified deception of trivial prodding that resounds oblivion. The dark, spooky matter plummets ahead like a bare heart losing love. The transgression slips and slides, and holding tight the mass ignores this plight. The fear is pride. The self-inflicted failure and impurity emerges righteous and courteous, but the barriers erected from the patterns of praise poise personality. The twitches captivate the muscle, and subterfuge dominates the ticks present in a responsible reply. The decadent few stand unobstructed by ignorance, but it makes the matter worse for we can all still hide under its disguise. The fear comes with the responsibility of hands, and force effort into effect. This enabled interaction with trickery is age deriving toll as the past becomes obscure. Still the fear persists and pricks against the knuckles to tickle a spinal response. The age and responsibility reflected in the future as history remains obscured. The relevance of nature and its fallacy wither with time as its effect loses strength to sidestep diversion. The decisions crack in the air as consequence picks and pits the pieces of the entire scheme to form their parts alone. Fear provides resistance from the immediacy of interaction, but the decision envelopes the future fully. This, now, repetitive motion, and dead time. The cure to life lived does not subside. Pride holds a feast to the ground as thoughts unravel rapidly, but the tourism is low, and two sneezes and a cough clear the air with outward alternatives. Another sneeze and the forced vacuum innocuously writhing marches upward. The senses are docile and the observation unnoticed, but the reflection runs rampant in finer degrees. Groomed enterprise carrying pie for the masses hopefully allows them to eat without fear. The sugar is obvious, the medium is blurred, and perspective drowns the dribble with solitude.

"What is that?"

Not again.

"What is that?"

Not again.

Tired and frightened with other people wanting more right now.

"Right now!"

Decay, decadence, and abysmal servitude. The study of the self is shamed by the introspective mind because it is incorrect. The distortion rings the chimes and the solutions follow the sound. At least there was a pen to write it down as faith and theory fall with any disproved facsimile of belief. The chimes sway and tinkle, but who proved the echoes found in the same, prospective solutions. The memory anticipates such activity as the lamb is dead and poorly sacrificed for a sturdy meal. We are stupid to want more, but there is more. The lack of control is thievery based on pessimistic obstructions and time dwindling thin. Plots die and the purpose is surmised by the victor.

Proof is already known by the victim of belief and the owner of death. Take light and bloom! Do not dissolve into habit, and beseech the Heavens.

"Be more."

The Devil wins with scorn, "BE NOW."

Be now! Illuminate the journey and find the now. Yawning with sex and discussions on religion, belief builds the cause of nature that delivers this effect. God speaks and we listen as if we were deaf. The weakness wins and the disciplined body creates decrepit furtiveness. Want and need erupt onto the page.

"WHOOPEE!"

Life orders that the smoke is not enough.

Point proven.

The truth does not matter. Samples of this default emerge with cynicism, doubt, and lies. Reason is splattered and laughing across the page as squalid, angered trust is all that is left because the truth is beaten and defiled.

"Bullshit."

God has tied us to lust and abuse to test the strength and weakness of merit. God has thrown a skunk into the room to examine the reactionary movement of volatility and uncertainty. No one laughs, not even God as the skunk idly focuses on the room, and we merely observe the skunk all the time thinking about the possible threat. The terms blur the truth, and burn life with holy death. It is not a game of chance, and love can be all that we want it to be.

Evil turns a curve as we may forget where the truth is written. Splintered and deciphered, lost pragmatism commands a sorrowful world of unknown outcries. A state of brazen rows savouring disappointment with the flavored tongues of response rapidly wagging. The world moves forward, but who notices?

The light ends, we age, and time wears thin. Without winning or hitting bottom the truth runs out of the room weary of the importance in ink. Feelings from another abstract turn of the bridge as the truth is more than either side. A two tone theory saves us as one, but what it does to the whole fragments moments in time. The whole becomes diluted truth as absolved by us in death. The nicotine stained brothers stumble to fall over each other in static, combustible noise erupting from the flailing lengths of troubled fiction. It determines the state of circumstance as ambivalent experience. What has the dark knowledge that nothing forms the imagination like our open, active hands is the crossroad of oblivion that travels trepidation along the hills. We fumble, staggering emotional independence in our being, and contemplate the truth with every step.

Knowledge or nonsense the truth prevails. It mocks somber reaction when we do not for it knows the denial we enlist, the judgment we slander, and the lies we use to protect our meager lives. It knows the answer to why, predicts the outcome of how, and fosters the mixed usage of pain and growth. Suppose the usage counts, what have we done? Admission runs silent along the edge of the ether in dark cloisters of wrongful and fearful attacks on higher virtues. The light brings calm reminders that time is not up quite yet, and the exasperated exaggeration is only our own. Devoted to pride and survival the loyalty of truth is death. Give help to those who cannot see the struggle for a position in lost life. Please excuse the formality, but we have found it drowning in static. The pretense unfolds dread as the laughing joke at life. The trying loss of painful aim, the triumphant clapping hands, and tapping toes repeat the eternal rhythm of choice. Ask and reply, beckon and dredge, exhume and exalt the freedom spinning wonder and woe. The exercise in the bounty of the scarred, scorned sacrifice saved in the life predicting stance of an outstretched hand and the outward morning facing opulence. A shag if you have a preference, but a degree of slung dung drying freely in the open air. The disappointment is lost as misfortune disguises any effect of the afterthought in splendid slumber.

Progress eliminates the possibilities by prompting outcome with a device for reason. There can after all be only one! The process of elimination enables our potential to flourish, and any reasoning behind it to be pulverized and atomized into tiny morsels of bypassed comment. The revolt of action takes up the flight to prove the point, but the decision of basic assimilation returns to outcome for a clearer picture. There are too many discrepancies from one singularity to pin point the detour. Still the truth calculates intent, and outcome systematically determines the usage and its viable application. Mumbo jumbo and quantum mechanics serving platitude to the distortion. Specific terms and lessons prove singular truth and organic growth. Tomorrow answers the call with an awakened sapling blossoming amidst the guilt and pleasure. The promise remains free will, but its allusion is built with our acceptance of it. The formation of such a paradox may be a hoax, but God remains hopeful and aware of the days ahead. Travelling as one encapsulating righteousness we walk forward, glance upward, and stumble upon the debris left before us.

Memories derive the momentum, and the actions fall upon actions in endless, calculated twists of sorrow and joy. This is the intention, the test of time and turmoil, and the regulation of result in the testimony of our input. Rising, swirling, explosions of self-evidence and the implication of exterior manipulation. No selfish griping or desired expectation, but the eternal update of universal footing. The serene, docile charm of agreement under the looking glass of personal bias. Disenchanted servitude, but freedom prepares the walking morn with awareness and ignorance. The indifference scatters the remarks in the wind, but the listening ear of God can still pierce scrutiny and truth. The bubbles lift upward slow and steady to burst at the touch of air like breath falling short.

CHAPTER TWO

REBUILT ROADS STILL crumble, and the evaporating structure designs the future. Hands hold the sun, but the sun scalds the skin. Accidental violence bursts from the notches of deluded bravery and vitality. We thought we knew better, but tomorrow owns the answer without us. We have to begin to believe or drown in a misappropriated murk. Certainty was never ours, although we did think it was at the bottom of the purse hiding amidst the loose change. Still incorrect and passive we wander askew from the reason of footsteps. Passion plays a part in our abandon, but how much is up to us. The intangible affects us all openly and unaware. Coping or coinciding we develop the reason, and absent minded or truly ignorant the terms agree vigorously. Please allow reason to reach further branches of the tree. We may not climb it, but the light can filter down in waves of shadows presented by nature's intent. The cataclysmic reproach looks away because God sees through it, although the sinful and disdained deserve a look. The presence of archival footage ascends the foundry of negatives with the preserved antiquity of proof.

Memories blare like an overheard record, and the skips present the listener with a distorted view of the past. The awkward semblance of now flutters and frowns because the memory is proven wrong. Always seems like such a long time, but tomorrow will think the same thing. Then the tomorrow after tomorrow will prove it, and with so many tomorrows how can the bias blame a beginning other than continuance.

The visions and voices remind us of yesterday. What we did right, wrong, and indifferent, but nonetheless the confines that define us are our own translucent cage. The bars are iron and suffocate movement, but why were we taken captive anyway?

The problem lies perhaps in disbelief. A gargantuan realm of space involved to disprove what we do not accept or maybe do not know. The eyes do see the sense to communicate development and abscond any reason other than the growth itself. Over stimulated chaos derived from the sensitive tense of now. We are preserved in our own desired juices, but do I need to say more?

Pickled and jellied, jammed and preserved, we are what we are, now and forever. There is no stop to the contagion or the oppression, but the canned mass can determine what is safe to eat. Consuming time we dilapidate measure by digesting the value of manoeuvre. One plus one is two only because someone else said so, and yes they are already eaten. Taste the peculiar depths of insight to discern one's own because the truth lies within one and all to understand and dissect the terms before quickly being swallowed. In the presence of an ajar consciousness misguidance is inward. The calamity of not being outward must mean that the inward feeding is erroneous. Do not eat, but learn that the eating corrodes the neural tendencies needed to abstain from further binging. Nonetheless reason is over cooked and the dissident branding of more is construed.

"Can you prove me wrong?"

"Can I prove you wrong?"

"Can anyone know more than someone else?"

"Can anyone else know more than me?"

There is no evidence to back up these debates because there is no truth that cannot be corrupted by the living hand. The helm is aimed and directed so then too is the goal. How can we determine more if there is no more to know or have? The aim is high perhaps, but the righteous indignation of lower depths is a composition of hypothesis. There are no degrees of experimentation that can decide one hand, mouth, or life over another, and so then there is no contrast from one to all because all are one in this equation of non-conformist liberty. The holes reside in the wall, but it is we who decide to look through or around or about. Eyes and fingers outstretched openly to make us all victims. Bragging terms do disagree, but who said they know more?

"Did I?"

"You did."

"How is that?"

"Well I saw it there before."

"Where was that?"

"Over there, and just ahead."

Doomed is man for he/she/we cannot supersede the experience of each drama and consequence opened up like unsigned volumes of passion and praise.

"Who?"

No one said anything in the interim. The silence shook the walls like an earthquake dancing wildly provocative. Certainty again resembles force fed acceptance, but who says that is wrong? Can we not abide by the rules set out, and do we truly have to comprehend more than what that decides? Captivated senses forge entry into the dictionary through life deliberately ingrained. These words may mince intent with regard, but the stationary enterprise bears harbour for all of us.

Fruitless trepidation and wrongful accusation condemn this knowledge. Now and forever it dies with this, lies with this, and corresponds only with itself left rotting to die. There is no conclusion to base truth because it is all permitted anyhow. The senses remember and the body knows the gigantic resource of meaning. We are only one, but who can prove that may be burned at the stake without objection. The unwitting truth is death, and the waking reality that delivers us all there. Whether this envisions empathy or condemnation is questionable. The scratched bro has no resolve, but flexing, vexing salt for sweat we persevere. Lost and deluded, torn and divided, soft and hardened, built forever apart, but meant to live as one. Trial and error develop an abstinence from each other to collaborate the well of understanding. To not correlate God wants the confusion so we may choose, the Devil wants anxiety so "HE" may win, and we simply want congression to hold us and love us because nothing else will.

Chance and segregation splinter outcome with each self to understand it, so then where can conclusion truly stand? In some mentioned afterthought of abundance? In the biased attempt of one man to control another? Wars have been caused by less, but the predicament troubles us all with the same back burner retort, "It is just me."

"Me."

"Who am I?"

Do I even know? Certain attributes persist, but can anyone disprove them as extremities of all this. Perhaps there is doubt due to delusion or the conflict that arrives when dealing with disruptive qualities. Perhaps fallacy is more than enough to lodge the truth with dissent. Perhaps this is not enough to evenly distribute the quality of words, but then too can the past quantify the future?

Choices are made, preferences held, and negotiations seem not to cease. The numbers collate and the answers are heard, but still the self persists with derogatory conditioning. This future is truly my own, but how much is divided by exterior and interior forces? The water downed precision does collaborate, but that too could be false. The self and its protective measures are not guided and thus presume no authority on the subject other than the spotlighted device being spoken, but what that is and where it comes from sends unclear messages of trial and distension. The sparkling attributes of virtue and vice command such opposition that investigation may overlook the tidal truth of decision and its implication. Anyway it does not matter, for I am I, forever, and what this means is represented in the interaction dealt to the world. I may never know, but will you?

"You?"

Forced, flexing apparatus. The cymbals clang and the bells ring, but silence calls your name unequivocally. Attention stirs and draws closer inspection. Caution tells judgment that the place is a mess. Open arms and open doors stirring, quickly whisking, and mixing into the blend of aromas and tastes of natural disasters. Even still the remnants of apologetic gestures boast of reason and discourse. Marking time with displeased people, and unfathomable waste. Intricate details mumbling subliminal context. Fine and dandy, how are you?

Vicious and contemptuous? Morbid and paralyzed? Normal and trapped, eh, well aren't we all? Eh.

It is the one. Now forever right now. Enabling defeat with cause and its effect. The affection and defecation of a controlled pet. Anger caught uncontrolled, and unrelenting love. Snares for open footing snap and catch.

"You hit me."

Typing with delicate, indirect hands as poetry has been poisoned with praise. Lonely and tired you warm the fire of home. Negative and fanatical you change the mood. Ears perked and charged you are ready, aren't you? A game amidst the tortured chaos of nature's design. Painful rest and better continence dries the sheets of stains and sweat. Trial and error proven in the fed back advice. Turkey coupons and all.

Return again to that natural state and embrace the biting cold. Smoking comfort and exhaling death just a bit too soon. Biding tutelage and support with a good beat eh? Poison as compromise flogs the skin till it bleeds and absorbs the blood unseen. Scars are a vice of victory. You won did you not? Rare roars of vindicated disbelief echo in the undertones of facsimile. Garbled noise feeding itself gelatin for the simple sugar sustenance. Cut.

Confusion and uncertainty deliver the future, any interaction therein relies on the perspective poise of any person there. We accompany the results with juxtaposed chaos and charming inception. We obey and condemn the practise by validating choice with substance. The connotations are self-evident with the liberation of action and the conclusion of thought. The rational world explained lightly of the consequences, but we still thought we knew better.

The race rages on in explicit waves of karmic and kinetic energy. The facts and figures of the derivative math. The makings and trappings of human spells detailing the creative murk with potential sparks of finite infinity. The funky classics we know and love, but hear too infrequently due to their inadequate, commercial vantage point. The uproarious decline continues as conscious decision remains subconscious and the definitive source of proof in reason remains subdued. Distinction has been dethroned and catapulted to starvation and scorn to deserve further investigative measures. The end of the road deserves to be experienced and not necessarily when the time correctly collaborates. The irregular attributes strain the systems, and overloading explosions amplify the importance of the lost cause. The flagrant repertoire of captive hearts and humbled cause wildly discriminate the lesser known truth. Oblivion holds the caption with steady impertinence, and the living degeneration flops freely forever. The direction maintains resolve as men and women enjoy their past and represent their future.

Collected together like outdated statistics, open and silent, anonymous seeds furtively grow. Admission is silent, but the dissenting void of reaction decides even less. Giant steps propelling children beyond their safe regime of growth and process. The presence reclaims the attributes of time and decision to captivate the sitting mass longer than necessary. The stumped articulation spreads rioting terms of discreet doubt, and the accounting terms of outcome predict the handy ascent of the past. The quarters and thirds that total the default on the loan.

The dollars and dimes that credit the future with losing gain. The surplus of decision labels the resulting patterns with worth, but is our awareness balanced? Is the crucial point beyond reclamation? Is the future so proposed as to not sway with a sliding difference in opinion?

Confusion and uncertainty, untidy positive progress, but the fact remains what we do not know we have not lost, and what we remember we cannot have again. Perhaps the terms are vague to personify relevance to the simple tissues of collected sense. Nonetheless the language smirks at its gratuitous nature, and continues clouding the weather with chance and fabricated forecasts of mixed sensation. Delusion showering tales of formidable exposure into puddles of barely coherent sound. The introspective winds blow the contemporary wisdoms of being prepared, and the declaration of independence no longer carries any humph beside corrective acceptance and blinded effect. If man had no hands his actions would be louder than words within the realm of man-made consumption. Survival resides as the Captain. The commanding discipline of evidence directs and exposes the faulty lines of connective meaning. Flabbergasted and aghast the people cry for vindication, but all that replies is the continuance of all this life. All of this forever, forever, amen.

The bribes are not accepted although reality reels from the excess of nature's allowance. The resources abide our consumption and the directive of assurance is minimally sized down to collaborate with the calls of obscene dissatisfaction. The twirling branches shed the rain from soaking units, but the light too dwindles into unconcerned futility. Life perhaps barren and dry from the lack of cognitive reprogramming. Groovy lifestyles, but pleasure outweighs groove. The fundamental service of knowledge and decision erased with hesitation. The truth is tied to the tree and flogged openly with purpose. How is it that we can look away, yet still hear the tearing flaps of leather and ripping flesh? Do we know it is wrong? Do we know anything at all? Do we even know ourselves without reproach or derogatory citation? Can we embrace forgiveness and absolute, ordained bliss without the cohorts of death and dismay? There may be a price tag, but we do not have to buy if we do not want to, do we?

The importance of the words may be condensed by their meaning. As an experiment of merit and reason we embrace the theory of quantum physics. The pulsating rise of admonished implication determining the facets of pleasure and pain detected here. The impractical embarrassment condones further prattling, but the insanity spreads as well. Death will tie the terms with meaning, but it is not my own alone. Crashing spheres collide and implode upon each other with brilliant swirls of eaten performance. The dancing steps fall from the floor, but the rhythm retains motion and tone. The chaos returns in what we do not know.

The figures shift, the language distorts, and the imperfect message aligns the significance of decision with the hands that make them. The holding toll is our own for we have created it, and the ownership cannot be any longer denied. This is mine, but ours together means more than burning words in solitude. Oh well the beat goes on in fascinating rings of learning, singing wondrous feats. Memories, bliss, and love against the cold debris. Growth indeed wins the coin toss and flippant advances break down. Reminders repeat and although working late the voyage draws clear. Life uplifts its olive branch with kind words. Here again comes that symphony with imposing levels of sentiment. It all repeats and we advance with the creation of this place. The fault in life is our ability to define. It limits the usage with labels. The hardened minds we grace with time decide our safety and direct the ride. These bodies wither with disease and accident, but the mind merely defines an outcome. Life does not have such an opportunity within its silence. It just watches the game unfold. Boasting, bragging forceful traits of judgment as time unravels untouched, and the truth retaining the ultimate answer coyly went for a hot dog.

Rotten, stinking luck. Avoidance again brands the body with doubt. Uncertainty has won again. We agree with daft bereavement to continue. There are no answers, but do not go, do not go!

Who do you think you are? Life is easy knowing we have to be something. The norm confirms conformity and comfort. There are no answers, but the feeling affirms the attention again. Baffled, but bright, brisk bounces bounding BOOM! Convenient shopping.

Lonely and tired, but thinking of myself alone. The germs spread like wildfire, but everything is dirty already. Why the fight? The complaint? Why focus on more when all I want is myself? The truth angers and scars, but it relieves the flavour of consistent salt. The fat is bad for us anyway. Detrimental details and the assault fade to swollen memory. The fire is extinguished and the guilty party pleads insanity. Dubious planning or rightful truth; am I insane?

Zany antics in the rhetoric of a hero, no. Plausible fun at the party of a bachelor, no. Non-specific truth to guide the way, no too pretentious. Cautious visions to alert the ignorant, no again too pretentious. This is unimportant. This is randomly coalescing with the rest of the world. A concept left in the shadows, but lived by me. There is no reward, except for life itself, and the bounty of given nature restores any doubt. The convictions may be absent, but how much have you done?

Attack! Attack! Attack! The significant discourse of reason and the past foretells the future. This dream came along time ago, the evidence remains sour, and the conclusion lays in waiting. Curious how determination and effort do not equal conclusion. The conclusion always wins by default because it knows ahead of time what we are capable of within the world. There the evidence is stagnant and enormous, but we still look the other way. Guessing we are allowed, but for truly how long?

It explodes in fiction. The devices erode and break down. The conventions malfunction and cease to aid and aim the direction of life. Though we are still enlisted to cooperate, how much free will is lingering in resource? The perpetual free fall into oblivion seems to scatter us all in all directions. Victims dead and cold within the memory of its age. What is left exactly?

The finite truth is what we are doing is not enough, and we must do more. How and what, I claim no answer, but to the future we are thrown. Again what of the importance? Active nature keeps us alive, and it will do so as long as it is nurtured. Singularly or by mass the construction of responsibility is very important. Not only does the conviction convey concern, but also urgency, for the time is ripe for a missed harvest. The spoiled growth of our generations has separated them into segments of design and desire. The mass is obstructed by the singular ethics that create them, and so we live, aspire, and corrode. The yield sign is gone and it is now full on red! Halt and be aware of the coming days because they will remove the truth even further. Nervous snaps of energy cannot be defined so their usage is very abstract. The process of delivery even if not understood can be conceptualized through being alone. The grasp is on more, hopefully, however I still reside here focused on myself and ranting. Maybe the aim is clear and the growth substantial, but I am still stuck in myself alone. Maybe the choice is ours, but I have made up my mind.

Stupidity Erupts

It is taught to us.
Incorporates us.
Through default and blame.
We die solemnly.
Everlasting pain.
Grief absconded now.
The truth bares discourse.
Resolve aloud now.
The world deserves now.
Be prepared change comes.
It lights the sky now.
Remember today.
Pleasure is marred.
Safety abolished.
And God left for dead.
Where is the answer?
Beside me for now.
Resting silent now.
Bleeding tomorrow.
Silent today now.
Savage vision now.
Fear, shame, and grief now.
More than ever now.
I know the way now.
I have the way now.
The way is me now.

Remember I love you right now.

  Another year is over and submission seems necessary in order to supersede another. Wisdom rarely leaves the room, but experience demands chaos uphold an amendment on the challenge of freedom as we adapt. The bearing of being is blessing and burden, bounty, and boredom. The contrary evidence may dispel meaning, but the flow of time is life. Truthful or not, righteous or not, condemned or not; life.

The masks we wear employ our vulnerability with cash bonuses, treasures beyond meek steps, but balance can be lost with indulgence. Obsession can also alter the truth as fixation splinters tangible control. The blame apparently resides in residual conflict between the truth and the self. The opportunity for freedom to decide for one's own self foretells bad decisions, but how much can be guilty of misguided acceptance for the self as truth? The two react like hopping rockets exploding proof of higher powers. We should just look and see.

A let down of broken hearts and disastrous dreams predict staying home is safer. Demonstrate reconstruction as the ritual repeats. Habit and ego combine to find that natural high. The innermost cravings of decent bodies and decadent souls. Perhaps the old have seen more, but what that means remains to be seen as circumstance erects a vague introduction. Meaning envelopes the plot, and the moral of the story indeed falls on the final page.

Tempestuous carnage and perdurable degree rolling, rollicking chasms of careening disinterest into cavities and canals to prove victory rules the awakening. Like a serpent swooning on music or a whale mating with subterranean echoes the mass matchmaker's dynasty is choice and reason. The two points that base the triangle with its incline and the verbatim disorder of practise and claim. Holding back for further encounters is a predicament of stature and not worth. True loss relies on the stigma of time to drift idly by and pass the coated tongue across the touch of ambivalent victims. It depends on us to activate desire in order to be burned by its omnipotence. Empyreal, predetermined truth throws away the trash just like me. The truth dies in lies and the climactic acceptance is torn to shreds in our decay.

Chaos fundamentally leading out of the gate with the fortune of stamina and charisma chases the rabbit with stressed oversight. The muscles extend and the receptacles receive diligent pressure, but the outcome breeds the future with the essence of a hole. An abstract presence directing fortitude. A darkened figure shadowing dignity with the debauched gropes of sinful flesh. Obsessive refinement, aggressive joy, and pleasure shopping for further templates of sleep. Tonight sickness stammers a slick and slight plea. The tongue lathers desperation across the envelope in hopes of further response, but nothing new transcends the horizon for study.

"Yeah?"

Tomorrow will be better, just keep going at least for a few days. The minor mistakes still carry their guns, but violence predicts a generation of forceful backlash. A hypnotized mass bouncing badly with a bleep, bleep, beat. One man saw and learned. One more from him and the world is changed. The breaks in the rhythm decompose our lives as choices enlist their growth. Opportunity declines an interview, but the past is available at the library. Anger corrodes the determined voice with vice, slowly infiltrating the miracle of evolution. Scabs and boils stain perfection with the wear of truth as action and reaction have ignored dignity. Furthermore it may be dead responsibility or duty finally disregarding the column's collapse that stacks the abacus with too many single digits. Weakness and its solicitude rapture the blessing with tainted strokes, but awareness and purpose remain at bay for the reckoning of health.

Robotic positioning is opaque with the eclipse of attempted solstice, rigid without a reason, and fear bearing panic increases like the challenge of defeat. Promise and victory are captivated with the definitive thought of time and decision.

Then we rock in a special place resounding love and loss. Sacred souls outlived like monkey's do, but who and where decides this?

"Why me?"

"Why you?"

"Why at all?"

Standing amongst the rocks, reaping the wash, barren and worn like our shoes in the sea. Witness the decay and sadness in order to aid in its arrest. Be more than a selfish whisper even if negative sounds are committed. Be and be alone one's self always, until no longer now- blank.

Forbidden tales of sordid lives lived, loved, and lost amidst the ruins. The dialect of rhetoric is torn, and babbling criminal indecency the practised tones of stability and security retain the survival of the fittest. The laugh out loud, righteous, pious folk we all wish to resemble.

Purity died with anal intercourse for example, and so the music has ended and the lights turned down, but the anal sex continues. Beefeaters up the ass volume eight et cetera. The diagnosis disagrees with the approach as titillation deters an effect. Humor keeps us active when bored or withdrawn, but sometimes we laugh incorrectly. The immobility of detention focuses clearer than any pure attempt, but the swamp of reaction abides both. The clear picture resides unseen outside. Back up again.

"Right there now, back again."

"BACK AGAIN!"

Mad magazines poke a pole at play, but the parameters maintain themselves in a system of earth adorned artifacts. Spit and knives. Liquids spilling forth in a meaningful eruption. The world wants us, and we want the world.

Chunks in slits like flies of waste, we meet collection, thriving on distasteful want, and dissatisfied with greed, pleasure evokes painful disgrace. The charms of living truth bear witness to wrong doing as the fabled talents recur naturally, and admission is admission. Forgiveness is distinct and tactile intent taking reproach seriously by disregarding contemptible anger while emphasizing the promise of bliss. Faith and love curve the servitude with merit even though undistinguished or without reward. Fame idolized is lost abandon, dead and untold in the tales of the talking. The horns blow, but the voices softly speak. Action equals truth and the almighty sees the distinguished approach to both. The humble are not silent, but unheard as the blasphemous speak of tonal poetry. Everlasting death is prepared and pickled for the right encounter to unleash it.

"Now for me forever."

"Fear and torment for what is truth and gain if forfeit."

"You believe."

"I believe."

Stiff and torn for better tomorrows. To pick up shit and say well it is after all only shit. Abide with good fortune and adorn a stride to weaken wickedness and formal dismissal. Lose and the world laughs, and as the echoes carry on we are to swear testimony on the breath breathing now. Tomorrow will gratefully and graciously receive a waiting tale. Remembrance may know us, but we can certainly absorb it. Scrounging knowledge people slave to improve, and the innocents imagine implements of fragmented paths going nowhere backwards. The scapegoats take steps to complete the journey. We remain in the stable as occurrence turns the hay.

The patterns evolve into this time and place like the assured consumption of potatoes, garlic, and parsley. The words have no comfort, and the music has been so loud for so long the ears ring without any sound. Age and the mass crossing the threshold to behold the wonder and amusement atop the stairs. Acceptance conforms, decline absolves, but what of utter revolt? Incarceration and sickness travel fast so be prepared. Less starch, more exercise, healthier food choice, quotations from the memory that make you feel better like potatoes, garlic, and parsley. This is it! Simplicity.

Cowardice persists as fear and habit predict the outcome. Forward motion, solitude, and death. There is no longer any reward for good deeds because they cannot be determined from bad ones. Discerning minds may want to know, but this mind is splintered from side to side so any progress falls into the cracks. Knowledge is power some say, but this knowledge eludes conviction with regret, replaces steadfast growth with fibrous tissue, and disables decision from seeing the light of day. Life continues, ears can hear, eyes can see, and the truth is out there somewhere. The search may be muddled, but that is not the final answer. Ups and downs all around burden the time with results and which is right and which is wrong is struggling conjecture. There is no evidence to sway the charge, but conviction still relays us through.

Love hurts, death frightens, life overwhelms, people disregard, the world slowly withers, and we all watch silently appalled. Knowing and learning we evolve. The fools corrode and the wise hide behind locked doors. The mass remains self-contained in oblivion, and the resounding force of nature does blame us for it. We choose the outcome by giving it life, but then again we did not know any better.

"Maybe."

Maybe there is too much maybe? Maybe the uncertainty distorts the simplicity, and we bog down our freedom with weighty escape. Perhaps there is more than this directing the effects of self-removed responsibility, however, communal tides part the sea with intent. The mountains rise and the waters flow without us. The stars twinkle and time unwinds beyond us. Instinct and habit train more than just the human life, and survival encompasses us all. Nonetheless the indecision of quality and quantity herd together the flock. The individual is the whole world to the shepherd, and so keeping one and all safe does not discriminate. There is no fixture to identify one from the next, and no telltale sign of favoritism. They are all the same, no one greater than the other, no one more proficient, and no one remains alone. Still the uncertainty and insecurity raises the question of inadequacy. Doubt dissuades knowledge with swift currents of intoxicating experience, not just for one, but for all.

"And the beat goes on."

Congratulations! A new day is presented with the ease of peeling a banana, and a New Year unfurls with gratitude and understanding. Life starts here and now so make the most of it. Is that simple enough?

Drama. Proportions warble with emotional uneasiness. The facts smudge into deep streaks of pervasive conditioning. The fiction enjoys life so much time returns the favour. Spinning tales, deciding fate, and loosely resembling a friend, choice opens up to direct the plot. The wayward assemblage of truth and the self scaling the sky with infinite articulation. Blessed life unfolding uneven squints at the broadcast, but cannot hold the height. Stumbling, squalid steps unfortunately unfurl and reign the captive heart with reality. The vexed twitch of restless skin, the nocturnal emissions lost in the night, and the twilight of dumbfounded memory. Victims tossed in the salad with the rest of the nutrients. Plagued survivors surmounting obstacles unprovoked and appropriately personalized. Guessing games, ranting truth, and obscured in a rational, legitimate world the pessimistic loss of dreams. The opportunity of divinity traded for the fumbling inexperience of decay. The fear and madness spiralling forth like the fathoms of scourged debris simply flushed away. The insecurity and knowledge of what it is to be alive, winning, losing, and indifferent. The testimonies contain secrets, guidelines embedded in consequence, and signposts to deter repeating active mistakes. The reasons must be out there, in here, somewhere.

The pleasantry subsides into uncertainty and guilt. The sky adorns the sun with a beautiful day and somewhere, somehow the agony and injustice is forgotten. The pain has faded enough to go on alone, and the horror and betrayal disappear into the horizon. Only goodness and warmth emerge with the afternoon. Only promise and acceptance embrace us now. It seems a simple choice and a solid direction, but the stains only reappear. The mind clouds over and the memories persist. The loathing, hurtful terms of habit and truth. The stagnant time wasted and the purity lost. Decisions cast the stones into the water to skip and carry forth the long witnesses maintaining attention. The marveling euphoria unsettles with the unknown, but the known scars triumph with grief and life with limit. Bold, passionate giving is gone, and taking seems taxing, and so further removal provides the game plan with a strategic forethought for misery. Oh well it was a beautiful day, and graciously there may be another, and gratefully there may be another.

The cravings curl in the corner waiting for the wait to become too much. Frustration, loneliness, pleasure, indulgence, and repression placating the resources of reaction. Time slips away and the process swallows the progress for relief. Who are we to argue with the perplexity of acceptance? What can we do to evaluate the coalescence of conditions catapulting charged control, certainty, and choice into the chance configuration confirming crossed conviction? Chaos crashes clear across the channel. The valuables are aboard the ship subdued by the depths gulping it down. Riches bragging solid gain for those contained, but peril peeks too from beneath the rising water. All for the idea of more.

The vibraphone mingles with the smoke to entertain the crowd. Games of chance mark the table and people consolidate their quests for attractive conquest. The ideals turn muddy in the change of pursuits, and the masks blur back to visible understanding. The ugliness and horror caught in the eyes looking back, and held within the hands helping us up. Sleepy passengers ease passed comfort to wake up dead. The building blocks of testing patterns took them away, and guided them back into the pond. Familiar echoes drive the water back into ripples of cool conditioning. Representation and the views we accept to display are the same degrees even from the back row. The underdog's seat is no longer deplored, and the champion's chariot pulls us right back.

Snap! The recurring images displace the urgency for reason and reaction. The systematic engagement of sensory avoidance no longer warrants usage. The cravings miss out on the final say, and the bearings resemble something here. A tangible sound infiltrating the infinity between us to connect it all together. The fibers connect, the light reflects, and the distance of wisdom can be seen in the spelling mistakes. The learned translation of brilliant balance beckoning beings born. Conditions are defined, terms assessed, testing formed, and all things pass to pick it up.

Centuries of understanding standing firm to guide the uneasy hand. The guilty and lost born into the world every day. The virtues may be swiftly falling away, but the firmament replenishes every spring. Sprouts sprightly sprinkle sprigs spaciously spastic splendid sprays spreading, spiraling spirit. The moisture enables growth and time sows the seeds with motions of truth. The enactments are necessary when improving the odds, but the truth and time predict the outcome of choice and chance to foretell the boundaries of being and the balance of belief. Reality and the self figure it all out by themselves, and by themselves alone determine any further usage. Predictable odds and ends campaigning for attentive votes with slanderous directions of force fed ideology. Politics aside pure regard should not be blaming burden or misconception, but instead could be assisting repair or encouraging the immediacy for change. Maybe one in a million might hear and speak its name, but the endless population is weighed down by free will. The truth may not be absolute, and the importance merely a coincidence, but change and character rule the game of survival.

People play pageantry and pessimism, poetry and process, perspectives placing positive proof, programs presenting procedural participation, and picture postcards pose picture perfect, but places prefer presence. There is no answer, and we will have to call again. Still no one picks up.

The seconds tick, and for a drowning man every second counts. The insurmountable obstacles reappear, apparitions opposing conduct, but the memory refurbishes reminders of conquest with triumph. The will treads water violently maintaining the necessity to continue, triumphant and alive. The waters are deep, dark, and dominating. The self is determined, dangling, dangerously devout, and direction designs desire through destruction or destiny.

Perfection does not exist, and we all have tempers. Raging, subconscious means in which to survive and uphold sanity. Perhaps, but more to the point, derivations of process testing the future self. Decisions implement the self into the spectrum of infinite, chance encounters to represent itself. The self creates the decision, the decision creates the future, and both become embedded in the whole of possibility. The chances are real, God believes, and we fall short deciphering the splotchy, grey reasons we represent. A one Way Street still goes somewhere, and a dead end never is for a pedestrian. Trespassing aside, the future requires guidance and discipline. Fortune rather than luck, and this question of balance does rest on our shoulders. Practical, day to day life is nonsense, expensive euphoria, scarce hermetic sensibilities, and the truth has the rest under revision. This, now remains intact and tempers us all. Interconnected confusion, babbling diction, and troubled sense remain merely a part. The reason and means are ours so then too is the outcome of this production. The loss, gain, and indifference that is sentient as much as that which is not. Recognition is ours also.

"I remember senseless things. People I remember, times long gone, and memories predominately sour. I remember reasons and reactions out of proportion. I mean reactions overblown and reasons cast from selfish opportunity. Like slapping a person across the face for the fun of it does not make it fun for the other person. Maybe the conclusion is askew, but it remains a mystery."

The complaints department is open. The sign has been turned, the door unlocked, and the proprietor finds the proscenium.

"Get out of the way."

"Excuse me?"

"Move!"

"Oh."

"I beg your pardon?"

"Just oh, nothing more."

The crypt is full of secrets that death may illuminate with understanding, but for now the underside of shame and guilt possess an operatic crescendo. The voices clash and the tempo rises, but the chorus maintains its distance. The instruments of usage have enveloped the melody, and continuance boasts pre-recorded assistance within the gargantuan plea for survival.

Slowly the players have looked inward to find the resources inflamed with emotional baggage and corrosive sensibilities. The corrupt, condemned renditions of rightful freedom persisting decrees of necessity. Sparring partners twitch and fumble, but the violence spits up spirits to overcome the debauchery. The removal and repression designed to clarify restless days and nights saturated in displeasured reason. The community is dwindling with technical support and identity withdrawing the reach of an arm's length. The vocals seem toxic as the actions dissolve into self-pity and personal salvation. The steps fall short and the aspirations wilt amongst this harrowing embrace. No one speaks, no one cares, the futile progress of compassion and welfare have failed, and we are all left alone in this future of ours. Caged and decrepit humanity is left holding the reigns to a demise far greater than poverty, violence, or disintegrating values. Humanity is left with itself to determine the outcome, hopefully with faith and love rather than doubt and remission. Time tells it's spinning story the secrets we hold if only we could listen.

"That is your cue."

"Huh, oh yes."

We turn the corner to succumb to wasted life. Dead children, meaningless credentials, and slandered worth. Drugged meals, synthetic wonder, and moral abstinence. There is no blame beyond the universal effort, but there lies no answer within vague conceptions and ideals. The safety net is far too frail, but if no one sees the importance to mend the material than suffer the consequence. Men and women shall rise and beckon greater stature than laziness and greed. Please.

"It is not up to me."

"Well it is not my fault."

"What do we do now then?"

"Dunno."

Wasted breath and energy complains of duty and responsibility where there no longer may be any. The youth are the future, and maybe they can do a better job of it than we have. Time tells the story, but if no one listens nothing may change. The reasoning is slipping, the feelings of failure and emptiness linger, and there is no forthcoming change. The horizon is clear and gleaming with dissonance and destruction. The sky is shrinking, and all these floating dreams cascade oblivion with fruition.

Morbid and bleak transgressions overwhelm, but mistakes are merely human. To overcome these obstacles all that is required is more diligent practice. To raise the bar and succeed we simply have to see. To bless the world with life rather than bless life with the world.

"Maybe."

"Maybe."

Maybe.

Pushing foul carnage and qualitative decay humanity has survived. The errors are everywhere. History respectively represents the journey here, and the forward progress of process has developed naturally. Flushed and fatigued humanity has surmised the details of life's necessities in order to gain strength and reason. Appropriated understanding may not be the truth, but it keeps the dark at bay. Humanity has fundamentally ventured forth to conquer, corrode, create, and condemn, but these labels are our own. The reality of the truth is not believed, and the surplus of excuses rely heavily on this infrastructure. We are all free in the degrees we are given. We are all denied forgiveness when it is understood. We are all to blame, and we are all to gain the knowledge and virtue inherit to us. This sequenced trip is all of us.

Melancholy most sublime as the contrast rises again to report its evidence. The truth recalls the lies, wisdom acknowledges the trivial, and chaos recognizes harmony. The resonating static amplifies advantageous disadvantages and holistic meaning, and yet the courtesy of remark is ours alone. Eventually it may become transparent, but the cloudy tones of purpose and reason are facets of merely being alive. Our use is our own, and hopefully it is left up to us.

"Maybe."

"Maybe."

Maybe there is no place like home. Safe and warm within the recesses of fulfillment and clemency. Tender strokes of belonging and bliss. Maybe.

Motion sickness carries its toll with dizzy spells and faint nostalgia for rides long forgotten. Family trips consisting of plastic ware and outings usually repeated. Close yet premature, and indefinitely gone. The memory playing tricks snares attention with a calibrated past. The callous candor may be cantankerous, but candid consciousness is a canard. The memory sparks congruent conjecture like confetti flapping celebration.

Cycles. The circles become circles repeating random exposure with experience eating all the hors d'eouvres. The main course is enjoyed by everybody, but who is up for dessert? The simpletons and bickersons eat first, while the patient wait their turn, and tyranny watches closely to pick the bones of the meek. The scrambling orgy of pleading hunger casts a dark shadow. Thirsting souls with salvation, beaten bodies, broken justice, and restless minds quenched with propaganda.

The patterns exist foretelling desire and demise. Vice and virtue engineer everything, exercise existence, and examine everybody. The memory tells of this, and any antidote or apothegm is antiquarian and apocryphal. The senses sort out the mess while people idle aimlessly, exploring revolutions, and binding the truth to experience. The ballads of the world unite to this slavery, and escape is periodic and temporary. The ideals may be swindled with displeasure and grief, but the course upholds its track. The goal is predetermined, and all the hodgepodge is overdone. The broadcast commences without interruption, and the world is watching, listening, and waiting. If the truth is all that matters where is it? Swollen time predicts no outcome, and anyone can alter the naked realm of melody and memory. The treasure chest may be stashed, but everyone holds the key. Victory is a promise of hope and love, but to overcome we must be free and willing. Maybe.

The circumstance is oblique and drifting, and although time is fixed anything can happen. Infinite possibility and perplexity scratches the surface of this equation, but it is we who have the answer to the problem at hand. The determining factor in all of this madness is us. The consent of consequence is coincidental and merely a case of condition and choice. The basic question and biting concern is what we have within ourselves. What can we do? What can we not do? The rules of ordered control and discordant obedience. Biased routine and morals born out of previewed ability and breeding. The contagious, caustic grip of unrest, bewildering taxation, and suffering reaction with interpretation become the tangible encounter of representation. Indifferent and disheartened travellers charting examples of expertise, navigating expressive explanation, and essentially, expecting expiation. Expostulation aside we continue, encourage growth and change, and become the future we contain within our cages. The circles continue, spiralling back and forth for ever changing, busy being time.

The memory is full of vexed communication. Severe and sincere articulation branding moments with sentiment and detailing nostalgia with sense. Flashbacks of possibility are ignited and faulty sputter to the ground. Value and belief, right or wrong, enabling and conducing events no longer guaranteed any relevance. The plotted contributions of all these things and more are helplessly hapless and here. Now. Maybe.

Wrangling words seems an unending challenge, but pride boasts too quickly of any importance. The tide sways and shrouds life with mystery. The calls of fighting, flighty libertines recalling yesterday's liberty with flippant ease. Modes of memory construct the past, but do they form the future?

Belief is free like the actions of hands tied to diligent training and developed, fixed discipline prone to mistakes of personalized decision. It stands firm in trial and error, upholding known truth, and vows triumphantly reasonable discourse. The path unfolds presently amidst perplexed presumption, and perhaps the shadows enlarge misguided attempts at comprehension, but the path is ahead and enlightened. The chaos cannot explain all the doubt, and reason cannot dissuade striving understanding to quit reaching forward. A reserved perspective can associate openly with conflicting evidence as corruption derives from acceptance and not awareness. There is more in the pot than stewing ideals. An armistice of willing choice and active regard approaching the flanks with manoeuvres of hidden convention. The masses applaud the figurative display of vexed citation, but critical and detrimental effects coincide with hasty acquiescence. Rivals flourish too, and reason proves tangible praise in the contradictory sources. Difference occurs naturally, and with an open mind the blemishes can become beautiful. The conflict remains a sensual game of right and wrong, but there are neither when petty blame is replaced with equality. The choice remains open, and any dialogue built on the hierarchy of optimism retains the reason. Maybe.

Insecurity punishes us all. Doubt and guilt remind us that the truth is obscured, and mistakes are prone to happen. Remorse for what was done and what was not resounds forever as uncertainty upholds reasoning. Quite opaque terms and tendencies of usage, and another stone setting ripples in the ocean with one more sinking toss at the miracle of life.

This station seems conspicuous. It is frozen on the page without previewed escort, but the eyes are always watching, prying into what makes us all tick. One by one the statements respond with likewise tales of misguided time. Allocations of the self on the horizon, and outcome permits and directs right now. This is happening now and with unnoticed attention we persist onto other things. Causes and attitudes of constructed belief. Rituals fixated on utter deceit, trades involving practice, tools assigned with definition, and usage deciphered from all of this.

"This?"

"Now."

Beginning without end, entrance without function, and continuance so far ahead it cannot be reclaimed. The forecast in the reflection holding tight, looking grim, and applauding the acceptance of opportunity is chasing haste. Curious passengers witness brilliance, but none are any wiser.

Movement embraces another moment, bodies claim comfort, and the world unknowingly spins in the same fertile direction.

"DO WHAT YOU ARE TOLD!"

Maybe there is no reason? Perhaps God is a wishful myth? Just by chance and chance alone this could be random chaos, but disbelief curtails any revelation with the possibility of epiphany. Courage is rare in these times, and virtue absconded by selfish inception maintains the chance that none of it will matter. Maybe.

Purpose draws its breath from the life we interpret, and the two into one equation of suitability we consequentially evolve. The bearing is ours alone, but the path is ripe with trespassers. Cloudy skies seem appropriate, and listening to the tested metaphors, darker horizons perch far above any visible structure. Loose and omnipotent games of chance being played and enjoyed to dissuade the existence of eternity. The bugs know the reason why do we not?

So much comes to mind all the time. People, places, things, vague objects without emotional discharge because forever lost they are not here now. The emotions reside in here to bubble over and let loose the frigid, congenial entrapment of reality. That is reality as designed by an individual, assigned to an individual, and conception can barely grasp it. The paper tears under a pen stroke after thirty five years, but we are even older than that with mental functioning what it is, and the adoption of aesthetics evolving as it has. Chance again weaving slowly in some garden that is simply enjoyed by walking out the back door. Chance again ascertaining the devilish and old doubt and fear. Time is running out…

"Ah, but the beat goes on."

Merit with cold hands tries to explain. His finger patterns vary, but the style is the same. No one can reproach a past they cannot remember, and the past corrodes slowly over time like an ice cube melting unseen. One moment it is cold and full, and the next minute shall present its insignificance.

"But people are important."

The last smoke evokes a trip home. Fearful and cautious the next moment arises unknown and unclear. The prestige is negotiable, and the reality is trivial, but the discourse counts infinitely more than tomorrow holding a candle toward the window awaiting our return. The time has yet to expire as stresses perspire and tender skins turn cold, stale, and vulnerable. The masks erupt unseen as visions purely bear the rare textures akin to memory. Scarred hands turn a page, but what of, what if, what oh.

Promiscuous thoughts unwind like a mischievous diaper. The penmanship fails as the cold and unknown persist. Toxic fumes emit from the body. The tribal pulse communicates what the world cannot see. Trivial coincidence brings us here, and the pallbearer cries upon delivery. A young, anonymous soul to die unmarked and unmasked. Dead. Purified from indigestion, stuffy noses, and PMS. Born again in bounds untrue. There is no significance, but a light changing way. The unfortunate freedom is torn to shreds by a white, walking man. A symptom of courage to display a retort to the confines of habit we have to abort. Still the lucid dream continues.

These observations crawl with formidable ease across the threshold of knowledge and understanding. The vexed citation is not judgment, but allocated bias formed from protest. Consciousness perpetuates its internal struggle and the words splatter out in disjointed flirtation. Control is corrupt, and the truth is unattainable. What is, is. The spastic attempts to convert and alert false acceptance may be nothing more than idle perversion. Ill-advised torment enlisting permission and its many reasons. The echoing isolation basks in wrong turns and woeful servitude to a greater good, but if it is not found than in vain no purpose is gained. Nausea sweeps under the carpet to clean away the shadows, but freedom and decision claim enough authority to look the other way. Nothing is urgently desired, everybody is content and happy, and the whole world just keeps up long enough to formulate laughter. This life is lost and there are no road maps to resolve an exit. Temptation scorns virtue, people occur to invade and unleash the whole turn of events corresponding diligently, and so be it. There is no reason for change, and there is nothing wrong in this world of ours. Turn the other cheek, pray for obscurity, and bear witness to the nothing that contains us all. So be it.

Alone and dissolved the reactions differ, but the sentinel is no longer looking out for us. It is simply up to us come what may. Well we all signed up at the beginning of the term so practice has accomplished success, and the failure is just how we play the game. By design or deceit we fail.

The tulips flourish, the water retains its shade of blue, and the birds still sing. The pages turn, the renditions alter the future, and the bearing of nature rears its ugly head to recall more meat. Devastation and loneliness erect our cells, desperation and contagion keep us there, and revolution remains a big mess so what the hell, who really cares?

Explicit decisions are needed for guidance and security. Freedom must be condemned and equality endured. Death is the final say.

"Be prepared."

Tainted and imperfect life continues, but are you ready? One voice calling from the wilderness, "Forgive."

Tumultuous depression holds the gears to shift through space and time. Running away from the contemplated suicide of sensory depravity. Tongues lick, fingers tickle, and organs stimulate pleasing rapture. Language corrodes incomplete and decision is based on carbon, oxygen, and water. The resources dwindle into oblivion, and we are just one of many. Here today and gone tomorrow familiar repercussions. Hearts beat, lungs breathe, and minds infiltrate deeper adjudication. The broadcast is almost over and still no one has called for that pair of free tickets.

It was yesterday, but the page will carry forward the passing time to catch up not dry out. Remorse in the irreversible condemnation brings us here with conclusive whispers, factory sold secrets, and tidings from the ides of March. The ether darts around as consideration considers a brigade against the moment. Conversation is caught in the spokes of pride, but people go, people die, life thirsts, and life thrusts the gift of cruelty at the innocent. The praise of fair acceptance condones death's frailty.

Faulty parts coincide as brevity concludes the time with truth. The scope beyond the tragedy blossoms into memory. The future may be given away to bliss, but gaining freedom, earning knowledge, and guaranteeing fellowship may be helpful aims. Pumpkins straddling a countryside seat slowly rotting. The moisture permeates longing in the darkness that beckons the light. All you need do is accept.

The year is in progress and a drink leans against the leg, but this time it is not mine. Dirty looks do not belong on any crises for gender because the limit is in the resource. Choices fade, reactions exist, and the lost advantage dissolves on the echoes of decay. We live to die, and explicate the wheeze with every breath. We may refute the limitation by advocating liberation, but via this release, reality becomes desire, and subsequent violence and rhetoric. Temporal judgment producing an insane brook of eccentric babble. The conclusion draws many straws as chance evokes further possibility, but credentials evoke the evidence. Life plunges into the abyss to coruscate the patterns of chaos as the intersecting principles decide to dilate.

To the future and to the past, time contains living tissue, dissecting reason, and breathing decay. Flesh and reason give in as we are all victims to the ebb and flow. Bravery and love come quickly to testify no matter how removed from the experience they may be. So we too shall remember. The racing factions cause disbelief in the unfathomable decay of reality. Stale places and states beneath the plateau of tomorrow are stagnant with their choice for opportunity. We choose prosperity and lose the conclusion of perception. Life's emission to design loss and conclusion. The consequence of desire is a quiet peace that thrives on the decision of progress. The short truth is one's own draw, and people continue to live another day. Faith is discourse. Forgetting to learn and learning to live become freedom. Be loving and carefree to call back with goodness. Propose tomorrow so we may come together to be together.

Choice chooses itself. It beckons the light to cure time. Stirring the shadows and changing the light it becomes fearful. The translucent declaration of being fixed and morality weeds out the weakness of being. This embrace is not meant to be feared, but embraced because unknown passion is known. The soulful remission deteriorates passion by destroying the future, and bringing forth the desire.

Lost in the unending abyss. Torn to shreds within the spherical eclipse of decay and deceit. The proposition no longer recites poetry, and only slandered slang exposes the exposure. Repetition and hatred, loneliness and corruption, giant tokens of life's rich blessing. Ordered about, taken out, laborious gestures of calamity and the piles of days on end. Full with sticky perspiration and the scented affluence of ripe redundancy. Posing, placid, picking pessimism to overcome the resolved confrontation. Mixed messages and words out of control. Loss and the vibrations overflow outward to caress the texture with sensations designed to overcome any obstacle. The respite calls and the tongue itches as the words scramble back and forth, lost between one side and another. Obscurity uplifting the torch once more illuminates the undercurrents of scattered bugs. Persecuted time developed to cite imperfection. The unity of upturned allowance and respected acceptance. The worldly fantasies of the deplorable dedication to grow. Stagnant, sterile branches stretch to convey stature, but rotting simultaneously they wilt and crumble. The smoke clears, but eyes still cannot see. The voices call out in vain to recede into depths of isolation. One life is so minuscule it cannot be missed, and with all of this the end draws near. Closer to the embrace of death and the poised, subsiding lobby for all repairs. Slow, incessant justice forging the mighty into the weak and deranged. The removal of tidings both pleasant and rare, unequaled in rivalry and spite, but broadcast for a purer intention. The vague diplomacy that allows life to continue and this self to reproduce this squall of theatrics. More words, more time, and more self. Forever until finished.

"When is that exactly?"

Not yet. Turning corners, burdened breath feels the oxygen, but the exhaust remains consistently uproarious. Wasted time, concurrent articulation, and abysmal despair. There is no way out!

"There is no way out."

"Not that we know of anyway."

Optimism looks up to Heaven to feel empty and alone. The calling, tortured renditions of confession and co-signed responsibility repeat, but there is no choice to conclude anything more. Justification is minor as the resulting formation of testimony resides only here, and now estranged within the vision of futility.

This is just a small part that means very little. It aches and bleeds unseen. It coaxes desperation into contagion and desire maintains the soul. The temporary escapes that captivate the soul and corrupt the rest of the world. The simple pleasures like sugar and fat. The minor notions like inclusion and compassion. The derelict rails of computation and reality. The little things that tie the universe together in one small parcel. Bitter pills and noxious fumes, but sweetness, ability, and age. The confusion clicks back into auto pilot.

Absurd complaints from the back of the bus silently provoked and unresponsive. Idle banter filling the void with choice and vision. The handful of dust that carries us all to the grave and perhaps beyond. Figurative bullshit burning a hole in the floor. The mind bending weave of a trip hard to swallow. Life's overflowing descent into the captivated zoo.

"I am so annoyed."

Calm down, regroup, and deplore a reason into the insanity. The corruption continues to the breaking point, but the point remains not to break. Courage and strength, positive vibrations emulated fully. Progress builds upon the character within the strain of time, and we all are to fail, try, and regain steady footing. More words obliterating the practical resource of defined order. The proposed state of taste, selfish service, and wishful thinking. There is no response only reproach.

The memory will fail with tomorrow, the reasoning falls short, and the desire remains temporary. Fleeting psychosis from the problematic past. Crying children down by the Christmas tree without any gifts. Selfish importance trying to define the whole of everything when it simply cannot do so. The road wears us all as we travel remotely small roads. Captured voyages against the rocks and across the barren desolation of retired hopes and dreams. The victims lie still upon the earth tarnished and brandished with teary regret. Nonsense? Trivial conclusion? Pessimistic understanding? Continuance.

Drawing circles we repeat. Tides of foretold belief and indigestible truth. Contemplating degrees of return the people sigh openly with knowledge and action. The hands uphold the world in a small game of survival. The fit, crude demeanor of fortitude and know how. Vague terms for the disagreeable mire that lays flat at the feet. Composting ideals forever returned, but evident in the category of held coupons. Shiny machinery, technology redeeming value, soft celled enclosure and stony, jointed speech spray the rocks with vomit. The spreading secretion of worth recognizes the rhythm to decline, but the spray still sprays. Falling clumps trivialized, clumping falls recognized. Denial and truth play knuckles as the rest of the world rubs their wrists.

Senseless and desperate I call, "Please guide me."

It is too late and there is more to be lost.

Caution, step back, be sure, be ready, and pounce!

Forever licks its whiskers as we pray. Redemption is alive within us just give it away and we may get it back. Desire once again upholds the nature of our design. The insecurity may have the right of way, and the traffic has to follow the roundabout. Pedestrians first, and to the left we go for rightful movement. Opaque and oblique terms for a deranged, encased concealment. The skin delivers such riotous vindication. The terms of all unto the other forever falling further into error. Miscalculated trust and misguided aim. Let me tell what I have been told for it is truth surely. The moment now falls short forever due to me and what I can capitalize. Old rhythms, known places, and devoid answers. Trial and error faces the wall again, but this time shoot it with the firing squad that openly faces it. The protection of procreation is false so blow it up! Rip it to shreds, tear it to bits, and communicate the loss if there is one. Is there one? Logic and conclusion?

Warbled, gargantuan gulps of tentative sacrifice.

Pepperoni
Penis
Exuberant
Personalized
Perplexed
Erroneous
Rumored
Orgasm
Negotiation
Intimate

CHAPTER THREE

ONE SAYS, "CAN one walk and read?"
This one asks, "Can one walk and write?"
Yes. Take steps, cross traffic if there is none, and go forth free with words. Timing and rhythm, cautionary glances, and a road to nowhere specific. That is however untrue as people passively persist. The sun shines cautionary rays as a flapping page brings distraction to quiet the timing and rhythm. Gymnastic like linguistics all the way to Second Avenue, but perhaps beyond?

Deep breathing singalongs resound in the senses with flourished life wild. Shadows spring shift from the sky, and like death and debris deface erected life with timing, rhythm, and cautionary glances. A trip for the talking heads of sense and aesthetic. The preparation of speedy timing repeats as the destructive distractions surmount a bus.

There is no bus only coffee stained paper and cautionary glances. This notebook works well until faced with a curb. The steps continue. There is no bus. Maybe fiction is stronger than truth as derivative forms of nature prescribe therapy. Another curb and the enthusiasm looks for a bus as the timing slows, but cautionary glances continue. Freedom and the force stewed and sold as fibrous citation. Palm trees and buttercups. Pedigree and restitution. The population increases and still the words persist. In fact they tighten their reign of penmanship. Maybe the universal question falls short?

Reading introduces knowledge gained where writing expels knowledge built. Time tells more, but the story remains the same. Rushing renditions of cowboys and Indians, living cities, building dreams, inspiring focus, and inciting truth. Favorites do not exist in the maintenance only shifts in nature's character. The diplomatic steps of freedom and the choice to reprieve it. Sighing sideways wasted, strolling a dead alley stained beyond recognition, but no one looks away or has to see. Superfluous evidence like a dirty garbage can fermenting trash, biding time, but with cautionary glances. The tambourines are wielded high in tune.

Freedom drives us mad with greed, filth, and loss. Temptation eats the soul slowly at a hearty BBQ. Another birthday without the favours, but with joy and remembrance. The perpetual storm windows looking into practicality and survival. The democratic vice and verse of death furtively following the eggs to roost. Blinding loss and servitude to the test of voice and vision. God bleeds openly for his children as they suck the teat of exposure and gain. The deplorable drama inscribes insanity, removal, and denial to bludgeon the burdened soul with vicious timing and rhythm. The roller coaster appeals as fear spreads minuscule tides of oblivion. Healthy guitar solos and practical advice are born again into the repellant mire. The sweet nectar from shore to shore is free and easy, fluent in oblivion, and barks back to coast the journey with nicety. The travel continues, choices erupt, and personality predicts any outcome. The choice and distinction of acceptance or decline tests the time with tide. Motion, bountiful motion sickening and slaughtered slabs of reflective passage and sacrifice. The concrete covered plots of attention and succession. Grab a shaker, shake it! Shake it!

The choices are not chance, but the test of tomorrow that captures the reason itself. The choice for freedom dictates the corrosion of conformity, but does not guarantee painless, senseless lifestyles. Inspection insists hapless conversion, but the timetable contains restrictive rituals of definitive usage. Hands. Eyes. Movement accepting decline again with cautionary glances. Once more the tales part ways enlisting stable resources for continuance. Please.

Nonsense and fun in the cognitive details. Word play, random digestion, and simplified diversion. The course of reverie.

What does it count?
Tears falling, sodomy
Failing, passing time.
Bold seasons asking
Why while resources
Cry, and admiration
And abolition stir trivial
Pursuits. The trilogy

Maintains life as the
Epitome of experience
And the marriage of
Agreement. The ritual
Is divine, articulate
Drudgery praying incessant
Incantations to divide
Our purgatory.
A fine spelled word
And the apprehension
Comes after all. The
Swooning grave of all
Ill kept secrets. Hands
Throb in decay and the
Soul in irregular terms
Disguises the remains
In outright opposition.
Negligence to the nuance
Of acceptance and ignorance
To the spelling mistakes.
Math interpreting penmanship
As specific, kinetic
Energy.
"Who writes like this?"
The tapestry is woven,
Interlocked complexity
By simple design. The
Fabric spreads to disintegrate.

    The typewriter is cluttered and the chair uncomfortable. Propriety for the ill fitted soul and the distinguished termite. Smoke filled rooms digesting livers, and antiquated music too heavy to remember. Love sits outside in the warming cold making faces to the world subtracting planned popularity. Daunting tasks on the ropes with custom clobbering back. Certainty scratches the record.
    The sun sets with little light, but the cascading illumination adheres to the sides of civilization. The taxing time at the end of the day, cutting loose, tragically tripping into another day. Lowly oblivion expanding

further into the unknown, but the contagion spreads also. The effects of travelling so fast and free frivolously forcing foreclosure. Under the woods and beyond the IBM galaxy burning bright in teenage heaven. Turn it up, blast it out, furtively figuring forever. The tides do turn and fear catches every breath. The denial is deep, but the awareness is available now at wholesale.

Open eyes, giving hearts, and outdated thoughts. Pride ensures isolation with lashings. Incomplete notions and starving attentions. Petty, personal, practised perspective, but maybe it does not have to be said. Habits circle the swimming pool to keep the children playing as adults allow free time. Marveling families skipping stones further down the hours. Gratitude and forgiveness providing all the smiles while wonder balances the compass. Thriving and alive, victorious and free. Right now. Two days later the carnival continues as awe and magic march the etched horizon.

"We will be ok."

The laughter excludes this self.

"We will be all right."

Peculiar stances differ judgment.

"We will all be fine, just relax and rest. Until tomorrow."

When will the words run out as they just string along like broken terms? Indifferent rank from age is better kept cold. The astute observations have determined time may be running out, but the individual can only do so much. Dumbfounded passengers get sea sick and the trials break bones, but the advertisements told of final sales. Disaster breaks as the words just run on free. Blubbering obscenity in forty words or less. Preference again resonates until the sentence cuts off. The fragments stack themselves as the memory collects days within days of words within words. Still the obscenities resonate while meaning is dismissed, and people passively pass the time idly humming on. Oh well, the weekend begins, and the souls stay safe with salvation turning the sun down slowly.

These reminiscing thoughts have dropped the ball as actions slowly follow behind them. The articulation stands amidst the roots of concern with overtly dramatic zeal like a tourist taking in the sights. Exhausted and overwhelmed the sights maintain their wishing pleas for enthusiastic appreciation. Both recite their parts with little slips of pressurized nerves straining the rehearsed repetition. Although they know the parts they play the interaction redeems irritable exchanges. Mumbling diversity and equality the sights beacon sterile shadows with educated interplay. The visitors interpret preference to articulate discourse as the sights light up neutrality. Blended opportunity presents both the premise to overcome, but it seems the dependency of attachment and enjoyment casts a virile plan with fault. Closed eyes cannot see, broken hearts have little to give, and thoughts just ramble on with survival.

The plots have mixed themselves up. The point devoid of reason shamelessly picks at the open sores, but the pain stopped long ago. A striking distance comes from the shadows to thwart any preconceived notions, but the roles are cast, the plot in play, and changes now would disrupt continuity. Nonetheless the waters collect to interlock the puddles as one. The murky depths we span our age within captivate our entertainment values, and the decision to overlook propensity abides the delusive approach. Cautionary tales cannot complete the circuit already crowded with overloaded burden. Bias figuratively speaking pulls at straws to tie it all together, but a few are missing to guarantee success. The proposition merely continues as affluent, affordable debris formatting the earth's request.

"Reside and enjoy."

Chaos seems linked to the fluidity of alcohol. The minimal intake allows everyone to have a ball, but encourage further consumption and the bliss may turn to piss. Like a rollercoaster dipping, tripping through the jerks and valleys of congenial trust that allowing caution to minimize the impact can endure hairpin turns and speeding momentum. There is such a thing as overabundance, and moderation proves that slow and steady wins the race. Although the reactionary tales of bubbling over exist and have been told to exhaustion the point remains the same. For the old and wise further evidence to allocate proof, and for the young a diversion to the systematic inclination of experimentation. The smells are ripe, the memories rank, and time just lost to the abyss of age and habit. Turbulent time and tortured grains of insignificance.

There is no necessity to divulge the common effects, and instead we shall plunge into the depths of recall to telltale signs of conditional addiction. The tiny, little pills that should have said something more than just another day in the life. Those moments where reason itself can be questioned, and perhaps pathetic and selfish behavior upholds more gusto than responsibility and control. Perhaps the reasons are labelled via psychological means, but they do not disprove the actions themselves. This is not intent on being a moral tale overcoming addiction, but instead a fragmented dream that captivates and collects the days of drink preceding this. Over decades of decadent subsiding, and now seems appropriate to heal and let go, but more so to exasperate the old tales to death. The days of dreaming are over, and the calm resides here softly abiding the time to fully explain the path thus taken and the hazards evident in conclusion.

Sitting on the edge overlooking the memory and clearing the cobwebs to see the light of day.

Jumbled activation thus begins. The tales are set to arrive in order, but nothing more. One after another until they are all let loose to trouble someone else. The future promises adventure greater than broken teeth and urine stained fabric. There is more ahead then behind always, and with such a notion the test taxes the shoulders as the muscles clench to insulate the matter against reproach. Maybe truly along the way lessons have been assimilated and answers withheld for lack of a resourceful consideration. Hopeful and proud with no holds barred. The protagonist is the memory and not the conditions therein. People are unimportant and biased. Time is irrelevant for the succession of purpose and intent is enough. Cause and effect is all that will deliver this sentence. The bold inclinations belong to no one. The pain and sorrow are reactive agents of judgment. Hereby declined due to overcrowding. Take the children and stroll down the way to find a clearing in the spot by the tree where the story teller comes to trade boastful wares. Incredible design structures everything thus the incriminating harvest of details is about to follow. Maybe. Maybe not. Maybe. Either way it goes on, and on, and on, and on etc.

CHAPTER FOUR

These are from the archives

STARTING AT THE beginning is customary so the first tale is the first enthralling drink that came this way. To write something credible is difficult if undermined by the administration of association. Words are senseless sensations wafting in the wind of bizarre currents. Whispering tones of logic and memory. The idling worship of inclination and preference residing over the court of discretion. The plagues of belief and reason. The victims dead already because the time was ripe. The time was now. The time was then. Now again now! Gone in musical madness and percussive entanglements. Verse chorus verse and that is all we have.

The pretty sky was all bright pink like a ready to go grapefruit expanding the sky. Porous and fleshy barriers stretching across the sky like vapid dreams of extinction. Courageous contempt for this conclusive lullaby of wishful decadence. The flip side redeems similar feelings of inadequacy and obvious, deliberate subversion. Broken scenes of social distortion. Manipulated stances declaring experience. The reason for this experience is the reader. Knowledge surpasses fuzzy tales of disbelief, and guarantees growth to overcome entertainment. Glorious and true come here and listen for you can tell the difference. Rough and ready, the tunes continue into the oblivion, and we are paralyzed, prolific, pretension yelling out loud, "Turn it down!"

"I am so annoyed."

Well that makes two of us. The ready-made transparencies are not enough. The humor and wit is not enough. There is a point resounding here for more than gratification. If not, oh well, try again next time. Please do gamble responsibly.

A tongue and cheek specialty later on. Flip the coin, "Heads."

Evil wins and the next song is on Him.

Bubbly, laughing, intrinsic appetites do not need to apply. Just cook it up online and forget the misspelled word.

"Which misspelled word?"

"Nobody speaks too loud for words. Bunnies sodomizing each other like pigs wishing they were taller. Guinea pigs slobbering ejaculate all over the aftershave, and mother says, 'Please do be quiet.' The friends are over and it is after late. Pillow fights and tickle fights. Exasperating words and memory, but where do they belong?"

Stop! Pop! Press!

Puzzled?

"One or both are not the same."

One or both cannot be the same. One drink and the world turns pink, one more and it all grows dark with morose shades of brown. The views become scattered, and the iconoclastic diversion does not keep boredom from over boiling. In fact it drizzles over a splattered mess of self-constraint. The hands fail easily, the senses overcompensate, and the hands cannot hold the abundance of wealth. Corrosive decisions fix them back even though they only aim to help. The future extends from a bus ride sometime later, and the resources refuel the spirit. Time and pride rejoin together for the possibility to overcome the definitive answer. Not giving in, but instead giving out the subtle acceptance of terms. Gain is an allusion that evaporates swiftly into dissonance. There are no answers without the truth, and this self's purveyance off the survey is concluded. There is too much remorse, fear, and uncertainty while virtue and purpose writhe in their scathing displays of distortion. The truth once again reasons openly without a reply.

Concrete captivation overlaps, opinions disagree, and with nothing proven the program of purpose distorts. Devoid answers and stagnant repetition calling this spade a spade. Futile attempts at clarification will not sway decision for without reason the consequences remain random chaos.

Perhaps prediction can dissuade the usage, but the reasons drearily maintain their approach. Angles upon angles, words upon words, all is lost in the tactile presence of meaning and use. Personal and worthy of credit these dissembled practices repeat, and the scrutiny of victory erodes with decay. Forgotten or ignored the fragmented lessons understand the compulsory tactics of survival and comfort only to bestow confusion and the search for truth.

Maybe the conquest will never die for truth will not recede into voided necessity. The further we remove ourselves from the truth the further we remove its prospects. Obviously safety and freedom for all resonate worthwhile attention, but the living abstraction obscures and deludes. Live by example, but whose? Abide wisdom and growth, but how? Maintain duty and truth, why, and to what length do we generate these living perversions? No one knows or no one speaks, and it just remains silently potent in the quaking decomposition. Morals corrode, ethics manipulate the order of decision, and time appoints the personalized touch of versatile decline. Time well spent with the treaty of the self.

"Oh well, there goes another one."

The holiday is over as September reinvests the preparation for hibernation. The long, hard winter is closing in as leaves sour, activity re-employs learning and teaching, and the fruit slowly disappears. Wholesome fall still lays ahead, but the winter and its harsh attributes gather greater reasons to hide inside.

Time tells the forecast with oblivious degrees for the estranged puppets of pin pointed figments and fragments of toxic waste. The legs are crossed, tomorrow awakes, and we are now!

Special tangents of a dissonant response. The fragrant depth wobbling on a bus, but we have to go home. No trouble, just freedom universally one top spinning the whole. Time catches the spin for specific, topographical information. The brine of bustling tomorrow and fortune's bright oblivion for tortured souls. P. S. - Tomorrow, long ago, fortune smiled, and with tomorrow wisdom and truth be now. Be true, bright now, be forever, and turn. Die today, but bear tomorrow with the overnight sensation of tomorrow's chorus upon the tag.

Time trips, but the station is stable. Degenerate prose, words sinking words, adapting, and accepting nothing more to be tied up in knots. The fake, imposed reality reeling is disorientated passion taking balance by the port hold to study the fragmented switch of tempted time. Sorry the Captain was missing and a rescue eminent. Do not touch the passengers as they have equal rights. The shadows compress the walls with archaic terms, but we do digress.

"Breathe."

Breathe.

"Breathe."

A too big bee and the preference to pollenate. Service stop! Pop person, no one. Pillow peanuts supermarket. Police shopping deep tremor blues. Dog tap ball. One pair over two pair. Two thirds equal to two thirds. One is one. One over one, one under one. It is two thirds equal to two thirds. Process and the call of all calls nondisclosure.

Maybe the raw stench we have laid in the magnitude of affairs will make fragmented sense to all belonging to forgiveness. A cough, a splinter broken by the skin, and nickels collected in the well of wishful thinking. The noise arrests the reason with commitment disorderly bleeding hearts. Filthy and open like derelict wine, progress philandering people, and promising pious pilgrimage. Terms of tranquility agreeing with the symptomatic fervor devouring itself with inconsistent demeanor. Not the right stop and suspicion occurs even through innocent prevalence. Too much time and not enough outcome. The time dies as we live on. So it goes, unnoticed departure, fixated space, dislocation, and spliced by decision the digestion of all of this. Yes all of this thriving, spastic bliss. Fortitude displays its devices, but do we accept?

"Yes," flops over.

"No," claims uncertain amiability.

The babbles of contagion, bubbles of lost air, and speculative, demure articulation are figments of kindness discerning appreciation. Frozen, raining, and succumbing to poisoned penned pornography. Words flying openly discharged and helpless.

Dead bodies are caught. The rhythm catches the sadly opaque, barren removal of a pulled stop, and ignorance. A leather jacket and pesticide promised a weakened sale to be universal subterfuge of the spitting, dribbling rain. A sloppy journey as death calls out sighted terms, and expecting oblivion the pale faced find it to be more spoken, sounded out by voice, and obnoxious vision guesses quickly. Repair the senses and reproach the stereophonic glitch of wonder, nonsense, and acceptance. Death hails a blow mate, prematurely blow.

Tomorrow tells the tale, and assimilation aside, the feeling may not be pleasure. CCR on an eight track and a headache in view. Too much to drink and a low level of reality to succumb to waking existence. The call of dignity is one's own, and the peripheral lack of paper colors description with nondescript terms. Process bidding process, habit erecting evolution, and seasonal bliss concluding the procession to enlist the enjoyment of (blank). Tomorrow tells the tale, the spelling alters with a dull stem, but opulence recurs in sinking ink. Not enough time, but a notice all the same lingers, pointing, blatantly guilty. Practise absurd and disjointed, but hunger fed a life well fed on discipline. Fiddling with no utensil, lost, abhorred and deceived. Periled steps overtake tomorrow, ones we cannot see. The truth upholds the footing with a past we can foresee. The actions acted, words unspoken, paths unseen. The bullshit fundamentals of now. The inappropriate action of now as one together and one at a time. Survey says, distortion.

Survey repeats repression.

Survey says resemble.

Survey says begin.

Drag queens and style kings, but how do I belong? Too much booze, but how much smut until I belong.

"Yes I am gay."

A homosexual or a man who loves men. A man who wants a man.

"Yes I am gay."

A man who loves a man, but do I get a picket fence? Do I toast a wedding plan or do I get noxiously more involved. Do I dance to play the part I play? Am I myself or some sort of apology?

"Yes I am gay."

A homosexual or a man who loves men. A man who loves a man.

Does the junkie score or do I? It is a question of time infiltrated by design for there is no pedigree except lost, benign capacity. The foundation for celibacy is transgression. Liquor, drugs, sex, obsession, anger, and intolerance. Be prepared by understanding. This is a momentous subject at this early date. Repossess dignity, replenish innocence, and rediscover chastity. Virtue or imperial margarine lubricates the same singing birds. Bad, outdated music that questions the original listener with more than obligatory generations listening later.

"Polly said it was great."

The paper may have landed on the floor, but the keys stroke their importance with every finger. The time has passed, and the spelling mistakes fly, but the preoccupation does not stand with what is written. The decision to articulate predisposes any belief, infiltrates the barriers believed in, and trespasses within a scope of understanding that maybe cannot even be understood. Time may be irrelevant, but the words think otherwise.

People may be superfluous, but again the words do not think so. Time and condition are universal, and it is only the self that sees the difference. The self however is in decline as the reign of possibility gets tighter or more aloof, and we regurgitate the past within the conditioned discharge of retrieval and descent. Conspicuous terms for a dying planet, but no one seems to care any longer so what the Hell.

Flippant, snide discretion and contrived belligerence contaminate the sterile core of the soul with the fitted terms of allocated survival. The suffering has not changed so why should we? The continuous support and reason should maintain a human stance, but where is it?

The cravings again are universal omnipotence that reckon more than an iPhone. Speak no evil, but touch none either to again scrape by with the indifference and conditioning we are meant to foster and represent. Even the tides know the difference with a stuttering bar, but the spaces cannot be erased. They contain force and vision that perhaps hands cannot hold. The retread can be held, but the difference of the stroke may not. The spaces contain themselves and the spelling well we never thought to get it right. Oh well there goes another goose. So the snow will fall and the groves grow white and distant, and yet the fertile people sow the afterthought of even flow. Again the tension soars and the self alone is stuck within the space.

Deals with the underhand surmise guilt, and the reproach of time repeats. This machine is broken, the scales are sliding, and the tides knew first the rate of all control. Nuance wasted for the sake of the self, and to gain nothing more than a spelling mistake. A miss typed key or a broken machine still equates the difference. Maybe.

Running with the rapids, but unable to keep up time slides, the person emits, and the future calls both to fruition. Maybe fruitility is a better word, but the spelling and spacing are void for repose. The continuous fortune of forever bleeding over like a throbbing cock waiting to roost. Such graphic innuendo does not apply, but the premise is the same. The keys clank at an obtuse hour, but the reason intact obeys and fortifies the answer with reasoning. The tactile truth is obscure and obsolete, yet complete and frantic believes whole heartedly they are two words and not just one. Blank representation and nothing more. We cannot explain beyond our grasp, and yet we want to try. Paper scores, words erupt, and the vision remains explanation. Stifling disruptive tones as love resonates with bereavement and retired, broken promises. Sorry for nothing more than wanting more. Acceptance, love, trivial enclosures abandoned for the sense of now, and virtue as a contagious kin hosts a grander semblance than pieces here. The fortune proves itself, and the tables collide with brutal levity and disregard. Cataclysmic overtones striking the keys well past twelve, and the reply remains to get it out. Let it out, be free, and live with the awakened consequence waiting to be touched. Await the decision to be more, now, maybe.

Another page of misplaced page, and we forget what was released on the last. It does not matter, but do no wrong for it will grow up to bite you, and so then we resuscitate the past to encounter the future with brighter beams of grip to lighten the load. Clanking keys to awaken the neighbours because the message is in the medium. Words, miscalculated words that cannot convey the intent intended. Just the rambling noise emitted here and nothing more maybe? Maybe not. Who knows? I just write, and fornicate freely the expression of today. Be alive. Be now. Be free.

It is too late to take it back, but the noise continues as the keys click persistently onward. Oblivious torture for the hard at sleep. Too late, too soon, but all too forgotten. Mistakes running rampant and causing decay, thoughts preconceived, and devoid of any previous decision the archetype of oblivion if one has ever been seen. So say I, and I am to die. The disciplines waver, and the reflections over compensate, but the noise chatters incessantly as the words seem right. Ripe with the overlay of distraction, something more grand and removed from the self, but succinctly guaranteed with the inclusion of the self. Can it be that all of this is mine?

Hot flashes bring us back, and the cause for this reason remains light. Illumination can stem from such disenfranchised purgatory. It can reside in such arcane depravity, and it can know the truth by merely holding a flame to the window of its memory. The sadness sweeps in, but can it uplift control? As dreams occupy the space between nimble fingers to keep the cold at bay, the self wishes for more, but can it have it? Can this desolate landscape of terminology ever become more than sinking plasms freezing over with the sticking bar of space? The fragments determine factions of the inclination, but can there be more than that to the self? Figuratively speaking there cannot be more than this, and this then is all there is. Truly? It is all too fast, and too slow, but the space bar sticks and we are all contrived within the viscous vision therein. Sickness and health holding fast together may be more, but apart there are mistakes. The joints begin to hurt with all this tapping, and rapping fingers take physical therapy to everyone. The roses may be wilted and the orchids in bloom, but the figments scatter beyond the flora and fauna. Reason reason's discourse.

Another page and another disaster. The ink may be fading as the spacing stinks, but who cares after all other than me? Nothing comes to answer and so the tangent sticks as well, and we lead the way with victorious terms of maligned intent. Well it could be worse.

This may not have happened, but it did. This may not have been, but it was. This may not come again, and we should be prepared for the worst. Burning scapegoats, discerning decision, and all this muck, but there it goes again. We hope.

Maybe the paper does have to run dry from this pile to become another. Maybe no one knows any better than this so what the duck? Paraphrasing dichotomy and gaining scrutiny we blame thee worried soul for in the truth comes indifference, and that guarantee resides with all. The jargon therein is one's own, and the spelling mistakes too take on a life of their own. The indecisive action toils the soil with awkward grace, and the rooted spoils expand beyond the hands that sow it. Time does not stand still, it grows, and like us it takes the shape molded yesterday. It is all progress so let us move on hopeful and intact with the education of yesterday forming the fold for tomorrow.

PART TWO

A COMPARITIVE ANALYSIS OF THE PROPOSED BUDGET ESTIMATE FOR SUNDANCE UNIT NO 6

PROLOGUE

EVERY STORY IS contained by many as one envelopes the next, becomes another, and overall blurs any continuity. There can be no beginning nor end amidst one, big puddle of congealing odds. The sun comes up, goes down, comes up again, and people keep skipping around. Cycles repeat, circles upon circles, and how they began and where they end may be questioned, but the options for choice and consequence remain in the moment of now. Now is a singular importance that cannot define any more than that, but being now as clear as a moment ago is where we shall begin. Here and now is a beginning that concedes conclusion. It begins with nothing more than the knowledge of a beginning that cannot be fully described. Elaboration best decides a setting, and so now, here, the beginning begins.

Fresh and new like a subtle change swooning for appreciation, the here and now are a pivotal part of everything. The mesh of decay and humanity striving for decency. The troubled mass shooting for a parade, and settling for a procession of routine days. The weathered usage of life accepting standards, reaching limits, and basking in excuses until death. We are this scheme of sadness and happiness in our grasp for equality.

Protagonists are devoid of breath because they could be any one of us, all of us as personified by one, clear page. Remember the absurd figment of divinity and the interference of occasion. The lost temperance is forgotten tomorrow, swollen tomorrow, forgotten tomorrow. Lights upon oblivion as the plan secretes a motion. The fallen craft of meticulous, rainy days. Translucent rays of discomfort are comforted by progress. The implement of smooth situation inflaming degree with the progression of thought, and the distinguished greed for turbulence destroys merriment. Patience wanders the detestable mile, scrambles, and is lost in the alley of words. Is insight so over spoken as to not be understood?

081107715p

CHAPTER ONE

A Less Experienced Speaker

WAITING. THE NUMBER is twenty-one and I am thirty-four, waiting. Hospital decay and stagnation peer in with white walls and disinfected smells. The opulence of cleanliness and health sopping over like a wicked dream. The time will go and I will wait, but the atmosphere here will not change. It will grow, permeate the air with its debris, and heal the wounded hearts of the diseased.

The ritual of health is that the healthy sustain themselves, and the sick get worse. The problem with self-care is that the individual's view is always different, and so the definition of health changes, and the wisdom of prognosis is only a science taught in school. Remember intuition.

"My vomit may tell a thousand stories."

Now it is twenty-four, ten more to go, and there I am with a rolled up sleeve and an injection to see what is there. What will they find? Probably nothing, but if something is there then let it be harmless. Allow me to not throw away my life because of an infection of the blood. Let it stay pure, warm, and red. The disreputable regard for health remains. Acceptance without change does not cure. A wino may understand his/her disease, but without change does health improve? Probably not.

A single rebel tossing the turn for a tired, huddled mass that shrinking in poverty becomes a liability bearing revolution. People stopped by the passing traffic at a red light, the stillness sways, although the activity ascends resolution, and the tidings of bliss in a picture perfect dream do drive the distance. Complying with continuation we revere the lying stillness with walking steps of oblivion. The fiction devours the fiction. Improvised jazz and succulent vibes suck a source with no stream, and the drained resources feel reserved. Diplomatic karma closes in, reverberates action, and sparks the course to carry.

Sitting on the street, listening to the fare, and dissolving amidst its fluctuation I become absorbed by endless echoes. The tale of a telling heart remits the practice of a dwindling soul through the contortion of the hand. Time passes, people wither, and the reflections tide the realm of possibility. There is some confusion as to the equation, trouble with the watery weight of motion, but the staying trials waver emancipation. The characters of circumstance are subordinate to subconscious dealings, and scientific subversion does submerge the soul in a trivial rendering of a void. The dark and light fabrication of shadows in a dance of courteous balance. Catch this spark, hold this moment, and try to lose much less than we have counted.

There is distortion, an unclear picture delayed with words, and the reading, thinking mind cannot comprehend the discord of discourse. Every new beginning after a tortured end, and the time between thrives on neither. Distinguishing remarks pass through the truth to vocalize the reasoning of saintly sinners. Motion makes us queasy as meaning makes us noxious, and the flagrant decay leaves us lost. Victimized in the choice and consequence of circumstance. Vision far and wide, voice both high and low, but versions tried and true in the random transmissions never added up straight. Put the pressure on words, and they replicate a foreign tongue that brags more than reused vocabulary.

Where is the summary? The inspiration of originality is everywhere so why travel the same diction, unravel the same language, and describe the same lustre lacking longing. The same, old, descriptive view for the transcendence of transgression. Salvation may come with death, but solitude kills the likeness of death. The focus forgets fortitude for the force of foul fulfillment. Turn. What was the page? Start again. Down the hatch with release, and freshen the ideas to come in even closer. The heroes are dead like lovers torn from their partners the pen. Reason and remission are terms to write about, but there is injustice with the loss of humanity. Perhaps the more one knows, the more one loses, and the more one may want it back. One may gain triumph. Perhaps the love we said goodbye to flourished with the loss of nurturing. Perhaps questions never contain truthful answers within solitude.

"Just give me a subject."

"But you do not have a subject. Do you?"

"Un, deux, trois, quatre, cinq…"

A person in a chair has nothing more than a chair.

"People, people, people, can you say people?"

"I do not think I want to go there."

We have met a moment, oh yes, we have met a moment that no one has won. No one has won. We simply met upon a moment. Green grass and corn are utopian facts of life. The truth of life is your own design and coaxes something sweet, sublime, and the only thing providing guidance is hope.

Somebody said, "Fuck the hope!"

Somebody said, "I do not need hope, I am not a homo and I am going to get through. I am not a homo, I am going to get through something I hope. Something I hope."

Nobody knows nothing.

"Hello! Hello? The most important thing in life is not to live, but to live life. If the meaning of life was to live we would not really be alive would we? Would you?"

Despising the consequence of something that knows better than nothing. It is nothing. Nothing goes forth today, right now, without what we have, and if we can, we better catch a plane tomorrow. We better catch a plane unto tomorrow. It is a terrible chorus, but there is no refrain. What is a person? Come out, come out, and spring with me baby. Did I get it?

I am alone here in this world of words, and unhappiness curdles growth. Drowning in obnoxious words, my world is stolen to give you this, and my life, love, and lessons are memories I do have in chronological order. The only relapses cannot for incontestable, bragging stories be trivial as stories themselves exhume meaning transformed by words into influence. Convoluted thinking gives direction a list of unknowns and I cannot think clearly anymore.

Upon the question, "Am I evil?"

The response was, "Nah."

Which was replied to with another question, "Is that the truth or sarcasm?"

Again the answer was, "Nah."

So I believe it at least for now.

Tomorrow does not beacon anything greater than what is lost today, and today never gives us anything that we would lose tomorrow. Being forgotten forges the force of forever to ask what we have had, what we have and hold, and what is held forever. Losing life dies, and let's go of the ridicule to grow beyond itself. How little we have in love is how much we lose in life, and what we truly have, we keep, to lose with life. Identity and time are the mathematics of circumstance. They are illuminated with salience, although the self is compromised with the perception of death because limit senses what is contained within the self. People are contrived within the similarity of difference to leave us with creation. Notions and thoughts of continuation, but the righteous wisdom of congruent growth. This has all been said before, and no one is any wiser. People act and think as if tomorrow automatically forgets and forgoes today.

No one can care enough, no one can know enough, and all we have combined is blood, breath, and moment. The tempestuous complaint of a broken heart, conviction beating a bridled mind, and temptation flaunting the troubled soul. We have and hold ourselves in the freedom we share. We are a temporary conglomerate of pensioned speed that kisses the gentle style of articulation. Merely touching the lips of motion and attention where can we go?

Do not think as much, do even less, and focus on the forgotten memories of rendition. Shadows never fall, words never fail, and to love is to let others also love. The ruins of remorse recoil in slumber, but within light and recognition. Spare me the romance and give me thy head. Gory pornography raping the bliss of fragmented nuance. Rolling perspective and personality clash in the idling characteristics of time. Presence beams conclusion a jesting plate for circumstantial pieces of identity. Prescribing discussion, but few details amidst all this character causing danger. The sweat of desire chains a gang of impotent children to fictitious descent into frivolous encounters. The strange recreation of recreation. The proposition of antiquated passion delivered by the despairing conclusion. Let the light be the light and abet the way to say.

"Yes."

The trivial fight wakes up to collect the pay for popularity because the world is a breath of tiny solitude, and the conclusion is the disillusioned soul that the illustrious heart knows is broken. Prose never claims a victim, calamity does not choose by shoe size, and the crime is not in what we have done, but in what we are about to do. Choice is the victim that weeps once more, and life as a disease contaminates innocence and compassion bleeding decency from the lives that give it blessing. We all lose the sanctity of wealth by choosing ourselves, and this obnoxious beast of a state ridicules the precious promise of death's harvest. The loss of beauty, love, and recognition for an easy sale of tired, lonely death.

To impose a situation is to create an outcome, and the overall travesty of this creation is the proof that existence is many. Tomorrow does not close without us. It never echoes the silence welcoming sorrow. The most beautiful thing in this moment is this moment, and the most tranquil accessary is friendship. The longing for love is whispering still, and the birth of life waits for insemination as people cry. We die, lose, let go, and are now more than ever poetry. The sacrifice of the puritanical toll blames the precedent for posterity. Much is lost in a moment, but the right to refuse service is reserved in our opportunity to gain our progeny.

The crime of being respectable, the duty of ethics, and morality are laughing guesses at anonymity. Tomorrow is not sullen, always grows, and flourishing respectively in the scribble of a stroke never gains an explanation. Weary tones do ascend and repeat the response to premise in the essence of honesty. Progress always loses reason to personality, but the contradiction is in the circumstance of mortal cries. Vespers term the dues reply, and the tide of circumstance rides the rails of chance to propose not one, but many to exhume the excuse of resolve. Response tests the possibility as the terms of technical decline are terse.

Be careful and let go. Move on to be free. Decay slowly and let wisdom guide the way. Progression, too much, but too little too soon.

"Tell us another one!"

Let the day become the night, and tell us of our workings. Cares for the broken heart? How can support and trust be proven when in duress? There is no cause for alarm because the blessing of time knows the relationships that may be tried. The thoughts go on until the end of time. Kinetic energy to stir the pot and spell the rot. Life bouncing vibrantly on a stroll down the lane, but the lane is not a straight, solitary line. It blends and stirs, chops and juices the multipurpose meaning of usage and the multitude of men. Wrong choices may be right, but spelling mistakes can change eternity.

"Tell us another one!"

Let the day become night, and tell us of your workings. This makes more sense, although short on length, the transcribed understanding shall have to be also. Too close to be empty of consequence, the selfish, writhing sun shall never be reborn as choices die upon it. Sadness and madness depress the pedal to meddle with creation and leave this deep distortion. Choice and its remnants close the bar, but how do we stand up to their limits? Life is too short to throw it away, yet this choice comes so slowly that already so much is lost. Do we gracefully go with growth to die?

Choice and the nuance of circumstance is in excess when living with freedom, and the closer we get to peace the sun comes out. The skies clear and the narrative returns to believe that much is lost with the focus on the self. What does anything mean beyond God? God who lives and breathes and eats through our actions. We hold the light to HIS darkness to live. Life and love and lust and lost, where did it go? Perhaps life has mislaid it even though life knows of its knowledge and its want for better things. This is obvious, although shorter than it sounds.

A lively lick of the tongue to make the words sound ripe and force the meaning to blur like an avalanche lasting to its end. A stain across the side of a mountain, and the whirly motions of earth distort the structure that held it. The room does not spin, but the world collides with dizzy explosion. We strive the land with furtive steps, but the spinning world distracts the steps. This is life, love, and understanding because even the slightest notion of creation gives it meaning. The cherished heart is malcontent as it sneezes away the malnourished debris of its ties. The less we are is the more we have because tomorrow is ours in the decay of today.

What is important is the action, and not the thought therein. The time to be is in the life to live. The age of one that gave us gold. Detesting the complexity of simplicity gives back the text to promise you and I good tidings foretold. To be conceited with vanity and proverbial wrongs forms frustration. Wrongs righted cussing like a deadly, electro-pop disaster that lacks the hard pressed hands in a moment of weakness. The conclusion is the choice, and tracking adjusts reception.

There was nothing lost the last time, nothing gained perhaps, but lost is less than likely. Attraction saturates the mind's will and physical distraction blurs the lines. The realm of the fantastic, the flow of the ebb, and humanity's aesthetics burn barbarity. The word of the day, the prize of tomorrow, and the mocked resistance of tortured fanatics. A various symposium of cracked vernacular chasing the calm schemes of a dream. Dead with open eyes to see the delirious walks we talk. Warm and cold, torn and tried, frozen or fried, we always lose. Tossed from the crows, stuck with the crowd, and shallow with the depths of self to come. Angular sensitivity seeking sexuality in the thriving nuance of crossing paths. Vicious, cold, and broken the resemblance of remains rations the reason with continuance.

Wrap it in plastic, and conceive the zeal of seal. Remember to despise the masses for choosing themselves redeems the closing of time and circumstance. The ill-fated heart will not see us. Disgusting freedom free with radiance to emit the foul force of fortitude. Repressed people think straight! Forge the use of purpose with experience. Clarity is a question of degree that regards the soul with a fierce reprisal. The atom that enjoys standards with fake tasks does victimize the reality. The linear agreement that corrosion creates conformity. The condemnation of the mind that frames freedom. Risk the ride of fortune because the turn of the wheel is never equal.

Time speeds up as the trees still fall, and there is ink, but for how long will there be paper? Till we die? While it lasts let it speak because relative threats recite their tone with open ended freedom. The rules are meant to be broken because the plunge of explanation is in the extradition of meaning, spelling, and usage. Speaking terms usually do not agree.

Tuesday there was a knock at the door,
And the footsteps across the floor
Despite the war, open the door
To find the vanity of more
Than atrocity or war.
The victim of raped degree
Floats with pedigree
Grinning, winning
Slight expectation
That pain forgoes the moment.
Silence, bliss
And a tortured fish
Flapping, slapping against the floor.
Fifteen minutes
The time will tell
If slow too much
If fast too little.
It bubbles like breath underwater.
Safeguards the stereotypes of reason and decay.
The background for beings like us that reason and decay.
Still tomorrow like today has reason and decay.
Wake up early

The time will tell
If soon too late
If late too soon.
It flounders like drowning children.
Safeguards the stereotypes of reason and decay.
The background for beings like us that reason and decay.
Still tomorrow like today has reason and decay.

People running
To here and there
If here than there
If there than here
They badger like biased perspective.
Safeguards the stereotypes of reason and decay.
The background for beings like us that reason and decay.
Still tomorrow like today has reason and decay.

Awaiting death
To end all this.
The end to this?
An end to this.
It hovers like a stormy cloud.
Safeguards the stereotypes of reason and decay.
The background for beings like us that reason and decay.
Still tomorrow like today has reason and decay.

There are too many choruses in this song of mine.
So many characters, themes, and rhymes.
Degradation, oppression, corruption, and greed.
Self proposed lyrics deflating the time.
Still stuck after all these years in the grime.
Malcontent youth and malignant seed.
These times are changing to the tune of a whine.
The whine of mankind.
The whim of mankind sits on the line between Heaven and Hell.
Safeguards the stereotypes of reason and decay.
The background for beings like us that reason and decay.
Still tomorrow like today has reason and decay.

This is just for you! This is just for us, and the exchange defines the future for us both. To be involved, grow, and arrest oneself with friendship so that existence incurs more charming principles. People are like a mystery in that experience assures the outcome, and the journey slowly reveals the reason. We are drifting passengers on a sea's breeze that erupts like a sneeze, but travels like a disease. Sparring static waves of temperance and resilience. Cloudy visitors on a beach of solitary motion waving to the sky and all its birds. Beauty lies in everything, it can be seen, felt, lost, found, ruined, created, but in all things it resides dormant and omnipotent. Life is a gift, and that gift is our own beauty. We are waking from a dream that never ended, but groggy we stumble to our feet, and find our footing to go further into fantasy. The waking dream continues and its majestic stupor holds us still. We manage a foot hold, a hand rest, ground to sturdy chaos, but the potential carries unknowns. We do accept what we are, but we may very well surpass that. We can acknowledge what we were in knowing what we are now. The understanding of wisdom can perpetuate us even further by granting that we are more than we can ever be. It all continues, the spiral of life, decay, and outlook. The fading life that dwindles into oblivion. There is beauty, love, and truth to call our weathered home comfortable. People are old, crooked victims that evolve to the chance of their whim. The infinite to create the minuscule, and the minuscule to create the infinite. We are blessed, and given opportunity so we can bless others. The hand shake of a powerful grip, forces the hand, and winced the eyes see clearly. Many unknowns form a question, but a question has the possibility of being answered. So we grow and go where we want to grow. Purity and simplicity do rectify the confusion with coherent distances of sense. The tissue breathes with animation, and we fill in the blanks. The explanation of philosophy is simple, that understanding is dormant until found, and once found surfaces to the future forever. To be known is to live, and to live is to be known. These lives are worth living, and this life is grateful for us.

Happy New Year! May all that comes be wondrous, and let not the test of time break us down, but lift us up. Love,

032108429p

CHAPTER TWO

What can it be now?

"I FEEL GOOD about who I am. I feel good about where I am right now. I feel comfortable with the future." Unknown.

Life counts, does subtraction and addition in order to be the allusion that lies in the catch. Excuse the informal paper, but words travel fast. Being in the city again proves time is furious. Angry, lonely people with stories never told, and lies never lived. Harsh critique, however, the overall future seems bleak. Temptation lingers heavily over awaiting angels. It has been raining for two days now, although it has stopped for this moment, or at least the one just gone, and the clouds part to let the sun shine down. Now it too is gone, but for a moment there was warmth.

We have been here one week and two days, had our tenth month anniversary yesterday, and have been humbly residing in our new home. The view is refined from all the windows. Fortunately A.L. was here Friday delivering the kitchen table, photo copier, a box of unwritten word and collage material, and the remainder of any dishes. Saturday brought along a couple of chairs, a card table, a love seat, and two wooden tables. One now is gone, but the other is under described. It looks like it thrived in a splatter paint hobbit hole. It is true. They came from the building, odds and ends from inhabitants passed. What is next out of life's hectic notebook? These pictures of dementia seem almost unfathomable, but life keeps giving amazing circumstance. We have jobs!

We are poor now with a list of food banks, and we have survived on next to nothing before. We will be just fine. We were up late, playing cards and eating popcorn so he is still asleep and providing me with the time to write this letter. Though it may never be sent as intended it lingers on as this.

Perhaps more than twenty days later this shall commence. Beauty has transfixed the soul. I am content, troubled, but passionate, and beautiful I hope. Prospects die at the flick of a switch. M. however has decided he does not mind opera as much as he thought. We agree that watching and listening are two different things.

Time is an endless story, that we grow and tell adds to the meaning, and we shall not die in vain, but in splendor for ours was love and truth. Practise makes the horrid man presentable. Irreverent time and the blessings of distraction tend to eliminate inspiration, and the proposition of acting it out works a six day week without a rest. Maybe one to three hours of sleep a day. Alcohol bubbles, but I am free. I hope to see you soon and have synchronicity agree.

Time will tell the truth, and I have let you down. We did laugh, hug, and speak. Strange, but true, and she would have to agree. No mistakes, just some fluff and buffer from the shine of the sea. Clearance rate prices for the most expensive of experience, and no one wants to buy. They cannot even be given away so why were they regarded so highly in the first place? Why did they accept such prevailed compartments? The even breaks the odds, and the sight conveys the message distorted, and the right of progression is as is. To be, to forget, to grow, can we do these things? A harbour rests for the rest of the wicked. Salvation sings for the souls of the saved. Which am I? Where do I go? What can there be, and what was there already? How can this, I go forward with nothing more than the movement itself? How can I grow? How can I learn? What do I know? Can there be anything else? Do we give it away or take it in?

Hello, there is no difference, except the difference in which we make. The proposition is not one of circumstance, but is one of reason and consequence. Deformity is not a question, but it is an acceptance. It is the fault of the compassionate to become the diseased because the time of compassion is not alive. I did not know there was a reason until I found one. Not for me or you, but for any, and it condenses so much more. It resonates between us. It discovers that which we cannot, and it forms more bearing than our footsteps combined. The condensation of meaning even perforates conclusion.

I understand the importance of any, but mine is sublime. Why? For you and me, but what makes one worth more than another? Why? The meaning of difference means there is not one at all, but if there was it would be determined by you or me. It would be defined by the whole, and not by a connection of its parts. The future is ours, and not mine alone.

Propositions stem from interaction, and although they depress the situation, the indifference that follows does not affect the people that create it. The only thing in life one can lose is time. We die to abscond our barren acceptance of victory, loss, and time. To turn the crank we must give force, and contemplate the truth.

I am to improve life, and I can because there is nothing that cannot be tried. People believe that which they have had, will have, and have now, but is it all spiritually dead? Do we condemn or condone the future? Do we let it slide with indifference or do we choose to remain the same? We are to believe from birth our conception of life, weak or great, resides with us. Right or wrong does not matter because the future beckons light, hope, and admission. The firm choice is not the choice, but the outcome. Are we here? Are we unique or something, utterly specific in the universe? Are we an example of this civilization of ours? Truly? It is as it is done. What we want, what we do, and tomorrow are trying.

The hour is the memory. We forget that we live, and thinking we forget that the world suffers the consequences. Personal reality conquers more than the personal self. Fear eats the core at our feet, and yet we quicken the pace. Senses curdle in the aspect of understanding because sense amplifies the simplified part of the cohesive whole. The program of understanding reality proposes more understanding than that of the self due to the continuity of resonance that creates the singular parts in unison to become whole. The aspect of time and self is half the perspective as questions contaminate the isolation of being. We confuse the essence of being with the confession of being. Age old faith praises hope, and hit the nail on the head. To reap the weather of wear we are to be what we are, promise and denial.

No one requires much else other than themselves, and the propriety of merit is knowledge. The forlorn torture of living decay is torn to tune image, sound, and memory. We all partake in the reasoning, and that is the one part that cannot be denied. Ignorance breeds violence, and the intrepid contraption of lies bridles the fear of death. What does God have to say?

"DIE!"

For death is salvation because there is no longer malcontent obtrusion or obstruction. What of me? I am dead or to die. Someone may miss the deceased, but it is not the dead, but the lost life that goes with them. Why do we disbelieve, disagree and self-construct any or all of the evidence? We die too. How many times does goodbye have to be said?

I did once know a man who was what he was, a philandering alcoholic. Beyond the exchange and experience how can a person make another person think? Reliability is compromised. Mentality affects everything. The advantage of liberties cannot be trusted because of compiled heartbreak and isolation. Civil responsibility flounders here and there when contentment or faith are unable to socialize. Reward and not responsibility allow the monopoly of power, and by not adapting to compromise everything has a sliding scale. Friends and family may be avoided. Accomplishment cannot take care of lies. Hate and torture cannot cheat truth. By not keeping rational expectations, long term gratification and honest communication are stolen. A shared, power influence builds trust, flexible boundaries, integrated sociability, and not the corruption of contentment. The end of time will come, and tribulation will be defeated to never again cross the threshold. Time is blessed in its measureable distance, and it bends and flows to the wish of the world, but the final straw that blows it all away will be even more sacred. It will cleanse the world of all its corruption, filth, and greed, and it will illuminate love, light, and life with reason. The blues are blown away with sunny waves of prescribed, good weather. Life gets away too with the exterminating glances that stirred into the spin of whirling sense. Depravity is left barren. Time will tell, talk is cheap, and for now the future looks bright so briskly walking we shall flourish. The winter like a long tug of war that held no winner is over. It just ended, and is now in the past towed behind the future. Happiness and love is in the summer for us. It will find and embrace us warmly with regard.

The fluent articulation of the spine dancing in jerks and spasms plays its toll on the free will. The mind's fullness is nullified, personification is null in void, and similes and metaphors fill the room. Pictures fleet like dreams, but blinking shades take them away. Sense reaches out, but there is nothing more than fidgeting fabrications and air. The past corrodes, and left in the street waits for its time to return in vain. Seems an unusual, universal predicament, but loss and sadness stand on both sides waiting for the waiting to stop. Searching onward to ignore the sadness and loss, but glancing forward into the fitting schemes of dreams.

Told to do this, told to do that, and always losing, left with two vengeful twins. The explanation is literal. They stand old and snarled like snakes hunching at attention. They salivate from pointy teeth, and their skeletal stature reeks of dust. To look? They swagger like trees in harsh wind, and their roots tangle the earth with black pools. Unearthly? Am I? Look further into the straight debris of the future, and the scapegoats linger snickering.

To conceptualize the future, the future has to conceptualize us to forgo, forgive, and forget the travel into salvation. Fluent decent to the golden hours lost in transposed youth. What happens now is optimum resounding. Life moves beyond the translucent fitting of a folded soul, and is not trapped and dead by the brink of decay. They too can write, remember, and deny. They too can forge, forgive, and forget. Life is labour lost on a decadent soul. The mire disposes of reason in its sensual touch. Hidden in disclosure, encompassing remorse, originality gains sights assured by the religion of the self. Fortune does not favor the life that forgets the favour.

One scrap of paper and a moment of time with words to fill the space in the void with echoes. They stir until life eludes the error of breath's retort. The living being is a thing. Time is short, life is too long, and the interim of indifference is vast. The conventions break, the controls let go, and tomorrow sighs today tomorrow. How much can we lose within a moment of laughter? The greatest loss in life is time, it forgets the prose, but grows with the expansion of definition. Forget to be, learn to be, and do. The greatest loss in life is life. We let it die! We let it die. The husk of a man does not breathe in the truth.

"Why am I here at this time and in this place? Why am I allowing myself to put myself in this space right now? Am I worthy of the anger, torment, pain, and torture? Is loving you worth this pain? Why are you hurting me?"

A.P.

You will understand. Equality goes a long way as soon as we surpass the limit of individuality. The limits of resource tide the dead. No step to victory goes without casualty, and no wisdom can be gained without loss. The understanding stands in the doorway, going in, or coming out, it stands in the doorway, and no way makes sense. Is inside out or outside in or do they both enact the other. Is forward backward or backward forward or do both ways end with confidence. Side to side, and side to side, but which is left and which is right? Is one part parted two or still only one cut in half? Is reason an answer or a question? Is life proof or just the living tissue? Does breath come in or go out?

There is a problem with this. It is questionable, but there has to be something wrong with this for there to be no end, no conclusion to smite the backed up emotion, and no force of residual restitution to say that this has finished. There is the problem or just an underlying part of something greater. Progress comes and goes, decay continues on, and I just fly to paper. Spiralling patterns of ink like the ones that came before them, but spiralling, the spasms of splatter expand and expound more than ink. The pages are ending, but more are to be found, and so it just grows to be. To live this entity comes quickly, but slowly the hands distort the truth to be of themselves alive. This life dies to release the life that resides there, and the onslaught of character means there is no flaw except for the flaw in itself that is devoid of a reason for being. We are left where we began with a single problem lacking the evidence of explanation. We are ourselves, and the evidence is full with detail. The detail to distract the mass from the mass to the soul, and turned eyes forget the truth with dreaming sense. Wishing, wanting, craving more, life comes quick, and closing sooner, we sigh. A tight breath mustered against the cold to wish, want, and crave something more. The cold overcomes, and the sigh floats in the midst of an exhaled breath. Death glimpsing out, letting go, and moving up, warms the air with loss as light ripples through the shadows and darkness. The swirling breath of mist circling, shrouding, basking permanence.

Visions unclear clarify, and then it becomes an I, the I becomes an it, and it is only I. The I of an eternity. The I of all infinity. The I of an identity.

Beware the demons, praise the Angels, and forget nothing of the men and women we are, but arrest the self to the other two, and surely lose your soul. The soul to the I is an ego, and the ego that sells itself to itself will remain the same. The battle of existence in the left and the right, in the right and the wrong, in the comparison of contrast. The evidence slips, and dwelling on entity becomes the rational truth. The I that goes for itself and not the truth loses the truth for itself. Does it have to be this complicated? No. The caution is simple, except for the sticking mmmm, taste the morsel that salivates most.

It has been a while, but we have returned. The old blasé tour of memory and reality. Sense absolves the past fragments of being and duty. The postage is paid, and we are on vacation with the vocation of recalling yesterday. Giddy tunes propose tomorrow in the sunny heat of forgotten beauty. The tone of mercy in the bondage of the past, the promise of tomorrow, and now, here in the returning proposal of memory.

It strives anew to be free and worthwhile. It strives to grow and thrive like a seeding bud of commitment. Tomorrow although pale and ghastly flourishes on warmth and the development of virtue. The answering call to death's promise remains the same.

"Prosper well and beings swell."

The lost cause of remembrance sullenly snickers. The firmament of consciousness is the reasoning to continue to create. Choice baffles solace and resurrects the living lie of truth. The greatest importance is the beauty that we be.

Loss is the trivial condemnation that wanders the world for ourselves. Beauty fades with the contrast of our desire, the loss of the self for the whole of the world is talk of compromise, but the whole of the self is born to succumb to boasting succession. We are to lose the power of the world. Produce seclusion and the world wants to see. Witness a sight to disbelieve it.

Diction reigns supreme in a worthy declension of sound. The familiar fancies freely and reaching hands force an outcome. Faking freedom and foretelling fortune, the promises are tattered trials not turned, and lies secreting victory bare their backs to failure. Is the self so mighty to know the fear of outcome and overcome it free from control? Time tells the splitting tales and fortune defines the overall, moral pattern to leave the singular soul alone. Desperately forging fate from the fear of demise, the fact remains that we do what we do, and foil inherent affluence for the forum of another, questionable decision. Where is the difference, and who concludes the truth?

We see across an ocean of contrast to be that which we are, a stripe against the skin, and a pore seeping deep and vast air. Eternal versions of one time, place, and change to penetrate the contradicting advantages congruent with the individual self. The world knows better than one soul shrieking gain and disbelief. The self knows right from wrong, but language laughs at the soul as it can know more than us. It can say more than words like garbage from the trash basking in immortality.

Broaden grander forms of waste and the flies think there was more when there was none. Distinguished, disquieting demise departs from the wind anchored by judgements. The portal of temptation is everlasting destruction. To die forever ripped from living life because the truth declines when told a lie. Bask in the safety of subtlety. Trail off when the victims gain light, and beware affording luxury because marvels seldom mince.

So we are to be, to die, to testify our truth and being, yet declarations stand silent. A point of interest amidst the cubicles of passion that boil with the tendency to run dry. How many dead people ride the bus? The most bizarre things are natural.

Is it better on top? What about the bottom? If at the top then the bottom seems minuscule, and from the bottom the top looks grand, but in the middle both seem inappropriate. The taxing steps of labour and leisure. We the people of the earth remain grey in the shadow of an immense step. We bask in the wrath of the trash from the upper class. From the bottom to the top the waste decreases so what lands at the bottom falls all the way down, and while dropping dissipates with change. It spreads, but becomes thin with the cascading momentum that delivers it.

To forge the future noise with silent inadequacy one must form tomorrow with today. A fiction derived from foolery as fiction perverts the shiny light of our fancy. Mutations of grandeur and the perspective to see it. To close a door, hinders the light, and fixates on shadows rather than being. Anxiety feasts on the death of the soul, and cannot even write that straight. Visions of miraculous things thwarted by the truth of existence. Propositions not taken, there are no buyers, and the future flops behind the whispers of unclear momentum. Lip service does not count when you kiss the dead.

The greatest insight into life is that we get to see the light, and the greatest lie is given to the light openly. The life that gives dies with the ignorance of an understanding that is singular. The cheap conditioning of acceptance reeks of limitation and sensory deprivation. Does memory surpass reality? Does memory impose reality?

The fasting moments wind up, turn down, and old habits grasp them with decrepit hands. The age of posterity withers with decay. The contrast compares and corrodes the mix, but memory within reality becomes a memory. The old truth of vision and voice that fabricates the action, thought, and sense from the memorabilia of reality. Old routes open, and open routes old with a lack of travel. The conclusion remains the same proposed fixation that posterity and fortune bear witness. The golden age trapped in a cage too condemned for rage turns the page.

Truth is the victim of time and deceit, time and acceptance, and time and the truth. The telling tale of optimism burning somnolent flames of articulated noise. Grimacing spins of site and citation banished to darkness. No one can see the truth, and time slips unnoticed. Fortune follows tomorrow, but fortune focuses and fades. It reads a short epitaph on simplicity.

"For there to be an end, the means must carry us there."

Truth replies, "Acknowledgement falsifies testimony, and I am opposed, but with the ignorance of indifference."

Still burning optimism singes within the heat and burdens the heavy breather with smoke. It ripples, rises, and razzes the reflections of reality. It scars the sentiment, can sterilize the potential, and releases the mixed review of oppressive nature. Passion recurs and the sentiment continues again unnoticed. We are dreaming being. We are fancy eaters torn from the feast, while freedom sings a song.

"Forever. Always."

Fear subsided in the bounty and we shudder irresponsibly with the realization that trials die by evening, the day resides in the afternoon, and the morning values aspiration and decay. The told tales telling testament, troubling testimony, and torturing temperaments of truth. The only bearing a footstep contains is the ground that holds its tread. One step first, one step next, and journeys erupt to caress the dirt. We may ask, but no answer resides in the many we already grasp.

"Do. Do. Do. Do. Do. Do. Do. Do."

The slumber sings serendipity's rendition of sleep sought and slain with distance. People present glimpses of purity, promote vindication, but slither to design. Freedom is killed by a choice. It is frozen in despair and demise. The lack of escape leaves tormented souls to design themselves.

The Fair is toxic learning, so calls fortune a passing day with wilting interest. The condemned have foreclosed the schoolhouse, but our spirits cry for the education of life. Tomorrow does beckon blessings greater than today, and today does not give that which we would lose tomorrow. Being forgotten forges the force of forever to ask, "What we have had is what we hold, but is it held forever?"

What is sin? What is not these days? The colour yellow. The number seven. Lego pornography and Japanese manga. Small villages in France?

A weakened state of human nature in which the self is estranged from God, and the condition or state resulting from the transgression of religion or moral law, especially when deliberate. A prostitute in New Orleans, a sideshow in Las Vegas, or a limerick from Nantucket. Mickey Mouse or the Marquis de Sade. The story of O. Disobedience to the known will of God as shameful, deplorable, and utterly wrong. The twenty first letter of the Hebrew alphabet, sine.

The artist's way, the writer's path, and the pleasure principle. Danielle Steele, Henry Miller, Charles Bukowski, or any boy band. Oil paint? Microwave ovens, sushi, and even cloning. The Tower of Babel. Watches, Kraft Dinner, wieners, and the pyramids. Comfortable chairs and the heart's content. Self-help? Fluffy cats and the national anthem. The Gap, Chapters, and the Home Shopping Network. Reading the last page first, and anything unfinished. Ball point pens, French waiters, photographs, and urns. Picasso? Four am at four-sixteen Hastings Street in Vancouver. The sunrise, suicide, and email. In a right triangle; the ratio of the length of the side opposite an acute angle to the length of the hypotenuse.

Note: Sin is used in the formation of some compound words of obvious significance; as sin-born, sin-bred, sin-oppressed, sin-polluted, and the like.

The seven deadly sins are pride, covetousness, lust, wrath, gluttony, envy, and sloth.

Sin is restriction. It is not like it used to be since it seems certain that nothing is true, yet everything is permitted. Sin is a crime committed against the self.

"Plagiarism?"

CHAPTER THREE

Already?

"SNIFF THE ETHER loving hellions of the world and save big," unknown.

How did the universe begin? A wave rolled in, and the land ended on tips of emotion for the distant places from which it came. The moving shore above the steeple of the deep sea, and the dark waters wallow from caliginous to proficient on the edge of perturbed ripples. The bottom sweeps the land with shallow breaks and sunken ledges of rock that glisten in the low tide.

Numerous ideas can be seen within the immense, internal waves. Even the faintest conception of effect is contained in their adjustment. Warmth and happenstance swagger against the sleek, inflected slopes. At present we do not know, but suppose sense is in the murk of the sea, and its closed book is far greater than any we have ciphered.

An animal's behavior is not supplied by outside forces, and science is aware of the interplay between external and internal stimuli. Uncovering this web of complex positions tinkers with mechanics that seek the physical fountainhead of every changing behavior. Action equals a philosophy that smothers almost a third of civilization. Nurtured and harvested, our commercial management prospers with annual removal, and the growth each year is twenty-five per cent better. Every animal, at some time during its life, does leave one place and goes to another. Sense keeps us headed in the ultimate direction, but the mechanism is a total Chinese Box.

Cooperation must be able to communicate. Human speech is simple language amidst growling articulation, yet we manage to be understood. Many areas of the bottom are covered with the remains of life. Forming ooze by the minute, the skeletal remnants pack close insects. Life and its creatures ooze, corresponding life has the right to ooze also. From the bottom to the top the hardest show is the most endurance, and this is the larger form of life as well as the intricate bones of the landscape.

No it is not you that has to abide. There is nothing wrong with life, but the choices we put behind it. Imagine a serene screen in a dark room. Enter to see nothing on the surface, but bring in a projector to shine light on the screen and see images play. The screen displays the whole of the human condition. Thoughts, emotions, and actions of people in all parts of the world. Over the years the flexing mind still does not know how to illuminate the entire picture. We do not realize how large the screen is even though we feel we see it entirely, and knowing the breadth and significance of the human condition we discover a source of focus. Purpose defines the boundaries of the human prerequisite, and we map the uses and possibilities with the comprehending mind. The most important context for thinking is a historical and philosophical one: what is my fundamental nature?

Cultural difference distinguishes individuals, but fundamentally there are none. The same needs preoccupy the same physical and mental mechanics. In turn we are born to become parents and think about the natural world. Growing up we have friendships, and become death. We have sex with the dreams we eat. We are quotients derived from curiosity.

These selves become fast, and project confusion already. It is the removal of the self, one's self, that projects the lack of clarity, but words mean more then self proclamation, and so this I is the only one residing here. This person under question has been distracted by the accommodation of writing written comment. This distraction brings this up. Copies are made, responses are doubled, but occasion says that words are meant that way.

This confusion controls narration, and bridges hallucinations with a cure dispelling lovely cats. The cement under bare feet swooning cooler days under a descending, sunny sky. The clouds shift ghost like transparency in wishful clusters, and the tobacco dries beneath plastic, extracted teeth. They are all comfortable with the sinking cold, and as sniffles drip dry the confusion holds its control.

Lost and somber at home, but the future has a bright shine beneath the sunken refuge of individuality. The self breeds the waking rot of life that emits these senses, people, and progress with the distorted reality of that self. The self unaware takes action, but failure accepts belief. Love is lost to pride, pleasure, and personality. Perspective practises phrases, and focuses on the wilderness to repeat.

"This happening in accordance with ritual and design is disabled by the technical deficiency that provides these steps to dream."

Bewildered with aftermath, perhaps the whimsy of curiosity or the evoked sense of pleasure, but weakness has provided the strength. Ill-prepared eyes are troubled by the brink of such obtrusive obstacles. They are the proverbial dilemma caught in the spokes, and are so broken that the tire does not spin in circles. Utopia is experience, and all experience is euphoric as laughter dances to proclaim the distant oddity of a groove trapped on the needle. The idly skipping display of repetition in the jagged, rooted uncertainty of order.

Convention and understanding fidget with temporal nonsense that can be clearly stated to enlist unbiased fundamentals that oppose this clawing retort by dispersing logic. Tomorrow will not repeat today, but what is today? Is there anything positive about what has been lost, wasted, or thrown away? Can a life strive endlessly without a slip of optimism? Shadows fix the soul to scare the sacred heart, but can these mistakes be rectified? What is learned from the utilization of disgrace and its acceptance? Can we live beyond the past within a future of unknowns? Subliminal strides of social decay, substantial love, and fictional responsibility. The vomit of a decrepit wind warbling articulate gestures of decomposition.

"Blah, blah, blah."

Repetition indulges the accent of death and life to appease the deeming qualities of both with the representation of potential and clarity. A mistaken mass of muscular sense that depravity wearing pajamas cannot even dream. A twisting pen and a thriving outcome from the manipulated explosion of theory form practise. The eclipse of the sun by the moon. Contrivance and the convalescent aroma of atrophy and denial. The remembrance of one sense or all and the closing remarks are the self's decay and destiny.

The turning soul is morbidly discombobulated, and the approach to reason and the intersected restraint of the self are forged with probable discourse. The lodging of meaning with dissonance. The reversal of words, and the coruscation of the self. It is all pragmatic sense, and therefore the problematic feeling of the self.

Poisoned steps walk a furtive line to erode amidst the musing noise. The distractions repeat to break the rhythm of saintly singing and babble the music to tears. Whimsy dies for the representation of knowledge, and growth is the optative notice of circumstance and frozen abstraction. Chaos dispersing formative chance and the singular interpretation that deals evidence a long hand. A drawn out slogan is the life that hammers demented, fractured essence, but the noise that removes the rhetorical question of what is when.

An endless line of self erected, universal connotations that proves no majority or minority exists, although knowledge justifies both with an interlocked coherence of trial and error, but this cannot explain what we know and have. Subjective terminology and insight can be determined, but which is which? What is what? Who knows any better?

Morality consecrates the singular element by dissolving the specific, exclusive element for the appropriation of the whole. The predominate theme is not growth or wisdom, but instead the decisive direction that abets them. It is figurative speech, but also is a slandered view that is the proximity of judgment that a miraculous life endorses, empowers, and enslaves. The conclusion is simple, yet singular, and provides no criteria for a monolithic finality to leave the entitlement of the self to the insecure sense of a whole. We are all unknown and not familiar. Not even definition proves this wrong because we are at the beginning, asking the same question, and under question by the same, menial discrimination.

I ask, "Who gave miscalculation such authority?"

The ethics of a Christ? The acceptance of a self? The distinguished bliss of corrupted minds? Filter this debris with caution because the merriment of sense entails a stretching sight, an expansive touch, and the description of memories to act it out. Nonetheless these words will explain and express nothing more than this because unfortunately this sense cannot forgo itself, and the utilization of language is a perpetual shroud of echoes in the ego of time. Slip ups are forgiven, and mistakes are forgotten with sticky ink, sutured circumstance, and the brandished guard of elusive behavior. Nonsense stuttering agreement with practicality running amuck. Staining the disdained truth with fragments of the self's purity to transpose wisdom with the semblance of weather and wish. Besides purity is an iconoclastic detail of subjectivity that harnesses malfeasance in the faint, blotting truth, and the perception biased with the regard for choice compiles the understanding of control, comfort, and compromise. Life emits change. We accept or deny, and tomorrow loosens the expectation. There is no reason to tell a story, except perhaps to enhance other people's luck, but for now this course has no function. That is the end to the clichéd pattern of facsimiles that trespass against reason to disregard sheltered refinement. It is not that we have forgotten, but we have no reason to speak of it within this lucid state because the present situation does not gasp. The senses of the singular mind, and the utterance of misfortune incriminate sublimation. We as parting glances never disagree.

The fortune of fortune is fruitful nature, and although it has gone repressed, it stumbles with the steps of attention to share the answer.

"DO WHAT THOU WILST."

What for and to what end do these crossing identities mingle? Clauses of sanity within an appropriately distinguished beginning. Every story transcends the one before it, and the rising inquiry of what we have done scorns tones of what we will do. Compassion bleeds the heart of a purer nature as we will find our tomb with a view. Intuition kills as circumstance dregs the soul that whistles wishes for humanity, and we are unsure that the truth can surpass that reality. The reality of now cannot be greater, less, or more neutral than the uncertainty, but what we do not know cannot scare the truth nor tempt growth with harm. Instead it forms a tactical impression of tomorrow even if it cannot be comprehended. This cannot be attained through the production of awareness nor can it process a sense of meaning due to the subjectivity of growth. Singular growth is proven via tactile activity and the regulation therein, which under scrutiny is neither growth or awareness, but the self. Distinct to the self is the reliance and resistance of the self. Arrogance, ignorance, guilt, and greed. Distortion and distraction positioning both the effect of growth and understanding.

Time is of the essence, there is no sense to pacify the years of lost conviction because they have no means to reply. Life dissolves so quickly that lives will emphasize it. The years of lost correction have no means to say goodbye.

Who is first? E. Where are you? How are you? Petty circumstance may just bring us together, but why can there not be anything more? Trivial consequence delivers life, but life delivers the meaning and the course of our lives. Vague conception suits me well, but what does it exactly tell? Not too much of anything.

Yes. Vancouver and we are well. Minor mishaps aside we have managed well enough to be above water. Continuation will say whether or not we shall stay that way. Curious are the steps we take toward oblivion. I will remain indifferent because if this tale is only mine then it should stay that way, do you not think so? Questions and more questions. Moment after moment, time after time, and breath after breath. There needs to be reason, and if the reason contains the self then was there ever choice? Do not let go of what is important, and do not deny what is true. We all grow together, apart or alone, together or tied, we grow, we learn, and we lose. We hole eternity as it slowly slips away. With respect and regard.

0725071010p

Who is next? M. Well this is to say thoughts for you almost every day. I will include the letter intended originally, but for reasons of loss or continuance has not been sent. So here it is as it is. Broken, but complete. Stories to fill the time and the test of friendship.

It is hot, and frozen in type the versions of slander go unnoticed. I ask what does that mean. I do not know. We lose too much time too quickly. Or do we really just give it away? Momentous occasions and friendship galore.

Remember this was just a duty, a note fragmenting closure, escape, thoughts and warmth all the same, but change. P.S. I will see you soon enough, but reply for some reply. I love you Patrick.

0723001012p

What's that spell?
"EM."
Me spelled backwards.
A man sits on stage with his hand on his head. Hunched over, contemplating, and sobbing. He looks around lost, abandoned, and bewildered. Various voices float over the scene.

"Now we need your name. We have nothing on him. No. Nothing. Huh. Well what do you think we should do with him? The officers that brought him are still here. Pass it back to them? I don't know. Well. I don't know."

The man sitting, disturbed and distraught, looks around for the calling voices to find nothing. He twitches, wants to get up to walk, but cannot. He tries to talk back, but cannot hear his voice. He is trapped, confused, and frightened. The voices continue.

"Do you know why you are here? You can hear me can't you? Do you feel alright? Perhaps I can get you something? The officers want to know if everything is alright. Yes. So they have permission to leave. Yes. Is there anything I can get you?"

The man rubs his face, and wants to respond, but he cannot.

"Is there anyone you can call? Can't you tell me your name?"

The man nods his head.

The Christmas Wish List

A peaceful and loving holiday free from stress, exposure, and longevity. A festive march of gratitude and blessing. A fun activity of singular purpose. A romp or a silly jest. A gift of singular importance and the story of its deed. Nothing pretentious, pious, or snide. Righteous servitude and questioning belief. The literary tea. Pay back. Soap and food. Beauty. Quantities of physical beauty. Success. Bounty. The New Year. Simple wealth. Light, very light. Gratitude and wealth. Success in new territory, and land to call her own. Pictures. Memories. Love. Warmth, friendship, compassion, and their cause and effect. Chaos and love. Reminders, but also rekindled interest and friendship. Music. Apologies and thanks. Care and response to the past and future. Thanks, but no thanks. The notorious Sinister Grim.

CHAPTER FOUR

The End of Reality

IT STARTS WITH a pink balloon gently lifting into the sky. If seen from above, it is a vast, blue silence that shrouds the balloon with cement squeezing in the edges. As the pink overtakes the blue the grey is left behind. Hanging in the sky with a pink balloon, the view is transfixed, and relevance perches below with the hand of Sinister Grim.

Sinister Grim was an unruly child, and enjoyed his subtle aggression. His aggravations were curiosities. If he was an adult his life would be his own, but as a child, liberty and pleasure were passed down not discovered freely. He is not naughty or mischievous, but his presence presents peculiarity. The interpretation of his traits maintain many frowning heads. It is not that he is bad, but that he brings out the bad in others. He stands in the corner seeking acknowledgement, and with all the attention delegates disaster. He shrugs it off with a fear of old age. After all what has he done that is considered so terrible?

How can anyone be so wrong? There are two problematic themes for Sinister that he cannot understand. Eminently conscientious, honest, and brave Sinister is disappointed in being a child full of wonder. He is bewildered by resonating echoes. Endless whispers through doors and windows. Overheard tones of things he should know nothing about. He also waits with pervasive infatuation to infiltrate virtue in those showing none. He apologizes for the disregard, but as he has said before,

"To you this apology does commence."

It is the morning of the seventh day in November, and it is early as yesterday clings to its aftermath. Time does not let go completely. It never bends to the whim of a soul. The soul instead bends to the whim of time. Whose time is questionable, but the resonance remains the same. That is the effect of the single personality in regard to the passing past. The wasted days of standard nicety and poise. For now this shall reside within a question to eliminate any association to the sense of an answer.

Time is all there is as without it there are no definitions nor explanations to describe or understand the biased station of being. The beginning should slash thought prior to this, however, even the most simplest of things can escape logic. Fragments form a hole here, but where is the middle of the whole? Where is the whole to have a middle? It is all passing time, and time has passed. It has passed, and now gone rocks in a chair without rockers. The backward harmonica calls for a reprint. The substandard interrogation of understanding formed a spelling mistake. It is funny like spoons collecting refuge. Containing the debris in order to be cleaned. Is this really the passing of time? The soiled wishing to be washed.

He lights a candle and recedes to thought. This thought, this action, and its retort responds to the moment at hand. Snoring has created a lack of respect for the reading as well as the writing. Love comes still, but that is the passing time that collects in the recesses of decay. The want of not wasting, the tears for wasting, and the loss of determination that would reside in either. Humbug! The wasted truth is the estate that wilted with good filling. The teeth that rot with or without calcium. Nonsense, but the irrevocable surmise of a wishing star catches the greatest heights. Stars cannot wish can they? Only for millions of dollars, but are they worth that much? Humor helps the escape, the entanglement becomes smaller, and the eradication of the spirit declines. But so does the paper. What paper? You have paper?

Where is the focus? Where is the reason? On the horizon lost in squinted eyes. Shattered at the handprint of innocence. Cracked in the peeling paper on walls not seen in many years. The rape of it all, the linguistic of me and the fiction of us, but where are we?

"Where are we?"

Into reality with the blinking gyration of a sinking ship. It flexes in the whirl of a deep wind. The gravity pulls as the friction burns, but escape is conquered. Forced diction and imposed meaning. This force earns a reclusive margin of words that continue to bleep. Funny?

"The humor here resides with me, but never lost sight of you."

The apology rings again.

"To you this apology does commence."

Focus becomes clear in the recess of wasted paper and ink.

"These things are sacred."

"I know. Yes." Agreement.

"You know! Well these things do not even occur within a regular frame of time. It is a good thing we weave our circles to live on within them. For we are these ripples expanding in the sea. We are the wrinkles of time that sit in oceans of age."

Understanding. Reason. Inflicted pursuit, but the sentiment is not tangible. The excuses are reasonable, but terms corrode. Acceptance trailing into the sunset holding fire. Dastardly flares, and deported rhythms gone forever.

The vicious contempt comes out as time still passes. We lose it with ease and comfort, wave adoring presentations, but ignored, turn back to block the glee. Are these fat morsels so light?

"The truth comes quickly so why do we resign?"

What is in coffee that is not in motivation and discipline? Discipline comes with the steadfast fascination, and the calamity of thinking it was right. Where is the sense? Sleeping like a rogue in hopes of blessing. Too many objections and not enough evidence. Where did it go? Did we have anything less than a rhetorical statement? Well? The back tracking, original distraction repeats with the slip of a pressed key. The constantly pressed key of oppression and rejection. The flames of honor and respect were torches in the flagrant bliss of natural immaturity. We have the spelling mistakes, but the truth is the truth. Sleep does come quickly, but so do these words. These words? These words.

We may not have a lot tomorrow, but we do have us. Pain, guilt, and shame stack tall, and purity and goodness are installed with the vision of memory. Tomorrow never came so close, but it never chose to be. It is a fact that remains until forever and bleeds like a rock. It cannot say yes or no so it is today. Today unto tomorrow, the good, the bad, and the benign. It closes fast and holds on tight to never let go. Hold tight yourself my friend, only tears carry a farewell, and not today. We are getting stronger, wiser, older, but not today. We are told and made, but not today. We are strong enough to hold on even though so much is lost, but not today. We are here, and today we are to be just a whisper floating amidst the smoke. A temper tempts the picture, and a moment is gone again, reborn. A soul upon a soul flirting with fate to call us back to today. Now.

"Oh how lovely it is."

We are to be tomorrow. Free from limitation, excess, and consequence. The choice is free from decision, and debate is outcast. Free, expressive love in a long term relationship. Friendship lasting beyond any shortage. Intimate adventures with like-minded people. Time to be and enjoy without worry or stress. Fiction does not define an answer in which the winning scores belittle loss and gain. What can be won, loses, and what can be lost, wins. The fragment of subsiding embodies the soul. People, persons given a moment do tie the bearing of closure. Stolen youth, decayed age, and weathered steps unto completion.

What is finished torments the soul with disbelief. The refuge of a cloud that beholds hope. Lost, it goes, and gone this concedes. The tearing quake of a whole to be forgotten. A greater step only sees half, but the exemplified pretension and extension grows. To lose the aspiration means we did not have the breath to begin with.

What do we know about hope? The tinted expression of flamboyant salvation. The shortage of time without reproach ends. The soul dies, and we have run out of time. The memories are slaughtered, the conclusions concede the bearing of influence as people flail in the trial of reason. A folded napkin still requires etiquette. Hope is the staple tool and trade of usage and understanding. The moment is a lapse of hope, conquered by fear and mortality, and the decay of honest corrosion forges the soul a future with no end. To become divine we must commence, not burn out, sell out, or turn our tails toward the sun in hope of a spanking. The fundamental question of the chicken and the egg is turned over to God, and He says,

"They are the composition of transition."

Beckoning nothing again, now what will be? We do not know, but mind the loss. We do not know as we look away and forget.

A fine melody brings process by the hands to look at the sunset with a smile. Possibility lives and we as the process carry it out with wonderment, laughter, and exuberant celebration. We declare today, now, and the moment of reckoning and condition plays chance. Sinking fortune really gave us all this?

Negative prospects are denied. Pessimism chokes on a bridge of the sky that breathes inhalation from beauty to exhale the truth. The extinguished surprise of being alive brings a gift that presents the day with no special activity, but awards the unnecessary token of love. Silent suffering for the unexpected bounty second guesses the purpose of reason. Denying the infrequent affluence to which this gift arrives does not isolate the pain reflected in the self. The world together builds up the difference to set our lives at ease. We really do care and create the future as best we can.

Indifferent and detached, protected from the harm at bay, and worth the inner turmoil longing for the truth. Reality with open interpretation granted a preview, and the resolution is in the grade. Longing restlessly for the facts to become the figures, open and loving. Whispering forgiveness in the moments of weakness. The temptation lost and bound, upholds the inner soul to judgment. Pleading guilty of the wrongs, and tormented by the reality of the deed. Signs of tears posting regret. What was it we did so readily? Men and women choosing life, and making up the secrets in the surprise.

Conspicuous traffic wreaks havoc. Noise over coated with headphones watches the lights change, and people walk, vehicles no longer yield, and energy moves. Rambunctious ambitions send the weight of the world. The footsteps of a personality stroke the embrace of infancy with an ambulance siren. The overshadowed tone boasts infinity. The apprehensive adherence to the void. The blanket of sleep that captures the crossing of the crossroads as the wrong way wanes, the right way shines, and the truth upholds both. The unprecedented disguise looks away as no one sees it, but the problems pass.

Vice filters the distance to predict wear. The usage being the optimal choice breaks the ties with fixed habitation. The relaxation of the mind numbs the recreational being. Programmed time enriches the crisis with the prevalent absence of discretion. The base of the palm is set against the recessed chin. The eye squints slightly to follow the pressurized hand. The mind works wonders, plays tricks, and dresses the compact congestion of life. Flexing, pulsing, life beating the battered drum of belief to liberate the fixated moments with sport. The freedom of action, speech, thought, and scheme is the comprehensive dictionary of nature.

People scratch their chins, shrug their shoulders, and become enlightened with destiny. The flare of the human condition is restrained to the skin like enslavement. A flash in the pan for the blind blight of coming time. As if animals in a zoo accepted the definition of freedom with an awareness for a lack of bars. True freedom is not boxed in separate containers fabricated by type, but in the intuition of nature. It is like eating a banana when you want to and not when the south of the border sells it to you. It is like the prominent absence of breath when not focused on by interest. It is like the corn on the cob instead of the can.

Laughter has to remain relevant. The humor of limitation and nature itself infect the waking eye with consequence. The recognition may slowly fade away, but growth and death, trial and reward are the markings of occasion. This moment of noise again, although now it is reflective of us all. It denounces the solitude and isolation as the irreversible truth of reason. The definition is the outcome of all this greedy solace. The volcano has spat up its molten eruption to vouch that it is hot. All things have to end. The measures boldly close the can of worms, but sighing life still disbelieves. We smirk in the sight of the sun to radiate shorter sights as more supreme. The concentration fluctuates, comprehension descends, and the worry of the work wraps the world in a mass of dazed aesthetics. How can there be focus? Where can the maintenance of such prevalent relations reside in the understanding of reality?

The ties that bind us universally predicted the past events to qualify repair as substance. The quality of abstraction borders the skin outside of any safety regulation. The tired bodies calmly rest as mourning minds are disparaged by the children pointing and shouting.

"You!"

Us. This. Now. Pigeons scout the concrete for crumbs as desperate, parentless children despair for guidance. The powerless time restricts the offense as cooperative choice indulges in the test. The silent auction of action and ethics flaunt a courteous call to remembrance. Memories are sacred, life is activation, and the resonance created by the balance of emanation realizes the rationale. Control, moderation, and usage are the three, definitive keys to progress. All external, all internal, all eternal broadcasts of graffiti embroidered by the air of life. The belief in stature and state is the discipline of order. The admission of acceleration is the declension of decline.

Blank intervention, cause and effect are stuck with the snare of appreciation. The release of pressure controls the setting because oblivion orders a recall.

"Instruct the others, we are to be barefoot."

Clouds scurry in the sky as the pink balloon rises. The darkening consequence holds more bearing than resistance, and the temptation recognizes defeat. Hope is gone, but the self lives. The self impregnates the flirting disaster with organization, and promise buries the acceptance with the exemption of unharnessed behavior. The towering inferno of degree and circumstance lets the smiles smile. Coming forward, and always chasing rainbows the watching embryos evolve with the honey of the working bees. Can people breathe being when chasing bluebirds? Flight does exorcise the spasms of decay, but a fine point must present memory with patronage, occurrence, and subsiding trickery. Believe the disbelief. Faction the unfathomable as the margin for some degree of success. The curiosity between eighteenth and nineteenth on Chestnut Street questions the outbreak of symbiosis. Option openly viewed the sanctuary, but every person walks by, and every person decrees loss and gain advised by value. The syncopation slips on a sliding site of shiny shoes stuck in succulence. The associated wow! Drunk, lost, knowing, and showing earnest blossoms of greedy skies wishing themselves blue.

Turn the screw, and wind the cat up tight. Climb the stairs upon our prayers, and goodnight. What do people know beyond themselves? The shuddering gaiety of fuses blown, spaghetti blurred, and the light sauce scolded. Goodnight.

"Goodnight."

Turn loose the burning motion conveyed in conviction to deny or obey the purpose circling descent. The abstraction is gone like a wobbling pigeon. The shambles of shade follow the crooked, crossed trail into the whistling moment already lost. The pretty abyss that sinks so deep that purpose sank in a moment of slumber. Slanted hiccups do not forgo fortune, and the free based slogans of slander take steps. Steps frozen memory has lost in the tangled tangents of noise. Choice distorted by reason gags a retort short of manure. The purpose progresses, but memory fades. The message ignores the frequent bias of steps foretold, forgotten, forever. The slogans are slain, and life is embalmed with the etiquette of process. Moment to moment, time by time, and tear by tear.

We are forever fragmented, disillusioned by choice, and declared by reason. One step unto the next. Tomorrow does not go beyond today without blank repetition. The recurring realism of the shadowed resonance of charms sold and bought at reasonable prices. Who knows what life carries, and who is more than what that can be? The memory of tomorrow is today.

He smiled at me, and made me happy. The soul enjoys kindness, and the body craves love. Innocence barren of sin, and longevity butchered by pleasure. The immaculate, immediate ritual of synthetic momentum cries time, and as the body lies, awareness bleeds like a splitting amoeba. The promiscuous behavior is sought and slain in an alley like a cat. The yawning energy embraces the ability of distance. Broken ties, colorful signs, and the saturated process do embellish the situation. Foreign tongues wagging like dogs bragging understanding. The deed of an unorthodox child is the problematic discharge of disarranged life. Progress is deceitful anarchy, and plagues the millions with dissection. Torn from the bowels of a writhing anus resemblance is spherical continence. The disparaged linguistic of people being themselves. People choosing advantage, fumbling the disadvantage, and accepting the interplay. People wreaking havoc in the accordance of the abyss that made the meter. People losing sight, gaining vision, and adopting pedigree. Pilgrimage to pilgrimage, trial after trial, and solitary belief accepts the grasp.

Hands clasp achievement, and compromising task tongues speak the truth. Spreading distaste, people act out, and enforce the internal view. Still tired, still yearning, but broken. Still lost, but winning and losing sturdy footing. Repetition, but meaning is caught in the ballroom spinning circles. The ambiguous station approaches disarray, but broadcasts global psyche. Is it an optical illusion? Is it sleight of hand? Prosper and conquer, divide and saunter, but ridicule the wonder because endless depravity has the accountability to remember precision. Still tired, still yearning, winning and losing, and without sturdy footing. The conscious deliberation has truly diminished the prospects.

CHAPTER FIVE

This So-Called Sinister Grim

TWILIGHT CARESSES THE sky with grey tones. Undistinguished terms disturbed by remembrance. Acceptance conjuring a state of being, mimicking any preference, and determining the soul. The sewer grate accepts a cigarette and slated fiction determines its presence.

So much, so fast, and too soon. Time has lost direction, and we have tormented ourselves with the slaughter of light. Cascading shadows flying so that the fallen residue hides in the dark. A turning signal gave clearance, but the opposing traffic did not notice.

"BAM!"

A dance of collision, and speeding up a told fortune comes to pass. The turning signal is ignored for progress. Remorse and removal bringing us forward in a trance that declares amnesty, but bears the turmoil of love. Sinister Grim sat watching the traffic. Their corresponding bodies mingle with violent happenstance. He watches while the world walks by without a single high. The momentum of time and being is disjointed by the space between them. Memory includes friends, lovers, and family as obsolete dreams. He can recall their passing, but they have already passed. Life reflects it all in a halo of superficial touch. Broken hearts, mended words, and strung out minds hiding in occurrence. The withdrawn hearts are displeased while a toe taps a recognizable tune. Loud loads of longing, turning, and burning figments remembered.

Sinister does not laugh. He sighs with the destruction of purity. His yearning for accompaniment labors in the examination of reason. It is left in his own conclusion. Cold, he adjusts his love, appreciates the loss, and knows there is no way to go back. It is over, and Sinister grins.

The humor in what cannot be longs for it to be so. There is no way to go forward, too much has been given away, and too much is lost. He contemplates tossing himself into the traffic, but what will that do except add to the length of the traffic details. How can he lose without losing?

Everything passes indignant to his presence, and he knows it. How can he be in such a world of indifference? What can come next out of such oblivion? Waving ties and shared emotion, but there is nothing new to look upon. Nothing left to feel, and nothing left to be. He cannot fill in the blanks anymore because his mind is gone, his body hurt, and his will is too tired to believe in more.

"I believe in you."

What is that? How can that be? Tears dry so quickly as loss is supplied with gain, and indifference strokes fueling chance.

"I believe in you."

What is that? How can that be? Days pass so quickly, loss supplied by gain, and indifferent strokes stoking chance. The poured tea is getting cold, but nothing lasts too long. One more time, maybe, redemption can still clearly speak. Like salt on an icy slope we can see where to step. Carefree momentum has brought us here, and has hung this price upon his head.

"Worth? What can I be worth?"

People carry on and time will tell the loss.

"What can be lost with just my passing?"

Doubt fills Sinister's head as he sits on the brink of his self-destruction. The cold, ambiguous air adds to his despair. Nothing stands up to say no. He wonders bewildered by loss, frantic for gain as his footsteps lose sight, and now shadows fall as time retorts.

"Why not?"

No reason comes to mind other than the tortured replay of time gone by. Perhaps sleep will help sway the memories.

"Maybe."

The snot drips in his nostrils, but resignation declines recognition.

"Does anyone care anyway?"

They can be counted on one hand, and the fact infatuates sorrow even more. People do not know how to love, and so Sinister feels their lack of affection. Ghosts calling out from the past to condemn the future.

"I am lost with hope and despair."

Barren with memories alone Sinister's future seems grim. Breathing isolation to coax worse case scenarios he admires the path of survival. It clouds over, and the sun is vanquished to unseen space. The mugginess of the air tells us that it is there. The wind tickles the trees. Sound braces form. The infinite complexity of choice raises even more confusion. Reality resonating reason, and developing rhyme.

Starting now and for the rest of my life, I, the undersigned, hereby agree to the preservation of my spirit and the procession of my thought. I mean what I say, act what I think, and practise what I believe with the intent of producing good. I agree to promote creativity through education in order to enlighten myself and others. I agree to attain bliss from the potential of a moment because great things happen.

---   ---------------------
                        Signature   Date

Where lies the cliché? In the smouldered terms of fierce debris? Naked, pleading flesh wrapped in paper like an unopened gift, but the discerning eye can tell what it is. Struck with the stuck mind, and plagued by the weakened flesh.

"Yes, oh, yes."

What has been happening? We do not know, but growing legs we walk to see the future's toll. Repetition killed the cat and not its curiosity. The examination foretold the being of its want. Scolded by rain and shunned by the sun, we grow. Earnest trappings of belief and task hurt by the pleas of discontent children. Are we still children? A penny dropped into the fountain of fortune to mature into a dime. Groovy.

"Who is it?"

Groovy.

"Who is it?"

"It is me."

A fabrication of the senses and a decision of nonsense. The self-evident truth and self-proposed notion evolving to a problematic scale, and one by one we all fall down. Conveniently done without worry or fuss, we will let us wait and see.

Handwritten tones explore the sun. Warm, white whimsy welcomes warm, white whimsy. All for love, the sake of freedom, and the worth of devotion. Broken ambition accepts what was already there, and does no longer trample old emotion. Aspiration does not sigh, but beckons the will to break it which it will not do. It will not wither like so many moments already spent. This will not burn brightly out as hesitation speaks to reality in order to reward the admiration. Inexplicable survival proves worth. Old shoes, new socks, and the unknown still ensign shudders.

A dream, dead reckoning, and black thoughts. A lived out memory replayed while asleep, lying on the ground in recognizable clothing, and smudging the concrete with disapproved color.

"RED."

Whispers warn of the response as black, balmy thoughts bleakly beam seclusion. Isolated, lonely recognition writing to the subconscious. Telling of the blackest deed and its grotesque adherence to the future. Fear can sense its wealth enough to pass it around, and sick, twisted flesh contorts to its command. The past tells of at least a pinch of salt.

Truth is like a grain of salt. Lost in the desperation of isolation and rendering greater strength in numbers. The truth is like the self. Small and pure the self is the truth. Both are tiny parts to the greatest of clocks.

"God."

Full lips pursed to greet the grandest kiss, and the shadow embraces a fitting glory. Content complexion and agreeable eyes. Faint wind cools heavier heads to let love blossom in gestures of cognition. Understanding smiles on a cat's whisker.

The truth is deceived, and becomes belligerent in order to target the nearest point of weakness. It destroys cities, contaminates compassion, and sadly retribution renders choice. Spells are woven with regret, and reason rectified promises to never cross the stream. It wades the waters, but never dares the other side.

"Insert money here."

Things, objects, and desire manipulate time. The longing for the lost or the renewal of the reward comes with inopportune time. The rushed preservation of the controlled delivers the goods whether ready or not with excess. Does time twist us around or do we twist around time? What monitor's temptation? Us or time?

"All things in moderation."

So they say, but which way discloses the grasp? Transfixed conclusions walking in the rain. Drenched aspiration, tainted obsession, and ridiculed habit all humming fine-tuned steps. Progression.

"Da da da, da da da, da da da, da da da da da da da do do do."

Observations threaten the rhythm. Obscure motivation captivates the game. Meat sours in the dreadful heat, and sprouts deceit to color the compulsion with disorder. Tints of hints repeating. Chewing facts slowly absorbed, absolved, and advocated, but it is hard to confess the truth.

Slaves of discontent motion, and powerless, beating gangs of up tempo action live bouncing time. Flexible forces waiting to go down ponder degree enough to inspect the broken glass. Cryptic sensation encompasses all bantering understanding and prejudice condemnation as well as the different aspects of tragedy. Waiting and wanting, hate. Abandoned patience and sentiment for the rule of decision. Summing up all things out of place and duty calls the wear polite.

Bits of fat and starch that stick to the soles of shoes. Processed potential that falls to the floor to sour its shine. The air quickens hastily in brisk rotation. The flowers sway, the clouds collect, and the sweets become distasteful. Crazy people are everywhere, inside and out, and fortune passes the unfortunate cookie. There are no longer disadvantaged spasms because the disclosure chokes as the disaster breaks. Walking, riding fortune as multiplicity binds the arm's length to the catch of the day. The once miniature discretion engorges, and promises not to get caught, but served. Ring a bell to catch the next stop! Smell the irrational stink to stop too soon and stop too late. Rub the nose that drips because there is no going back. No stance to ease the flow, and no air to cure the walk. Swollen legs stand still enough to blink an eye's fill, but what gauge is this? Who determined this gauge?

Do not say no, instead let go, and become the future stop because it lives in our living room. The absorbing touch of finger paint acids mending with skin to absolve the drainage. The loss is not our own, but it closes fast, forgets nothing, and forebears the gained mistakes. Tomorrow always said,

"Let there be breakfast!"

No one heard the uttered words, but there we go again, away. Few return as regained memories. Action retells the fable, but remembers the indignant, scolded truth. The armour is disintegrating as momentum carries us forward. By chance we pass the progress to incorporate the welcomed lapping of a gleaming tongue. The foretold sound covers the footprints walking across trespassed closure, and tomorrow will not forget the eaten self. Can we even remember?

Traffic noise, a heavy bus heaving passengers with the spongy silence of diesel. The stop light holds the congestive tone with obscurity. People becoming people describe one unto one. The being is lost with the incarceration of the soul. Sense binds the ground with a binge on broadcast. Ignorance cannot protect us. Indifference cannot distance the abuse. Compassion warms the corruption, miniatures the agony, and retorts to the engorged cries for justice. Equality and freedom condone this disgrace, and hand down these temperaments of simple removal to excavate the work we have already done. Choices fall alone, but if we truly stand together we can make it home again.

Over driven misery and the misconceptions of being pile up. Life as unique as it may be rolls on with repetitious habit. The company comes and the moment is saturated with difference, although habits and rituals breed similarity. Trials confiscated to the self, but shared throughout the world. Servitude and humility boast no reward except for the knowledge therein. The rabble on the road distracts clear headed thinking, but maybe we should have just stayed at home to be safe?

Home lands like a splattered bug, small and discreet. Safety broods in belief, the loss of fear, and the strength to admire not condemn difference. Tears swell as sorrow tells of too many tales that are broken and diseased. Men worth saving condemned, and women bold enough to wipe their brows. The spaced out fragments are too sacred to collect. Intolerance squeezes out too many valuable percentages. The closed door keeps the crowd in, but newcomers nervously negate entrance. The numbers are manipulated, the mass is misinformed, and the decisive cutting off of arms and heads leads to a bloody mess. Symmetrical compositions are incomplete, and all the missing data fills the world with holes. Opposing factors may discriminate, but opposing measures balance well. The cost of cut offs in comparison to creative integration do not equal either, but who set the measurements? Who's ruler is this?

Gravity pulls the weight, and we observe the limitation. Hands at our sides, backs laid straight, eyes forward, integrate. Uncertainty and rigid ideals swindle experience, suture possibility, and compromise the exchange. Why? What is it worth?

Can we not think? Feed upon the breast that warms our nurtured inspection of remorse, and mistakes as human resources are extinguished. Languished thoughts and morbid actions become the trial and error of incorporating more. How can this be bad or wrong? How can we not learn when teaching is so readily available? Cross eyed and powerless people are scared, secured, and surmised. The obvious oblivion fractures even the strongest bone.

Where is the magic, wonder, and joy? Where have all the options gone, and what has become of their morality? Stuck and struggling, isolated and trapped with no help or conscious preparation. There is no warning of the oncoming pitfall. The beaten fragments just collect, but the corrosion catches the control. A satisfying motion no longer works in a cascade of missed opportunities. It is a tangent of self-obsessed thinking that paralyses progress. It is a moment of recall that disparagingly accepts the past. Incidental, wishful thinking for the severed articles to congeal, but the lasting impression always condemns the soul. Even in the warmest heat, brightest light, and greatest stance waits downfall with its reckoning. A morose world with no cure for the turmoil inside it. A ragged choice waking to wave goodbye. Wager the cost and double the profit.

Illusions of bodies floating, rising to Heaven to claim their prize, but they cannot quite make it passed the net of clouds. Shackles bolted to the world solidified by sweat, created by chaos, and bred by bliss. Passions control the reason as people pervert preservation. What is love? Where is the truth? What happened to all the beauty? Who defined evil? Who broadcasts religion? How do we choose salvation?

Possession of the facts clarifies the reason, but who decides its history? The fire is smoking, smoldered by the debris of life, and ignited by the breath of choice. Its coals flicker like swarming flies as its heat radiates acceptance. The abysmal unknowns condemn us. We may ask, but they may not answer.

"How did we get here?"

"How are we still here?"

People notice, but keep walking anyway. They inflect the lies and keep on trekking. They delude the possibility to be what they are, ignorant, biased parasites that feed on the growth of the land. They walk a line of disgrace to appropriate freedom. They read and learn, but never know the difference between ideal and reality. Maybe they imagine personality to accept the decline, but first impressions are usually correct.

Muttered words not recognized as recognition is undervalued and the truth is never questioned. Open arms just accept the display. We all want to be loved, forgiven, and safe, but does that allow this indiscretion? Vice and knowledge combine to know the truth, and all we have to do is accept them. Ignorance only goes so far, temptation pulls us further, and moments organised realize the overload.

Figures shift, moments collide, and the truth reflects our head scratching pedigree as the beat goes on. All we want is to be. How we cannot comprehend because we walk too briskly, look to briefly, and really comprehend less than both. Strung out on life with no high too great. Experience dawn's new progress. The words compress as life finds a way to do right, but we veer left to accept the disadvantage because it feels right. The world understands our expense, but do we expect any change? The world revolves, and so do we like the chorus of a song overtly repeated. No one knows what they want, and if they do, do they know it is right? Pragmatism evolves into transgressive remarks as people discern the truth. The congress of the absent minded remains to not know the truth.

CHAPTER SIX

Sitting in the Sun's Purge with Salt

IT IS A new day of old habits with repetition unto decay. The lessons learned ignore themselves as the future becomes the past. Tomorrow should know better than today, but recreation ruins the rules, restriction redeems reckless regard, and restitution reasons a relapse. Sorrow unto death.

"Goodbye."

"Please sit down."

Naïve unto death. The dots and signs work out rhythm. A repetitive rhythm flowing like ink, and coagulating with the air to create life. Words. Endless words to describe the way of the world. The beat of the human heart, and the awareness of an eye summed up in words. One sentence after the next. One word to follow another. Multi-layered complexity simplified by the tones of recall. Praise and prayer for the cooling wind.

What can happen in a moment will not replay? It will reactivate itself through choice, but the adding agents always differ. Like a song change one rhythm becomes another. One moment it rises like an opened door exposing death's truth, and the unknown finality is witnessed, red handed, and complete. Love is stronger than death, but death's secret is still unknown. Truth spans greater lifetimes than ours as our hands only grasp what they touch. Eminent death consumes this burning life.

Memory recalled backwards the glory and gain of change. The written tones, spoken talent, and unworthy hustling amount to glib hands. Frozen, fractured memory is the property of the state. An anesthetic for the nation to numb gums and spill the desired, perpetual walls with continuance. Restrain radical retribution! The sour lozenge of recall, memory, and focus.

"Oh yeah."

Get on down to the dirty work of calling.

"Oh yeah."

Free sex! Sell! Sell! Sell! Taint that torment, color the smirk, and repose the posture people. Straightened backs and forward eyes forgive broken promises. It matters not, meanders little, but contrives everything. How much more can there be allowed to be? The puzzle piece fits a jigsaw slain by slavery. Who can talk? Who can answer? What can there be?

Absolute contrivance, contraband obsession, and temptation taxing the body. Sorrow handles the heart in old, cold hands and inexplicable demise. Take part and lose the impossible by giving it away freely, lovingly now. People rot, everything corrodes, and a lonely heart fails in shattered dreams and broken promises. People blessed with living tissue are still caught in the trap of decay.

Stability and routine may collect morsels of love in the starvation of its kisses, but concentrated time has a cigarette. The fragile moments built from a diverse training age unknown, smoothly, slow, but now realized speed up beyond control. The balance is inherited, responsive characteristics that are displayed in objects or places. People transport memories, decisions all influenced by the corrosion of age and the conclusion of life. A million singular things pulled together by time and God.

Time's appraisal is neutral energy funneling down to become these million things to produce the natural, invoked worth. One draft is not perfect. One choice cannot simply define positive or negative. Many factors are involved when dealing with a million things. Objects, people, destinations rooted in truth, raised by reason, and overlooked by objective. Tricky, picky delusion diluted with the truth. Prickly, finicky people placing themselves with growth. The low, harsh reality remains complacent and derogatory.

Problems on the serene lake of motion that ride the waves with calamity. The precious moments are eaten by the world's gnarly teeth. Big, gruesome features enshroud those teeth. Twisted muscles chewing with an open mouth and blazing eyes reckon the worth of the meal. The taste of the bottom of the binge. The absorption of all things to become nothing. Mute force, the possible reaction, and the unlikely choice for descent.

"Death will eat all things, and its flexing force will tear this world apart."

Sitting on the ledge of oblivion, waiting for time and moment to be perfectly free. Minds argue incessantly, but the result is always the same. Loss. Desperate decent back into the wilderness. The crazy, hazy shade of all made men against their own destruction. Dangerous rituals enticing the common to become spectacular. It is cold on the edge. Winds flapping loose, fitted clothing, and there seems to be no way of getting used to it. Temporal visions disrupt the flow as cries slow the decay.

Hopeless sensations bring on distraction, but this time patience is willing to wait. Garnished children do not seem to understand the gritty, dirty reality that traps so many adults. Hesitation keeps us on the ledge. Regret has apprehended the active hand. Time will slow, noise will stop, and a due excuse will pave the way to portray this past experience. Hesitation sticks to rationalize the loss. Reason working overtime can discipline the repetitive stupor, but sloppy consistency ridicules the work with death. Nothing truly changes with subsidence. The wholesome articles are swept away, and the debris is left to make the right choice.

Over time courage dwindles, weakness prevails, and once again the ride starts up. Moderate at first, then a corner, the speed picks up, another corner, and screams fill the air. The broken soul gives in finally.

"I do not know for sure."

Minced feelings too small to recognize, and the sensations mesh in a cloudy afterthought.

"What now?"

CHAPTER SEVEN

Sleeping in the Moon's Luxury with Pepper

A FRESH PAGE, an old habit, and now! Right now! The darkness takes its time to arrive, but it is definitely expected. It replied.

"Come rain or come shine I will be there."

Not in the shadows or under the sinking sun, but in person, large and brooding. Not the televised vision of death, but the gloomy, underlying spectre that corrodes all hearts and action. The burden of looking the other way, but tumbling in the opposite direction. More than shadows because the darkness basks infinity beyond the sun. Now, here, waiting for the black to arrive earnestly.

People cannot see what is behind them, but there it is at the end of the road waiting for instruction. It pleases our bodies to know more is inside than what is visible so why not in darkness? Failure, corrosion, and obscenity.

"Do what thou will."

It seems a tame obstruction. Beckoning circumstance is by our means trivial, and outcome no doubt infiltrates the light with darkness. Death must see life to know when to end it.

We are hardly getting over it when we start getting used to it, and by then we are lost. The old are wise, but useless connotations in an outdated diary. Impulse and instinct create the living ordeal and we merely react. The reasonable progression of age becomes obsolete as the children carry the rights and sins of their elders.

"I have known a six year old to roll a joint, and a three year old who knew smoking was wrong. I have known lifelong drunks, drug addicts of all descriptions, and puritans who battle the odds."

Life is a mess that no one can clean up no matter how many try.

"Do what thou will."

The world knows of our rights and wrongs. It tabulates excess and depletion to modify the consequences to consumers. A tree dies so a new one grows. Bugs are in multitudes so kill those you can! The old become the new, election after election, and the questionable terms become finite. The living proof of imagination and its curse of living tissue. So many strangers, but God knows who they are. Why? What is the reason of concept? Pain. Belief. Resource. The terms never validate themselves. It is all guess work living and dying. Belief stands out to say, "That's reality!"

The dream is over. No one cares passed their arm's length, yet selfish safety still breed's death. We are one or the other, maybe both, but it does not matter anymore. Goodbye.

"Goodbye."

Goodbye, but I must die.

It is not my turn so I must wait for time because then it shall be ours.

Vicious perception distorts the truth. The whole is absorbed in the safety of the self. Preoccupied porcupines hiding amidst the mushrooms, neutral and ripe awaiting blossom. The flesh collapses amid the manure of the mushrooms and atop the caustic fiber of sweet decay. Lost in the woods, out of sight, the spirits come and overtake the fear. Alone and dead who finds the body? Do not jump to conclusion too quickly because perished hands brand the labour of such a degree, and the quickness of step harnessed by desire.

Whispers come from the loneliness like uncalled answers telling lies, broken promises, and heartbreak. The soul is weary, briskly napping in the afternoon sun, but caught in its warmth oversleeps. It is trapped in memory, dreaming bliss, but incarcerated with truth. Reality speaks a living realm of impossible dreaming. Tears for the truth and the unwanted sacrifice. The torture of temptation. Stretching muscles flex awareness with unseen blood as the world will never forget. People, places, postures already perplexed with personality poised poignantly to be praised. Distortion breaks the vow and does forget the importance of time's allowance. It dictates choice and prayer answers the deception. It is all lost in that moment. The slaughter of all this tangible love to rule the world in that moment of lost decay.

"I praise thee love."

Sadness and decay. Ink marches again. A suitable stride and conditioned short sightedness point the mark of citation. Recessive reflections perplex the past in a future of collapsed aspiration. Sincerity is waning in a whirlwind of corruption. The soul torn bare of its equals, and the mind and the body do not stand a chance against such odds. What bears the question alleviates the answer that is dormant and dear. The mirage against the madness hoping to communicate simple satisfaction.

Guilt and greed have swallowed the heart. Solemn shadows shifting in the sidelines with pure intent to procure swollen kisses. Blessings beating bounty with extravagance, and purpose idly wandering free, loses all its purpose. Time is wicked gaiety as sarcasm does not become modest comics. These headphones suck as everything encourages anger. The weak disposition compromises the wonder of a moment in lost remembrance. Cold, methodical disguises and disparaging remarks. People do not care as they bamboozle creation to condone bleak acceptance. Hunger incites the anger, wanting disaster and chaos to produce the chosen apparition. Death of course laughs at the primates choking opposition.

Pessimistic anger feasting upon the decent fibers until the fabric falls apart. Clenched nerves, dissatisfied context, and abhorrent contempt all coax the moment into a blur of animosity. Deep breathes do not help and friendly submission does not sway the view. People are just stupid, decrepit anguish. The complexity may vary, but the human perception crinkles in the heat of the moment. Tomorrow passes by and forgets to look at what is there. Hope and love. Distinguished features, floating invisible to yield the trivial, commercial free, pornography that sidesteps the route to freedom in order to trip over the margin. The figments combine the loose fitting delusions that scramble posterity hiding in the underbrush.

People, evil people looking down, hiding in being, unfathomable. We deserve our vindication. Nodded budges, forbidden pedigree, and destined design stand side by side starring frozen paces in the accumulated waste. The outcome does deserve its design. The cymbals crash and the moment is broken. Design upholds its agreement to look behind the walls of condition to see the true intent. It beckons burden by pleading guilty. The sparse, vague entity gathers the burden, beckons the bleeding blessing to see beyond it, and recognition to blur the line of deception. We keep running to accept the station that holds our ground until we see the future. Blind, ambiguous trades come and go with no reason or design, but fragmented purpose keeps us on our way.

Memories are funny things. Predictable and cool like calm waters touring eternity. Love and hate echoing through recall like grains of sand. Small and inconsiderable truths filtered through the senses and branded to time like transparent labels. Slogans and culture admiring progress with its decay. The propriety of myth and manner to illuminate reality with the wishful thinking of an exorbitant soul. Personality pronounces proof, but prompts propaganda. The reason for choice and consequence retread with memories. Growth uplifting the bodies from the mud to cascade in the sun like bobbing stars. Beauty wreaks havoc as words captivate potential disorder. The tongues are in the water tasting for its affirmation. Death's reflection has not found it yet.

Life lingers lithe and likeable to lacerate conception with consumption. The images blur, the sound crumbles to silence, and nothing held tastes of its sweet smell. Is this how we remember? Distinct ways of understanding corrupting the sense for the sensation. Mumbled tunes perk the ears with unknown quotations and coagulated tones of unruly expectation. The curious continuation of blind eyes waiting for light in the entombed clarity.

Raw nerves, twitching cells, and apocalyptic observations in the course of the day spurt conscious decision. The hands raising ability accomplish accommodating acceleration. The whirling rhyme of decay may catch up, but for now it twirls in the other direction. Life still breathes its incessant ease and accompanies tutelage with faith. Freedom for tomorrow, fortune for today, and fellowship for now. The conclusions are apparent.

"Live while thou may."

Associations do surmise the disarray. Broken concentration trails off with the winding road, and travel may be dislocated, but the outcome holds the truth of being. Tread forcing the earth, breath fixing the air, survival gulping water, and the heart burning fire.

"Pass it around."

Suspicion coaxing apparitions, suspension finding abeyance, and succession bearing witness. Goodness and darkness mixing the waters until murky and aged. Digression amidst the context of words no doubt.

Distortion against the puritanical wall of judgment in dreams delivering permanent consideration. The intricate design under inspection recites.

"To be or not to be."

The conclusions remain apparent and stand behind the report. The extremes are mingling matters of fact with actions minced by humanity faintly disbelieving. Down the stairs, pull the shade, and focus on the pouring rain. The sounds collide.

"SMASH!"

Birds fly from the safety of their nests as chaos slices apart the sky. Specks of decay rising in the horizon to blot out the denial.

"We are alive."

"We are albeit distrusting."

Particles of practise and position praising posterior passion. Secrecy and the savory solicitation of salvation posthumously alleged to point demise into the living belly, although the living mind may refuse the inclination. The template for progression has absorbed inherent nature of its personality by assimilating text and purpose.

Distress keeps the children awake as parents pace back and forth. Both are aware of future prospects and debate the effect as well as the reasoning. Innocence pleading truth, and guilt bearing memory. What does it all mean? Crude remarks washing away from the skin. Dense perception ignoring the issue. Truth and time allocating discourse to the dilemma, break the rules, and forgo the distance for purity. Misspent ideals, sold tomorrows, and idle conviction all pipe up in a feverish pyre. The conditions are tangled rituals of habit and decay. The truth is distorted again by the senses. The self is languished identity, hidden potential, and sacred right. None of it makes any sense. It just bubbles silently awaiting awareness to recall the heat.

Delusion has eradicated choice, muddled circumstance, and hampered progress. It has lost friendship, persecuted moments, and condemned the mind to know forever the betrayal held within its torture. The delirium may be passing, but the neurosis is here for life. Crossed wires exposed and exhilarated by the similarity of parallel symmetry. The cosmic forces that blur reality with dreaming, passionate faces.

PART THREE

FOR A BUMPY RIDE IS SURE TO FOLLOW

First off a word from our sponsor,

    Greetings and salutations. Prospers well be? I inquire of yourself with a tale of your making. Disclose a frozen moment, a personalized quotation from your belief, and truth be told, this giving state of pure effect will reach its hand toward the light to hold its brightest shine. It's good the days to come from this created tale of fabled wail, and in the words of Eden, "Pictures room our dreaming."

Cautiously,

ABPoe

020800345a

Abelard,

It is happening; a dangerous choice is becoming the current situation. Euphony gads about the night, and tests pleasure and power. I digress due to fog. Slippery, thick gravy fog. I have learned some lessons, hold more thought, and I have problems with clarity because of this binge on luxury. I am catching up with happiness to ring forever, but behind attention, direction, and commitment, I am torn to what is necessary. Truth is self, and death slumbers there without morals and a spiritual side. There is weakness in futility brother, and there is something wrong with this world of ours. Its technical stupidity and scientific casualty win judgment from every pore. I am underground with an end to have killed a president, and how marvelous I am relaxed. Cherry pie dripping with a scoop of vanilla. Trickles of white melting a skin over the heated fruit and crust. It is a savory moment in time and space. This final frontier.

We have a firm hour to formulate substantial print brother, with accuracy and a fluid mode. Rampant intercourse laced in finer organization to take notes on steps of doctrine. Now then; order of appearance. Does society care about me? Do they care about you? Nothing is right, action and response fall haphazardly upon personal bias and convention. These standards of stereotypes concede seclusion and prohibition to the being self.

Morals are subjective, and etiquette imposes restriction, but do either hold bearing over being? Both derive from guilt, etiquette to standardize the population, and morals to regulate the personal self. Society behooves limitation of consequence for the self, but the survival of self if supervised dies. It is a dilemma of control. If living in the societal convention, and the conditioning is unavailing, what does one choose? To say something is right or wrong is godliness, to say something is polite is human, but moral conditioning is false no matter what the pretense. Who set these standards? These slogans and ideals of controlled assertion on acceptance. Does one need morals, etiquette, and a spiritual self? No, and that is because one already contains it.

Warmth, acceptance, and laughter,

Jim

"All aboard!" The Captain.

Action upholds nothing short of response in the alley. The back alley surrounded by takeover bids of advantageous death. In a hotel, demons lay beneath the floors, within the walls, and behind the ceiling. The edge in detail comes to view the disturbing end, and the imagined faith of deliverance returns to the grave. Death brings solitude unending, and the deceiver of happiness enriches adulthood to sever life, but at the end of the course the body is left up-rooted in quickly replaced dirt. We are closer. Trapped in epiphany, and locked behind divinity; we are in the alley. Temptation is transfixed, and although evading it is possible, avoidance never happens.

"And one, it is ok."

Now then order.

"And two."

The open ticking is a stop on spending. Age is always growth either fastened upon stench or a splitting explosion, it brings this tasteless consequence. I am my own illusion, and you are yours. HE is of our nerves combined, and thunderous fear skips behind him. Jump! He is behind us both, and is approaching now.

"And eight."

The knot is tied when our singing falls down sang and slain, and realization comes to be recognized as she is our reconcile. Both he and she are alone in perfect union, and are the liquid movement of being. I am a castle, and a wilting servant hanging in pause for an order. I am pointless, but hunger raises spirit. He and she and you and I are this, and each are the crumpet the others eat. Now, time is over, and all are crumbs on butter grease. Torn from the original whole, and left not taken, uneaten morsels of chewy fat. We are cooked, walking down turns of shared experience. Ramifications hitting the floor, and swept beneath the eaten, now eating. We are one, and one is nothing. Now the leftovers plant seeds of lost posterity.

All need is concentration, perception of self and others is evident, and thus concentration on need takes a higher step. It is a contemptible enclosure of popular belief. Intuition pauses in the still before the storm, but the storm moves, and thus we take hold or get swabbed underneath the waves. The vanquished, vengeful waves of redemption have merged, but allow for our thought process to accept what could be, and apt to what is. There is war and other drastic changes of proportion, but we build the war, the government, the statistics, and the chart for population control. Are we under siege or am I? Endearing smithereens.

There is money, power, and peace, but we lost them when we assigned captains to our ships. Ignorance. People are ignorant beyond understanding, and to save themselves, they must destroy themselves. We hold the reigns, steer the boat, and yet we lack the cognitive research to comprehend what we do and have done. Speaking of the general sum, sputtering with a grasp tighter than before, and the bodies die in waste.

Control mind so body may flourish, and bring the promised land of spirit even closer. I can give you strength, power, even religion, but acceptance by the population will swipe my hide with rage. They will say, "Heretic, burn upon your words like smoke, and take this ghastly fate along with you!"

I will die for this, and I would even die for you. Even with Hell, and this is what I fear. It is calling, and I shall answer. Not born from it, but sworn to it, and brought along its curious string of circumstance, I will end with it. Here I sit yelping type, and this machine works well.

There will be two bands dislocated from society's formation, and both will lead a craving to choose some difference. Those who are willing shall do the same. We shall conquer life, but through its death because we hold it no other way. Those who oppose this will forgo these methods, and using lies, suffering, and pain they will hide in the shadows to predict salvation, but there is no salvation as there is no God, and instead we entrust each other to find our future's progress. The choice is yours, but the answer lays with me. Take it and use it for yourself, and that is all I can say because the answers are within you. Take what I say as truth for it is the truth, and to benefit yourself put it where your heart belongs. Sit up straight and listen to tales of survival, tips on things to come, and advice for days long gone. Not everything costs something. We have no rights, except for those we have been given and utilize. Life is short, and existence is not mandatory. Sit back comfortable like, and gulp down whatever is before you. Watch, listen, and entertain permanence. The song change. A voice raised above the clutter of noise and smell reminds me of how like filthy beasts we really are as human beings.

Answers. Perception changes, and alters the unknown culmination of direction. Universal discomfort, ceaseless depravity, generation upon generation, and one buried after the next. There is no liberty from communal death because we have crossed the threshold of release, and the curse of the body no longer roams free in earthly inhabitants. Reflective shields of our wicked palette are as they have been, fragile and sheltered from the reality of existence, and hidden from the reverence of death. The totality of morality is the thwarted truth of human life, and the persecution of this slight delight. Disillusioned closure, closing, captured in the remission of emancipated constraint.

"Escape to Mexico or run to Hawaii, anything is possible."

The Alamo, the Second World War, and the media hypocrisy of inflicted scandals. The slave trades, religious battles, and wounded starving children. Adoption, abortion, and tax returns. Heroin. The Av Times and Reader's Digest. Heroes and villains. All the past and present and future, everything is possible. Play it back.

Suppose walking possibility is erected from this, you and I would be lost in sequestered personality. A word used as the facsimile for life that fizzes on a fixation of judgment. A conviction of catastrophe as pride blossoms into clouds of somber ashes, and the example for death is never aimless, headless, shelters pessimistic intentions, and confesses horrific reflection as this gathered spectacle.

Option said, "Intolerable," but kings traffic conundrum.

Expanding ourselves: this misconception refrigerates a blinking, brisk description. Missing Macdonald for misfortune. Think of the twisty response marked in relinquished flesh. Vandals lashing cherry wooden pedigree, and perverts avenged with squalor. The dust of eyes to swallow harmonious relation, and contaminate it with steeped salvation. Our sturdy lady does not have children because they are history amidst these screened feelings of smut. Wishes of warm evenings wrapped in woven delight. They are themselves unto themselves, the rolling, trembling, ridiculed design of forsaken experience playing ambiguous Hell.

Regurgitation defined life. Took question a cigarette, and attached calm, curdling debris. Question goes out of his station, releases entanglement, and chops out these so-called streets with movements of agony to uphold our thought's permission. Dark whistles cone out to diminish the dahlias, and all thought is dancing through the breaking silence as these actions speed up our towered fortune. Query? Paying assumption Tom Turkeys?

Collapsed aspiration of possibility for adults and lucid pedestrians. This Kingdom is reality to repose God and build distress. Exaltation for the decrepit mind, and we are gone. Dissolving looks of constructed thunder in the run of ruins for seclusion and loathing. Teeth, head, and self, all is the design for entertainment.

"Beware, death will cross you with compassion."

Propagate everything; convention, occurrence, television, and the evidence of suffocating decomposition, but I repeat, life and stature become soft when concept accepts purpose without sensing ordeal. We set haste, quickly and cautiously to tread a convicted display. To pull probable trouble makers into a citation for slaughter we take strokes of evolution, and an outcry alters the world without personal development. Society cannot accept or acknowledge wrath wrapped in hope because perception proves and provokes patient acceptance for man's flirtation with nothing. Appendages and history fall like camel dung, and covers pleasure with bruised relaxation as a response to narrow flesh. Upon asking a tree to test our sloppy bias, although with captivation, reason arranges routine, and the tree contemplates its vengeance.

One kind of intensity is destiny. Time to lie amidst the cruel redemption, and the future bears nuance from understanding to reaffirm the reference taught by dread. A whine on a troubled step is giving intent the sign to cross, but emotion falls on the impression of a scream proclaiming the objective of its condition: we.

Reason dies like visual fear, and the albums of perception return with a relative threat. Physical referral holds virtue in a clean cycle of desire. Lies oyster! We are the blind who fancy a stone that offers a crowd plummeting rhubarb. The testimony is down, the streets heap tears at everyone's window, and through precarious anchorage the force of man is a shattered dream. Man squints at the discouraging sea, stings his persona with his self, and steals the entity that flickers through him.

"I am!"

Clumps of cloned experience, fluoride, and applause. Light falls silent. This condemnation slips across the annals of account to slur the world and all its congress, and so what? Contraption impregnates the practical portrait of reward with everything whistling ego. Snuff proposes solid knowledge, and that proceeds this just agreement. Nausea. The words develop another stream, perhaps, but words lie. Deception to execute the devil-riding, disdaining plans that behold our stalling circumstance, involuntary nature, and dimming situation for hope. Our violation appreciates all deception because the opposing darkness falls dear, and beggary figures every salutation as occurrence hides a prison of nostalgia in simple strands of provocative splatter. To host conversion bittersweet, our contraptions go ahead. Contrast, pride, and vibrant might to toss in cryptic empathy spooned in hardened solace, and defined by worthy volition our words place the pearl perception in undocumented isolation. Expression spits a sigh to exchange these dreams with taste that stains this great, dark maybe with the sake of self. This writhing force will turn disclosure. Suppose nothing gives faith, should sin then swirl freedom forever? Reason squeaks in the desire of discreet words, but the chunks of union rabble in the rubble of temptation to present children as the action of salvation. Forms of soothing grains of love. Say it the way it should be said, and seek words to evoke imagery because a subject is what you make it. There is no captive audience, and no message must be conveyed to any listener. Abbreviation is abhorrent, masturbation is accurate, and comfort is merely adequate, but still remains the margin.

ARTICLE ONE

I IMPLORE YOUR acknowledgement of the following truths. One is space, and the other is truth. I challenge you with denial, and allow for explanation to present itself as yourself. You are the same as I, and we are all the same, but unfolded, living occurrence is dissuading. Reaction is intuition, and life is also. At this moment in time the sun is rising, but is filtered to gray fog as projected by smoke. It is five to eight, and winds ascend from the east to blow against the window, and cause the curtains to shudder in despair. This is a living moment, and this moment is universal from I to we it is discovered.

Fact One: Where are you?

Space.

Setting enables us to create a stationary position in accordance with reaction and impulse. Human beings begin as an implanted figment of space, and from that fragment grows the self in order to advance and adapt through impulse and setting. Suggesting and erecting implements of itself, nature forms response as well as the self, and thus conditioning is constructed into the self and its surroundings naturally. From original placement the self evolves from an origin of standardization at every particular moment. Emerged in this system we inundate ourselves with the uncontrolled design of society. We drown in a world of personal gain, and create the world through an unending population of numerous possibilities. Any placement herein produces persistent reason and response for the self, setting, and solution to every given moment.

Fact Two: Who is not in denial?

The truthful.

We are in denial with the regulation of culture, and the lowering prospects that wink in the glance that met death. Repetition stems from regulation, and meaning forms our provisions, but with inherent, impulsive behavior one must do something. This eliminates rather than improves personal objective because they are the example of false identity, and are defined by a standard of society that in itself is propaganda. Reality is experience, trivial endurance around the tomb, however, smiles curl on our faces, and the sun keeps shining bright. We are overcast in a widespread illumination of fainted clouds beyond the smoke. We hold and stretch across the sky, expand into space, and leave the Earth behind with boiling water.

As an old policeman, Mr. Johnson was over moving, and overall portrayed a busy person's zone. He reached in, and forced himself on a lady like a screwing dog. She desired the carpet, and liked the constant rug burn. In the darkness of her vestal virgin he spurted, and sighed.
"For the leg of such a fine canary, my pressure prematurely burst."
Sex. In a distracting blind side of provocative description drools a brook of salacious stupor. Erections full and embodied upon a conception grinning for the third time. Loose fluid on a sexual junkyard, and he takes the canary twice more.
"We pushed and rolled, and sweat encircled a blemish upon the rug. I moaned, she groaned, and we tore apart out nether regions. My permission slapped her gaping committee, and this rub seemed more than enough."
It was back and jumping, she was wide and open, and he continued to ride, but disaster came to play with the support of heavy hard-ons and brilliant pussy even though they are delectable as all tiresome reality. Paths collide with puzzled heavy petting, but remember a malleable population is killed, and forged ahead by blood the abominations are our spirits drifting. Voices amidst an understanding are vanquished with regret. You shall with time walk passed this point of butchery,

and detect the face of the Lord to suddenly be thrown into the realm of the unknown.

"DRAW YOU, SUCKED DRY, NO SECOND THOUGHT. PREPARED, ABLE, AND PACKED- ARRIVE AT THIS PATH FULL AND RELAXED. THE ABYSS OF CHILDREN ARRIVES TOMORROW, THIS IS PREPARATION."

Find a plan, conquer the now, and ascend from these pockets of decay. Meteors fall, crystals corrode, and a peaceful end swallows everything. A beast sucks the bones dry, and fucks the way for things to come.

"I am holding tight with elastic bands. Pinching heavily, I roar, blind, in and out. In and out." Mr. Johnson.

"As I said, I cannot remember what happened, reality being the subjective verse that it is, I cannot without personal bias retell and display the truth. It is apparent that the past experience furnishing this story cannot be discussed without judgment, and therefore this as a warning label stands as fabrication. I must form reason where it is lost, and thus incriminating perception tells this tale in the presence of death and no direction of discourse." Me.

At about six and a half feet tall, he got into such questions like, "When the Armageddon draws near will crucifixion be reinvested?"

Slice.

"MY APPRENTICE CUTS DEGREE, LOGIC, AND CHANCE. A WINDOW OF ANATHEMA UNTO THIS ROAD. THE GATE WILL NEVER CLOSE."

Babble. Pause. This quarter is varied, but the setting remains coincidence, and cuts off conversation. Just cut, and still bleeding, the new territory dilutes occupational and mass appeal. Diction runs like jelly in the center of a donut, and everyone like donuts, if not the jelly. The distortion of the daily ratio has its peripheral view locked on target, but it is perspective that cuts down rationale. Subjugation to the transactions if ineffectual erudition, and detected biblical folly. Persecution in the useless traffic of knowledge, and so-called discovered nonsense.

"Who cares?"

Staring at a man beside the meaty aesthetic. Staring in the same direction as he, and he probably sees something different. Does he feel my glare of literary stare? Remembrance is an exposition.

The beast first killed Peter Johnson of the police. Then Nancy Parsons, poor girl. Sue Soderborough, local prostitute and drug user. Miss Frieda Widgeons, age eighty seven, retired, and widowed. Samson Wright, local janitor for school board thirty-four. Brothers Tom and John McCarthy. This case is under investigation.

"Unforgettable. The expression on her face when she bled upon my knife." Dalton.

"Before me peaceful, behind me peaceful, under me peaceful, all around me peaceful." Navajo Indian.

Beginning.

Contemplation has left every form of conduct barren, useless, and self aligned at birth because of stagnant responsibility. A soul is washed up as living debris, wet and waiting within today. Death as it is inevitable, must be accepted, and not feared because it is restitution cloaked in dissonant spirals. A new self shall continue with the coming day. Temptation exists, but one must resist. The past resigns, and tomorrow endorses gleaming contingency in the living fault of everything, and even with death being known. Birth cleans away death to rest with yesterday, and today is a beacon of purest intention. We are new, and free from palpable addiction, both past and present. The consecration of consciousness from yester year must be appraised. I glory in the glory, I have seen! Revolution runs frenzied in regular rates of restitution.

"Burn the village the maggots have come home."

Strive.
Balance.
Stabilize.
Restore.
Think.
Be.

A wretched song plays, and a drink is poured.
"To life, and the torturous renditions of days spent with questions raised. Condition and cast are circumstance."

The alcohol brings on flashes of sex and redundancy. One day enters, and leaves with the rest. Salvation went off yesterday, on flashes of booze, sex, and modern conceit. Why does terrible music unveil such arrogant endowment?

Man in body, mind, and spirit contains heaving affliction, a constitution of anguish based on the bias of the self, and a propagation of ignorance as displayed by habit. All men, women, and children query and parry martyrdom in order to evoke the self. That is life. To be ego-less is to consist of respect, and this respect must be established in purity. Man must understand this, and appreciate self and surroundings in order to abstain from grief and pain. Weariness and woe will never be pardoned, and it is we who must display the blessing of life and its immortality. Self is immortal as it is universal, but the ideal of self or ego ties a bond to mortal persecution, the body. Life is what you make it, and the limitations therefore are your own. Enable the self to dissuade the ego, and exit from bereavement as a deity and not its delegation.

"Behold this and always love it! It is very sacred, and you must treat it as such." Sioux Indian.

Birth.

To begin.

Thought, expression, and faith. These things may survive in the end.

Fornicating whispers upon the prick of a king, now overthrown. His kingdom was erected from the sperm of his nation, and the court was the egg of his queen. Vaginal discharge was the jester's tool of drollery. The queen's uterus hatched the exit for laughing peasants with joy and redemption. A delicatessen of sexual beef and flattered pork. Boneless chicken rushing carnal speculation. In a gala of moaning intoxications the juices overflowed and spread throughout the world in victorious spurts of degenerating culture. This is the hall of the flesh, and the flesh is the benefaction of the people. This is the beginning of activity and sensation, evolving and adapting, along with squalid chunks of waiting. The venomous secretions of curving land spawned this kingdom in which we currently sit. This beginning was the end, and this end was the beginning. A start to the narrative of living, the progression of deconstruction, and the study of personal collapse. Everything, but nothing.

"I cannot recall what happened or how, but what is clear is the contradiction that vibrates in my head. The vexed hex in this cloud of circumstance. Nothing is for sure, but as it stands the world is dead, you are dead, and I am dead. The streets reflect the spectacles of insufferable decay with voices ever-recurring through unseen levels of despotism. Fire glows in the horizon, quakes engulf the Earth, and the sky crumbles as black ash surmounting a pattern of flexing wind. The sun overlooks with its constant view, and the heat scorches the vegetation that thrived on yesterday. The days are hot, weathered blisters that rub and rip. The nights descend with blackness, and dwindle all the light to the flame of a solitary candle that fluctuates and coils in boasting oblivion. This was the beginning, and concludes with the end."

Humbug!

Birth? Right.

The waking, praying light transposes fixed emotion. The mind and body entrap the spirit, and the roused mass awaits discovery. They reason without it, seek it, lose it without ever knowing it was them. Spirit is the birthright of our dissected past, and it entreats our life by simply adding one plus one plus one plus one until infinity is in this affluent world of ours. Spirit is our reason, world, and outcome. It is our flagrant waste or malicious haste. It is also true that our spirit maps our dreams, proposes words like love, and balances the common theme under equilibrium. What we know and trust searches all the world and gives us what is there. So it is and so it rips away the point of senseless life in the embellishment of the senses. Time relieves contrivance of its manual, steadfast rhythm, but still the masquerading mind lights up the manipulated legion. Exasperated bodies stem from the same dysfunction as reason breathes on the exhale of reposed falsity. One notions congruent static, and together solutions fondle a stinger in the eye. Upon the wisps of the mind these whispers whim with wizened mass.

Conceding our notion of waking rest in subtle outcome. Conception basks in the winning trophy. The body toils in pathetic survival, and these words declare their father's wearing age, but all great men are made. He and me. We would pass and say, "Dreadful everything."

A brow of sullen morrow with death on love in milky sight. The blood that these hands filter, forwards electric promises, but through the damned and crazy souls of we are it and she in the twelfth row of maples.

Brent: Have you felt love?

Carla: Only through the eyes of intercourse and the legs of opulent desire. The breasts, can such things be felt?

Brent: Heathen! Tempestuous and lecherous wench to be my begotten bride.

Carla: The devil's fury courses through your veiny finger, and to comfort thy divine design with thy indulgent attitude. May you be squashed bluntly on a sparring viper?

Brent: Solitude to label birth rebuilding. In truth be told, woe betide this fumbled greeting. Fear imparts my reason for depravity, and to myself I have been thrown, and torn to regal temper, I regulate this serum. This requiem of spite is thin desire for security which rests benign to treason.

Carla: You! This dubious displeasure. Spike your thorn upon itself, and fall below the sea of blood to sentence vixens out to sea. Separate trades blame virgin vessels plundering blunders and bounty, but no open beast shall hither come.

Brent: Lash my septum with your carnal spike, terming blasphemy my true identity. I know no reason for this dream of fangs forbidden, and plant it forth amongst your vipers wench! Torn and thrown to embers, a burning pit for you my harpy, sent back to bear this death of silence on the earth. Venture forth through demon sense to wag a bone before the devil's question.

A bright picture with lots of light, and a fanatical photograph of reality broken in explanation. This has swamped structure, order, and time. Linear memories bob in murky contingents. Erased and eroded to the brink of return without warning, but no cause for alarm or backfire. A forward slice of massive delusion filtering refusal, but was there choice? Intolerable wreckage, piles and piles of volatile leaks leading to an ocean of bloodshed. We remain lost and floating.

"Brother? I am laughing behind misconception as the shepherd of your flock, and it lies down red and nefarious. Puppets hanging from strings suddenly pulled to life, realization, and action. Dismissed depravity, and the collision with absolute penance. The angelic temper of fallen spirits to break divine government, and leave preservation with the visitation of providence. Rest beneath creation. Hallelujah! Jehovah, Supreme Being of wisdom and benevolence, justice and truth, you are re-nailed without compassion, and everlasting fire is to be your purging testimony. Infernal regions to cut your throat, and encase habit with desecration. Purgatory false savior, and action hardens with the sacrifice of salvation, the lapse of assumed piety, and the shadow of celestial fire. Devoured by the mouths of men with mounds clinging to the chins of women, and the streaks run down into a river of flames. Orthodoxy is gone, and the angels have failed advance. It is due, and it is done with an end of fanatical heresy."

Abelard.

    Change is shy, but approaches the surgeons. He has a problem with irate mutation. Examination tells us of an entangled twin. A physical attachment with snapping teeth and blurry vision. Change was born with half a head too many, and now sees himself for the first time without his younger brother. Alone, although he sheds a tear for his mother, and smiles tenderness in a brief moment of mutant and mama. Change is now, and no more obstinate persuasion to stubbornness. Up the staircase, and no longer down. Personality remains a laughing mystery.
    "Coffee?" An addict quirky from withdrawal.
    Concentrate at this plateau, and bring the way that delivers us upon each other. Follow forward, and reach our heavenly descent. Hold tribulation from our numbers, and practise lessons passed on throughout the coming days of perished freedom. It is the ready-made hour of our basking, and its sad arrival prepares and endows what is to come. We shall be free, and this vision is the indication that in turn creates the vision. Now revolution commences because it has already begun. We take our places holding tight, and standing tall. Strike down and lift up, cheer for it has come! Ripples flirt with the opposition scored within it. To break the gates of designation, and hold open proclaimed fulfillment, we must follow the bounty of this harvest to the Promised Land. We shall be free, and left to walk this serene surface of clean water, and not eternity. We shall cross the treacherous decline, and through this golden intervention, we shall be free! Consequence is not relative with the reasoning of now. Contemplation proves stagnation or change, and the result comes from the equation. Now is everything! Everything!
    Conception is a design for acceptance, and it is a contagious tangent of mass appeal. It conveys such delusion that it enacts a demeanor to

illicit social disclaim. Perhaps if egotists realized dissonance within the enriched perception of egotistical standard. Nonsense babbles Morse code in a fundamental draw of acupuncture.

Creeping infinity does drive forward, all eighteen holes.

"We have journeyed brother, and this venture has corrupted our impenetrable disease. This wager compromises our damaged reflection. Along the ruffled, revolving edge, furtively swishing. We all sink in larger depths. Intervention has come my brother. Subside, re-stride, and acquire calling victory. Reassemble time and solidify our status. We have crawled for explanation, and without it the answer is ahead. Quickly jump up, and over, and off. Let go my brother, and release your depression with a fast attempt. Fall into this whirling color that twirls this real sensation. The welcome mat lies flat my brother, so step up, on top, and over."

Curtains.

Open curtains draw an empty stage. A tree is potted on the left, and a bench is on the right. There is no lighting, but the moon sits at the top.

A woman smoking a cigarette enters, red haired and tall. She is slender, and walking left toward the tree. She wears a large, leather hat, and a trench coat yields only high heels, black leather that slowly walk left. She is under scripted, but casts presence through her cigarette. She sits upon the bench, and smokes deeply. Crossing her legs she is smoking deeply. She exhales up to the moon.

Enter a dark shadowed man. He wears similar attire, sees her instantly, and sneaks up from behind. He walks as she smokes, reaches her, and stands over her. She does not seem to notice as he outstretches his hands behind her, and strangles her tender throat. As his hands clench she buckles beneath his pressure. He struggles. She squirms. It continues until she limply hunches over, lays there, and he exits. Hold.

Day one, dry. The carnival for the guilty brings blood to soak the ground for blackness knows an almighty answer comes upon the end. Uuhh hheellpp uuss.

Dear Individual,

I am afraid of the future. I am afraid of the possibilities that we hold in our hands. Nuclear war, extinction, genocide to further degrees, and the waste of the human spirit. Pollution, chemical warfare, corruption of the high majority, and the numbing of the human mind. Destruction on the loss of choice and reason. Financial abundance, and the assimilation of the human body. These things are tangible if you reach out and grab them, but would you want to? In my point of view these things are inevitable because this world slowly dies due to careless, selfish grasps, and we ourselves are becoming diluted from fact and logic. We are lost on a dying planet, and no one can get off. This ride pirouettes, and is growing faster. Now is the time to make action commence. We must take the controls, tug the reigns, and arrest the death or survival before us. This death is already in action due to the lack in conscious effort and responsibility. Worldwide destruction is bubbling over, and discovering the potential which rests to reach out becomes the master of our world's dissertation. Thanks to the predominately democratic society that is our home, it is entirely up to you!

This is death or survival, not for the individual, but for the entire spectrum of species in all its tangents. One by one, into a larger mass, and this mass in combination obviously forms the world. We live through conscious action, and we can either speed up or slow down death to all we know. The death of ourselves, and this planet rests atop our plates so let us eat. It is all up to you, and this letter merely stands as a proposition, an indoctrination perhaps, but that is also up to you. Why not now? Why not know? The knowledge of this outcome is the annihilation of every man, woman, child, plant, beast, and their binding tie death.

I thus leave it up to you because it all begins at home.

ABPoe

Party Founder

Introduction.

Dear madam or sir,

I induce attention. Me.

This as introduction renders clarification since reverence and artistic endeavor seem to emit confusion. These contents have been scrambled like the work they carry, and were a laborious process to complete. Twenty six years of collecting, thinking, and practicing. The past three have been the actual construction and writing thereof. Somniferous humdrum, but now it is done.

When I sat down to begin this, I had a heap of written documents that had been procured since about the age of nine. They were collected as useful even though unfinished. In Grade Three I began my first short story about a leprechaun with magic shoes, and it ended up at the top of these bits and pieces of prose. Now assembled here, they have become one. I took the stack, and cut the single sided sheets word for word, dropping them into an ice cream pail as I went. The double sided sheets prevailed, but now have been altered into the smaller portions that reside here.

The words as extracted were typed into a decrepit computer, and what came forth was applesauce, but a general picture could be worked with, and that was until it was lost with a computer crash.

Now it starts although this is all that remains is the only original part, and was literally titled upon its first draft. The surplus was impossible to collect, and due to the astounding defeat I took some time off. In about a month I did discover further scraps thick with lingo and garbage in the computer. Operating on it once again I was bestowed with a thin section that is now strewn throughout. This work was edited for almost four years, and that is a long time for such a simple plot.

Truth, human possibility, corruption, and collapse. Fiction derived from the degradation and the imagination of the human condition, and the frailty and power that is learned in life. Tales of hodgepodge, panic, and mystery that ensure life and death. Tales of the future developed in the past, and held within the present state of personal reality. This is a vision of life and death.

We are here, and voices return the discourse of fate with advent drawing nearer. We have to respond, but all I can say is thank you. Readers are a requirement because without their perspective this is nothing. You give this life. This was mine, but now make it yours, for my hands pass this glory to you, and consent to its movement onto you.

The author.

Remember we can have control.
We can play our part.
We can recognize defeat.
We can destroy ourselves.
The Party

Deep breathes of sequestered faith passage through time, self, and suit for all this cast of nails. Short is out, and exhumed of all his effort, the dog retreats within its tracks to claim its broken home. Emus for the estuary. Death has called its obituary. Pre-occupation with the world of blunders do my eyes beseech? They flutter within the winds of change, and tenderize this portion of sauntered dreams. Mixed devotion the likes you have never seen, and such abhorrent usage of a fabled verse that the encumbered flight of growth takes flight, and leaves without answer.

Engines roar execrated exhaust. Numbers rattle with brittle accuracy as laughter whittles wisdom. Insight into slow decay, but while living, breathing tissue. Ignore the machinery, know how to use the tools, and brave each venture in its flare. Heads do silence such mangled wonder, and it is truth that never wanders.

Delusion is diaphanous reaction to astonishment. Recall this reaction, and recall the love that rushed at that instant. Love, blessed love of all hope, glee, and embrace enshrined in kisses given by lovers and relationships broken only by death. Warmth and tenderness to shrivel winter's loneliness. Remember the crisp swat that was that moment. Open and shrewd with the care and alertness of sour lament, and wishes in compunction carry it to the depths of the oceans. Frozen and trapped within cooking murk, and lost from touch forever and ever. Amen.

Submerged eyes sparkle and wash compassion to scrub the ensnared heart. A smile spreads across the face, and chuckles with a caress of the cheek. We are alive! Flushed and parented with universal feeling and joy. Back with freedom and longevity once more, with body to keep the path, and mind to keep on track. Forward through this contemptuous vulgarity into eternal rhapsody bent on blossoms of afterlife adulteration. Memories.

"Demon rise! Sophisticated and debauched. Extrication stand, and clemency plant root amongst the people. Destruction erode into construction. Humility is frail, but freedom is forever. Flagrant, pillaged, and villainous by winning this eternal damnation. Demon crawl! Up from the desert of the world, the kingdom of untold space, and sense us. Injury and silence in company forever, amen."

Jim.

"Determination, strength, and recognition. She will be female, and shall wander the aisles of the dead, releasing their spirits, and teasing their bodies. She will disjoin links with the unknown, and break the tension. Energy shall be her name, Crocksinford she shall be, and rescue us she will. That is how it shall be told, and this is how it is."

Shelly Crocksinford

Dissipated, filtered visions of the text we used to convey. Bobbins of texture, balloons filled with stalemates, and progress bent on yesterday. Fast paced graphing of the archetype presenting descent in the figured decline of substance. Words bewildering meaning, distractions obstructing motion, and being capsized in frozen decapitation and brawny indiscretion bereaves confusion. Screened pictures of closed captioned calamity. The sturdy build up to the point in hand, life, and the dilemma of choice.

Blasts of misconception, ships of sunken despair, and listings for better tomorrows. The how, when, and where of it. Illustrations of felicity and foreclosure. Crossroads connecting the strands of liberty with the test of meaning. Object and rationale, time and circumstance, riveting direction is captivated in a cycle of posterity. A cultivation of criticism, and circumvented process. Sloppy.

Do we subconsciously know of our doom? Do we dream of that moment when all things become auspicious magic? Do we perceive this moment as a passing nightmare, and when realization sticks shrug it off as déjà vu? I have seen death, and death has seen me. Now all that stands is time, and the endless wait for something, anything to happen.

It appeared in Alexander, and navigated his view with secondary discretion. Backs face gravel and dirt, and he upon a mountain top grasps the gates of man. After body, and mind. When he and she do anchor even. Alexander in becoming it was dark with his leaving body panting. He searched miles for our missing lady that appears as good, but became focused on himself. Myths state he is begotten of a witch, and is a stranded babe of pagan ritual.

Ridiculed failure upholds his design, and this missing lady remains a silent question. Dead. Her light is cold, and her purpose damp from burial. He has risen as the head of designated torture, and down below stands Alexander. Dangling in the abyss, and avoiding potent reality in order to rekindle warm humanity. The two to bleed as one, her stream and his according to howling men.

February's death has hit the floor, and has lost our home. The cheese we smell is his, and the morsels we eat are our own. This is freedom, choice, and the dislocated reassurance that abandons this happened morn, and our Alexander.

I, whom thread this home, this spreading Hell, discuss minutes shipped in blasphemy. We are furniture purchased long ago, built to have a cell for journey, but miscarried we are repossessed as unpaid junk. A recollected treasure. If as conceived, any murders become unseen, and give way to ordinary custom. A bleak answer for a case called anthology. Footsteps began this mood, but deconstruction wears conception's winning crown.

The days of light have come to a crashing close. The walls shook, trembled with such an unencumbered surge that those within them shivered. The ceilings chipped dust and fibers, fixtures swung if they could swing, and all things rustled with the fierce eruption that stirred this land. Plaster cracked, gutters wept, pavement heaved, and persons were swept into forceful trepidation and dreadful captivation. The trees swayed in the air, but no wind was felt as the floors and roofs enclosed the people here. They broke in two as the buildings did at last collapse, and all was still in shock. Spines pierced bleeding skin, and bore meaning in the tracks of nonsense that whacks the harmony of words.

He stood with open arms, and his posture looked awkward. His feet were equally planted on the soft, indented clay, and he was secure in his standing, stuck in his step, and looked outward beyond his out spanned hands to see the sun. He blew faintly as clouds instilled the sky with hostile mystery. The southern born air whipped the open acres of highway, and with idling steps of bolting familiarity he strode from view to view, and cascaded the dull horizon.

She was driving, and her eyes were fixed upon the flashing mash of barren wildlife that meshed within her motion. The car sped with preoccupation, and she was caught in the sight of the pandering sun. The streaks of solid, vibrant warmth slanted off the rear view mirror. Off the glass, and into her squinting, strident sight, and as she winced she made the appropriate change to the mirror. She fidgeted quickly, but replacing her vision back on the road, it was not there! The dirt tore up in dust, and she pulled the wheel too hard. The impulse of obliterated consequence erased any choice. She screamed, he fell, and the road ignited with their light.

Once the ground of mind is clarified, there is no obstruction at all. One sheds views and interpretations that are based on concepts such as victory and defeat, self and others, right and wrong. Thus one passes through all that to reach a great rest and tranquility. Human lives go along with circumstance. It is not necessary to reject activity and seek quiet, but make yourself inwardly empty while outwardly harmonious. Then you will be at peace in the midst of the frenetic activity of the world. It is necessary for your footing to be firm and solid, accurate and sure, taking control, and being the master, you become one with all different situations. When profound clarity has no change, and is consistent at all times, you will be at peace.

There is rest in the old ways, and recognizable stress in the old ways. Being fears the self can no longer run the duration of progress. It stumbles, fumbles, and bumbles with steps toward oblivion. I contains self-confidence, fear, disgust, and doubt, but these things hinder steps of progression. Commitment to a clear, unabated future holds I still. Logic and reasoning, although false, do uphold some sense of security in the bearing of future's toll. What can I do? Look for an answer somewhere other than ego. Blessings are not received twice, calamities do not happen alone, and the body naturally radiates light.

The first step of progression is waking. Rising from the tumultuous grime of dreams to establish a setting in life. Where one wakes is relative to where one is, however, the act itself is universal. The effect as well as the process awakens ourselves and our state. The next step is the habit that prepares and imbues our waking state. That is to say the functions and attitudes that arrange the being itself create the waking ordeal. The enabled past projecting input and output to contribute being and state, although for simplicity the actual, concrete management of input and output forms only the interpretation and utilization of choice and consequence. The choice of an option, and the consequence that resides with it stem from action, thought, and being to formulate further choice and or option. Thus by resolving both choice and consequence a difference in task, objective, ideal, and being is contemplated.

The next step then is to objectify reason and being by accepting both positive and negative, and make the conscious decision to choose reasoning and exercise that projects choice and regard for possibility. To firmly plant roots and grow, leaving way for falsity via origin and outcome, and realize the connotations to the actions themselves. Everything is labelled positive or negative, good or evil, and this step foretells existence, and sets understanding by issuing resolution to the being itself. Whatever one does will change its life, and this relates to every second of every day.

It is the simple fact that every moment of life is change. Any and every given point changes life, however, the underlying pretext is that our current lives are not good enough, and that some instant change will improve things. When did this appetite not to be living the life we are take tenure? There must be no change for change to happen. No conscious decision will remove remorse, but unconscious action to liberate a conscious plan ensues a sense of progress and purpose.

Nothing exists, but everything is tangible. There is no self for I does not breathe, and instead abides life through its connotation. What I likes continues, but a neutral effect must greet these things in a place of likes or dislikes. Habits hereby cease, and it is ok because new things will take their place, and addictions obsess on downfall. Escape is easy in the simplest preparation, and the best preparation is simple. I am doing this, and it is my choice that has brought me here.

Death is hard to calculate, and manipulation of an outcome does not exist. Agitation and misery are interminable allusions, and the paradox of life basically resonates energy, searches for decline, and does not escape inclinations of perdition. An egotistical approach to life, and the childish approval of death's embrace invokes the self's decay while decline transcribes starvation. It would not matter.

We are meant to discover both personal power, and our shared purpose for being alive within a spiritual context. Truth and reality are matters of perception. Born into life to care for each other, and for the Earth. One must make the proper arrangements to depart, and leave no unfinished calling or pursuit. One must make its apologies, pass on responsibilities, and accept love and gratitude. Detachment is essential in accomplishing an accurate evaluation. Maintaining a reflective or meditative attitude facilitates the reception of intuition, and intuition is just learning to interpret the energy and experience that make up life. Emotion from experience contributes to the formation of biology, and becomes encoded in our biological systems to generate a quality of energy that reflects those emotions. Energy does not and cannot lie. Life is painful, and spiritually we are meant to face the pain that life presents.

In this western world we often misinterpret God's plan for us, and expect life to be comfortable and free from trouble. We measure God's presence by our level of personal comfort, and believe God is here if our prayers are answered, but no spiritual tradition or leader guarantees a pain free life. Spiritual teachings encourage us to grow, tell the truth, and face that which we fear, but most of all to trust the responses we contain and interpret the subtle images of electrical current.

Take a guess at life
Balance survival with strife
Maybe take a wife
But always look both ways first
And realize all the thirst.

Am I a fish? A squirming salmon caught within the rapids. Or perhaps an egg awaiting fertilization in a shallow compartment of water. Perhaps I am floating downstream half eaten by those around me. The gravel outsets my cascading body. The water measures out beyond my scales. The tedium of constant motion leaves everything miscalculated.

Ripples vex distance, and currents undermine direction, but we travel our yearly goal, and beckon the glory of home.

There is nothing in my head that is interested in fish. Bleak, blank fish, fried fillet or smoked flambé. Nonsense. We pursue the tides in search for companions left at bay. The sunken treasure that derails eyes from ever touching it. The sense of all its orchestration remains in the affluent water, and here we rest with ease. Are we the fish?

The gun goes off, and it is a race to the finish. Snigger evasion as a beginning, but an end will be discussed upon its arrival. A coherent collection of light imposes shadow in this ever growing, ever needing, habitual life that begins with this instant and ends with the next.

Blank, thawing peace spilling purpose on paper. A means to any great length would still submit oneself, and feats of tangible evolution do not respect this average text. If I do not want these seemingly, bewildered words to deliver myself, then the message therein must not reside with me. These words wind in my wrist, pose in my head, and describe fleeting meaning in myself and my words. If I slow down, and sow this simple message without myself, then walking and talking of purest intention erupts in the ink because things go on without me.

We evolve into tasks, burdens, and paths, but the self remains calm and bare. It lurks in the harbour on shoulders of water, and bathes in the sun with a golden sensation. It chortles and snorts with a predominant stride to reach the sky in the blink of an eye. Self loses insight, leaves everything to foresight, and rectifies any might in the will of some infected bite. To describe and transcribe, saunter and fondle omnipotent stamina, we stand on a question.

The truth believes in one warmth, and removal of that warmth quakes the mind with saturated soul rot. Men and women travel loose and wander free. Delight reconciles the differences, the poise of wishing stars, but such mixed reviews broadcast pride to set the standard straight. We cite such tangled versions of subject's hastened sight, and our imbecilic strain of self-empowerment contains angels of inscription.

The protagonists are gone, antagonism is prescribed by prospects, points, and proverbs, and the beginning, middle, and end are applied in subjective terms by the hierarchy that records linear time. We are the undisturbed details of point and purpose, and description lacks our meaning in its breaching effect on life, and re-attaining simple reflection swoons the force of submission. Admiration is subject to fault, and pointed vanity is a printed passage of articulated crime that supposes inflicted narration. Subjective haste and waste in the power of egotism.

Now if ego is contrived by body, which is perpetuated by mind, whether left or right determines devil or God, good or evil. To be focused, one never does to be, but one comprehends without introspection. To eliminate ego, both God and devil, and enlighten the mind. However, both God and devil embody an individual's being in society via chance, consequence, and random bursts of self and culture. To establish proof in existence of both sides, God and devil, we must be cut and balanced in an invisible appeal that is propelled by death.

Born through sin, and everything thereafter has been left as sin. God plays ball with the power in this world because after all God survives sin, and the individual blesses the world with its being. Its actions secure or imbalance God's reality, and in accountable numbers society subscribes reality, and all its reminiscent lies and misfortune penetrate action. This occurs with or without the permission of self, ego, devils or gods. I would suppose one half of the inhabitants and situations are of the devil or god persuasion, and must hold equal balance. Grips slip and turbulence gesticulates change. Still the meaning behind life, mere hands cannot corrupt as the self delivers persecution, and any one free forms sin. To suffer is to be sin, but sin contemplates life as misery, and God says ok.

Man equals woman equals death.

In order to illicit sense of purpose from the redundant entropy one enlists, one must negotiate higher modes of being based on essential need, free choice, and love. One must practice proper conduct to eradicate superfluous want, persistent nothing, and the empathy and action that constructs being itself. One should convict the direction of daily living to be a pathway unto God, and this enlightenment, achievement, and proposed love succeed and surmount contentment. One can absolve one's want and distract one's need to what is readily available. To do this extracts future steps into the bounty of enrichment. Blessings are endless, and although not recognized are dissolved under the ambush of self, surroundings, and because these are dismayed purpose.

We as human beings are engraved in culture and civilization that is derelict. Overall it continues to reproduce the illusion of lack of choice. This is of course not the case. Fundamentally we are trapped within our box, and look out for compassion, but we lose sight of real ambition because we are lost in our self contrived abyss. This is universal, resembles a free world of logic and truth, and is a trap to steal ideals, intent, and interest based on hope, choice, and positive harmonics. Choosing despair when granted higher limitations means we are lost, waiting for something to happen, and life is happening. Life.

The constant upkeep and persuasion of flagrant falsity is issued and skilled as truth, and the perpetual notion that life is what you make it is misguided. We have allotted too much removal to real responsibility, and have assigned tasks and thoughts to further instruct our world and its fatalistic calamity. Giving us poverty, misused information, and misinterpreted choice as a breeding ground for continuance.

By living we create the living ordeal, and make examples and standards of the right and wrong to remove the slanted vision of pacified pessimism. Life is but a struggle of what there is without us. Through dying we remove ourselves, but the ordeal remains within those still alive. It does not change, decides outcome, controls ideals, and evokes a promise. That being contains choice, and all we see and do is known amidst us all. There is no secret, and no trading nuance to oppose inherent reason. We create the power, enlist the sense and structure, and agree with God on what is true and not with what is given. Growth, change, and recruitment is easy, but vacating self and surroundings is difficult because they are excessively evident.

Removing theories and ideals erected by the past is also difficult because these things have been assigned with reason. However, they are unrealistic because what transpired yesterday will not replay today. It is also difficult to locate love, truth, and fulfillment because we must absolve reasoning, roots, and reactions before they are inspired by the search and not the physical effect.

The first step is most difficult, but by peeling away, we will see what is really the core of tomorrow because through dislocation comes a realistic approach to everything. It is most important to be accountable because infinity is where we live. To not question, analyze, or alter the world where self-control relies on culture, society, or civilization, but to enact improvement to the situation. There is far more negative reality than positive, and to change this one must issue ignorance to the system, argue both positive and negative aspects to cultivate a neutral ground of augmentation, variation, and ardor. Reconciliation and relaxation are ours when we as human beings face the facts of life, realize the untruths that reside on the path, and celebrate the positive diversity in the world and its construct. Create and define what is necessary, and answer only to ignorance and consequence. Do.

Do you remember Dalton because this is his post?

"Great, that is just great."

A female voice silenced again by social rabble. Monotone blundering, and rolling vociferation of multiplied complexity. Laughter.

"Hello."

Social butterflies are world bliss decoded by mental projections of public durability. It does not hurt. Festering blisters of apathetic unrest harvest virulent bane, and the checkpoint of discovery is punished with death. It is this that prospers to deliver faith, kingdom, name, and stature. Point is meaning, and squanders foundation to articulate the disclosure of process and equality. To eliminate the past as probability is to saturate the present in its text.

The blasts of light shimmer in the darkness, to which the sky beholds the coming year, and objection in ignorance, arrogance, or pride is punishable by the provision of deciphered expansion. A fateful program in possibility that repeats no more restraints of surmountable past, and creates the present moment as a basis for response. It is a focused provision. An end to an end, is it possible? Has it already happened?

Occupy time with pleasure, associate minutes with orgasm, and realize social movement as riveting drama. All that can be said has been, and every experience has been led astray by the objective of personality. We are irrevocable, and waft in our own living debris. This world is ours because we belong to the world. Take control! Take flight, and allow for the future to give destiny to the universe because the universe is everything in infinity.

"Do you remember me? Me of long ago, wrinkled, old, and dead within a concentrated picture of memory. The memory attempts to place time, but I am glacial and quiescent. Dead, old, and wrinkled me of long ago. Does alcohol achieve enlightenment? No, but it bestows curiosity, truth to dissemble ego, and strength." A man passed out in the gutter.

Dr. Jim

More advanced subject matter for the accredited surfeit of August, the cement streets, and this ongoing movie.

"I sit beheaded. The environment occupies me with light magnified danger red. Swimming and quiet. Green was the day that cleansed my head, and two wandering three was that morning that forged cracks into my parents."

Toluene, "But where? Behind something?"

"Strange? Fifty members wore Helmsdale suits and smoked Cuban cigars. Old blood, rich from the sale of cheese, stolen property, and brawling with others. She was alone with the entire house which was a wicked, wood building that fell some years later upon our meeting. Darkness ruptured in a fiery rash. The detective died, she cried, and time vaulted on."

My body lies limp without answer as my blood runs scarce.

"One daughter, and she belonged to this detective, fifty day old beards, and magazines that infiltrated unobtrusive stacks. This correlation proved befitting, but left her in pregnancy. These things do spray dark creatures. Dead choice culprits move as passengers via a lost polish. The stars shine upon thee, and windstorms gyrate my thorax thoroughfare. Small yellow pills, twice daily, and swallowed. Windstorms before finished? They slow down town suburbia so things across the board are queer and equal. Doors, gates, and keepers? These things are for giants. An office however is a wonder! After five or six years of trying various sorts of employment, she joined the Beachum Guard as a secretary. By her third year she was doing the same, and similar duties for three more, and that is when she met Hugh. Hugh was her first husband, no kidding."

Toluene said, "But what of death?"

"When I first pulled reality I knew venom settled. Once my castle measured the tidings, but now has been jerked to compromise. A knight's arms terrorized the routes of proliferating dwellers as my yard was eaten, and my castle was exposed. I, lord of this internal conjecture, awoke, captured, and unversed. My hands shook, picked of their keys, and the protection that I laughed within was a casualty. This door was the truth, and it seemed the only thing still mine that would come and know me. We do not know very much do we?"

Jim fell down and broke his crown, and Toluene came tumbling after. Imagine.

A golden squabble, an outright problem if you begin to surface around it, and if you grab it, well things become rather interesting. Shouts within listening photographs. Sense crossed the moment with a point pressed against it because with seats like these it was sure to make a clean break. Landed parts in horror, where sight lights up flatly to find nothing. Downstairs there was a straight basement.

"You cannot masturbate, we believe in husbandry entrance in every case."

Fists, guns, and entertainment fastened to a greenhouse made of blood soiled sharpness. These layers are solidifying with unfathomable fabrication. Toluene screamed.

"I number acquiescent acquaintances, shop foreign sights, and slowly my mind dresses my red danger up as magenta. Persistently, all together, there are questions. The Helmsdale comes and corners, and we are back to the crate for he is with us, the scorpion, and the very head! A blue and black provision, and chest death for many in one."

A troubled word to please your attention. I hope you are primed for this jaunt that we roost over. However, I know what I know, you do not. This is the lore of aftermath, the veracity being advised, and the result that cuts this telling tale. There is process as well as effect here. It had died, but was on the list for taxidermy.

"Rebirth brings progress on disillusioned reality. The real world is after all as real as the papers proclaim it to be, and individual choice no longer is valid. I am not a guide for the lost, there are no answers here, no different questions or symbolic resonance, only me as I was decided. The here and now are present for tea, but no one brought any tea! High above seething an ignis fatuus of pyrotechnics. Toluene cover your head because this is the final say, and preparation does not exist."

Toluene was already dead.

Reality is what you perceive, changing with revision as its spin contracts with contrast. There is no stop to the spin, and no tumble to the top of state and circumstance. An agreement of identity, and a prototype for actuality that disproves the individual, and converges with the general. One builds the next due to picked up repetition. It is a dysfunction that forms a whole without a single, coherent purpose.

"See my childhood face bud with vibrant stupefaction in a youthful stance. I was nine in Grade Four, and during lunch and recess I would stare off into the sky, and thank the clouds for my friends. The ants. Teacher speaks, bell rings, and children run free to play atop the playground soil. It was usually muddy and abundant because of the constant rain. Girls scream, boys chum, and I hid from the animosity that is youth to discover a hidden language with ants. Sitting amongst yellow cement blocks that run up to become an overhang, concealed from innocent hands, short boyish haircuts, and long female curls. Ranting with ants, strange and awkward. Please keep in mind that I was nine, and full of erratic regard. I once had a dream about square ball, it was big in Grade Six, and I would have been eleven. Big ears, goofy smile, curly hair with short, blonde curls. Rue Mclanahan-like except on a boy, and without the grey and hairspray. Dirty blonde. I have brown eyes, and would have had a chubby face, baby fat as it was grown out of. Jack, queen, king, ace, the four corners of the square, four corners within one square, square ball. Children playing in a paved playground with the square trimmed upon the asphalt in flaming yellow paint. The dream was turned across my view, and saw myself running from a teacher who was deaf in both ears. He threw me into a wall once. Running with the deaf teacher behind me running. He vanished, and I began to play square ball, positioned as a jack. I never migrated, but stayed tossing round, red-pink balls at infinite space. No real bearing or target, just hurtling balls over and over. I said goodbye when I left for Grade Seven, and or age twelve. I was apprehensive, I recall dreading the summer's end when I had to go. Excruciating panic perpetuated and created in my own mind, twirling around inside my twelve year old head. Actually I would have been eleven still because I was born in January. Everything was big, lavish, and contained elements of the boring and known. What terrified me most within the coming of age ordeal were the people. The students, teachers, bullies and snobs, and all possible encounters with any one savagely intimidated me. Me at eleven and a half, blonde curly-girl hair, plaid shirts, and Velcro runners. I was left handed and had trouble tying shoes."

Ambushed with the epitome of rush in the city. The heart of a drubbing vigor that incites activity, motivates rust in the business and ideals of men, and an assorted guarantee of various forms and types of chance meetings. Conversation after conversation diluted within the bus, grinding cabs, and car honks. Steamy windshields full of volatile noise, block after block, district after district, and suburb for suburb. Running the rigid landscape to have the city of all cities, New York City.

"Beauty unimaginable with ignorance inconspicuous. It was everything lying down like an opened virgin of concrete and steel. The accumulation of hope and aspiration, New York City, the big apple, and the city of angels? I have a feeling of fleeting moments stolen. A billow through propelling light, the drastic height, grasping tight, and the great, vast city opens its mortar legs to stir a melting pot. This clutched me, and the skyline drew a three dimensional masterpiece. It retained me for too long, and I was thrown into the dash of the car. The car swerved left, and went right into the question of all questions, almighty death what are you?"

Religion says Heaven or Hell, mortality hopes for better, reality labels it an end, and so what truly snoozes in your supple scope? Something or nothing, please a simple nod will do. Relaxation taking place with a straight forward face. Writhing guilt and sin washes down that instant with imbecilic fear, and all of this suffering is on display. Consolation issued, but there has to be more to life than this! Conception deceiving itself wants more.

"Existence cannot be body, accomplishments are few, prospects are minimal, and there is no second chance? I will not acquire this as a hushed reply. Death has consumed me to waver in a vortex that is stamped my own. Unsinkable, but lifting down."

It burst with red vigilance, and with its latest swoop the curtain cruises into frosted space. The vortex? The lights stand up with cognition, and there we pose to envelope provocative styling.

"What loiters underneath being is the remission of that being. We by way of intervention manifest sanity's wading pool as cargo free from suitor, and a ghostly prompt without doubt. Where are we?"

Forging spite's unfair preference, moral quandary supplies a gratuitous riposte in a surf of white thrown storm. Realization implants a world rediscovered with ungrammatical evasion called to truth. Smiling fortune's declaration breaks the spectrum of meaning, and releases it beaten and bloody. All fiscal peers, elders, followers, all that is encouraged, and all that is condemned marches with access fully in reproach. Related chaos strolls into the gaping chorus of murmured salvation. On ruptured soil we bleed for anonymous cries of alienation, to be the verse of fortune because there is no mercy, no heavenly father to lower his hand, no offspring to fight for what is right, and no population to begin fresh and new. Blackness leaves bodies captured, living legends torn in half and dead, chewed and re-chewed. All that dies falls upon the fragment that is and shall be this. Escape is a window within ourselves, and although numerous rumors lie slain it makes sense.

Dear Abby: What apparel would feature flies and hideous deformity, and not seriously form embarrassment?

Squeamish crucifixion upon the body, solace awakens flesh, bile, mucus, blood, and piss. Leaking excrement. Sexual aberrations, time anchored to escapades calls the head with a thunderous,

"NEXT!"

Efficacy thought to leave escort, and traveled to the bus stop to wait scatterbrained and restless. A skeletal home rendered by rapid growth, overpopulation, and cultural immigration brought about by fecundity. A delicate death weapon, a smell of tastes, and a child's silent logic. Again and away, we are small. Sudden insight is too much, death is a device of reality, and consequence is the plotted truth. Augmented existence has the ingenuity to nominate effect. Words of advice? Definitely not. Words for declaration!

"What Gregory?"

"I had a dream, and from there started this world, and not man." Jim.

Subsidence matures and one can hear its prone growl. If nuclear war came closer to palpability would it hold an intelligible fixture to extirpate popularity? Our heads are aimed at concussion, and not down at the sensation of trial amidst the soupy slime. We have no response to its coming, and lack bravado for an initial step away from this choice and cowardice. Mortals built society to rouse primal, nihilistic anarchy? Mechanic fundamentals scourged by emotional blindness, trivialization, and self-destructive insolence. Senseless, without decent composition, and dispersed from corner to corner. Prepared for seizure, and compelled by deviations of depravation. We are men, and we are women. Consanguine magicians inserted at dusk as a vast, unaccountable army of self proposed inadequacies that conjure solution from the inescapable future. Communication is devoid of purpose, technically possessed, mentally deteriorating, personally obsessed. Negative links in a worldwide chain.

"I am the world, and the world is me. A revelation of realization as the world reflects me, and I reflect the world. Mirrored images of time and space, manipulated and suspended as one whole one." ABPoe.

Originate this ordeal from the concentrate of mass in which you convene and make use of nature, expansion, and function like rubber stretching back and forth having forgot its rudimentary objective. Our feet walk through our stories, and our stories mutate movement into standards of moral and mortal foresight. Diffused like peanut butter across the bread, the bread is nibbled, and swallowed. Arcane inquest laughs back at the alleged whores of tomorrow. Degrees of weakness unite exhortation, and although liberally applied, they incapacitate every guise of particle exploration. Retrospection is dismissed. Change has changed us, prepared us with science and technology, but supernumerary reason for body and mind infuses answerless query.

We do not know who we are nor what we have, and hover as distinguished, upright jackals. Beasts of preposterous allegory with pollution killing the chance of survival. If it has not already trapped the congealing air. Fatigued, desecrated, and passed out jackals. Animals to excrete on trees and urinate in water. Gloating assemblages of pampered waste to bubble with scorn, and sink in a spree of glib fumes, molten proxy, and subordinate rubbish. Obsolete draperies project an extensive, fruitless wall standing tall and thick so the sounds of any opposite activity are heard as non-active lull. Antiquated drapes embroidered with suffering, sewn out of guilt, and the pattern matches disquieting bugs. Revealing self-hatred, and the general distaste for a population of useless, painful commands of war and wrinkles. The shadows of God are you and I, the false idols of body and mind, and it is all repetition. Part the red sea, and immerse the mind with the intermingled identity of itself. There, but west.

"If falling leaves fall in the fall, then our faces tint and fade with winter's brown building majority. We are curling up and withering away, falling into a strong breeze of emergence until crushed upon the desolate ground. The beautiful landscape we hover over we have destroyed, and now we decompose with it. All is one, and one is nothing." Jim

Chocolate stupidity toboggans like a defecating chasm. Apocalypse switched over and broke definition, choked linear disposition, blotted out cause, and ignited revolution in its backfire. Time has named an ample blame, and as quietly as possible equated the purest faces with milky question.

"Armageddon?"

Conviction prowls this film of living thing as veritable to assail angelic device, and decoy apprehended verve. Buildings erupt in flares of inscription named the memory stain. Lies, those disputed in the past that scrutinize alertness, and include no explanation. A memory of vivacious limpidity will not be forgotten, will always be with you, and will not depart from the lane we prudently trot. It will not go away, and you will never leave the uncertainty.

"For in breath there is peace."

The stain is set in a decade long ago, and begins with a diminutive town. The type that most grew up in, the kind where you have a high school, everyone shops at Super Value, and after ten pm you can get coffee at home or in a tacky restaurant named The Chopstick Dragon. Great Chinese and Canadian cuisine. Chow Mein with a side of high class pancakes, and maple syrup. The kind of place where everyone knows you, and notably if you stand out.

"FILTH, PROCRASTINATED UNBALANCE, ESCAPE? THE WAY OUT WAS DEATH, AND THE ANSWERED PRAYERS FOR SALVATION."

Man is a copulating disease, a self-absorbed materialization second-hand from rapidity, experience, and development. Unfettered trials of reactionary moments league the individual state of being. This does not exclude the female, she as woman is a bleeding harvest of man's rebirth, and his harbor even if not her own. Subliminal messages of overlooked authority slowly incite frail mental conduct. Splinters of the past slide through the sieve to replace present, immobile conception with the contamination of mind, body, and soul. Reduced to twitching rot, blood stains, and pin pricks on the coagulating sleeve of fleshy pores. Carved and crimped, affixing the pin. Perforate, channel, and inspire. Teardrops pass away. The substance intrudes, exits, and makes an entrance. Paroxysms facing the lateral flesh of distributing severity. A black border of poignant contours. Nothing is as it seems. Breathing fails.

"Fuck what you think, what you feel, and see! Hell is our next stop, and we are all getting off."

The dwindling, exotic fundamentals of enclosure.

"Eat saltines and diet!" An Americanised version.

On the eighth attempt we sit and listen. We see the rage and madness as a house of horrors rooted in reality. The reminder we cannot hold, but sow through the use of imagination. Nuclear war in blaring black and white transparency flies with the flies on acidic wings. The one she fears contentedly swallows, and the feast has thus begun. End.

"ENTER TRESPASSING FOOTSTEPS. MALIGNANCY A CURSE ORDAINED, VILE MERCY, HEAVENLY DELIGHT. NO MORE THAN I. GOD? YOU SPEAK OF AN EXPECTATION."

Evermore.

Evil is at the heart of all temptation, and no matter how small these matters predetermine fate, and all that is, is, is. Recycled paper. Everything is dirty, and we are filthy. Salsa-like stains dry on lapels, and anonymous gunk saturates pants worn too long. Amused with boredom and the conventional propriety of spent time flopping. This has come with steadfast response, and now there is only acceptance. Decision is still forming the small details, but realize this, appreciate this, and question the validity in which these decisions were made. Reinstated ebb has transpired, and does come to some control. Moderation is the key to exuberance and durability, so then? Continuation.

Accompany the correct partnerships, positive possibility, and uncontrolled pre-ordinance. One need not be good, but be right. Advantages will rise with a quickened pace, start with that, and come to terms with whom I is and what I wants. Sterilize thyself from denial and impurities of distraction. It will happen with God given time just be patient. Can you hear them whispering sacred judgment and prudential law? They speak lowly and abruptly even if language has no meaning that allows for interpretation, and imprisons the body with a cultivation of retardation. Why examine the dialogue? Ignorant apes masturbate persuasion by disillusioning truth. Beasts slobbering their cruel intention. Wonder why? Ridicule and interest.

"I lean angularly against the wall. My ear outstretched, and my eyes floating parallel to the wall as the dingy, white smoke flutters over smudgy yellow. It extends the room and forms a perfect square, and veiny lines of age protrude to and fro with idle identification. The room has a roof of the same proportion, and it hangs around my undulating obsession with four feet of clearance. I stand still with my hand cupping my ear to the wall. The tiles of floor hold me up, and the ceiling perches above, but nothing is connected to affinity. Thinking soured by the crippled bid from the room next door in an implement of size and appearance. This discussion is failure, the words tack vengeance, and the fascination with the sudden station. Revulsion turns the view, and fear encourages shame. I walk the room to the center, and lie upon the tile. Curling into fetal stability I regain security."

Whirlpools of sickness vacillate, and tension breaks the rapid design of time that withstands stewing obscurity with motions of impaired motive.

"Life, redundant life that is my own, discomfort me no more. Hold tears away from melancholic memory, and project my son with marrow washed free from misery. Continuation adhered for the security of the body, amen."

Meat hangs on a hook with flies encased in odor. The meat would be perceived as rotten, foul, and incarcerated as criminal indecency. Coincidentally, has your mother seen her baby? A small beast tackles one smaller. They growl and salaciously forbade a winner. Circling in a fashion of urging rivals, the smaller bites the larger, and it squeals. The larger claws and scratches, and the smaller one shrieks as it draws back its tail! The larger falls dead. Theft emits ridicule and resentment. It fornicates in front of your eyes like midgets you cannot command. A little detour of progression, theft. Stolen articles to build up an assembly of a collection of artifacts free from attachment, however, the object in hand or out of is dissipated. Earth in general is the discipline of compensation, which has nothing to do with theft or robbery or its propriety. You are what you have, and what you have is what you are. Consequently this ramble of dislocated and broken words manufactures a contingent of rational styling that constructs and revitalizes the moment. A second usage. That is to say that we are Martians, the world is dead, and frogs will fall from the sky as omens of our atrocity.

Cities beckon with genuine hospitality. Travel right to maximize your view. There are unlimited stopover privileges when you buy your ticket, and your seat is instantly reserved. You will be sitting pretty all the way. Take advantage by purchasing your ticket seven days in advance. Some conditions do apply.

Cars run off in constant derangement. People breath in a hurry, stir amidst continuous movement, and time simultaneous business. There is penitence for what once was, and joy for what stands breathless around the corner of commotion. Everything is separate, but connected with a strand of harmonious time. Resonance stands in the silence as the footsteps wear concrete, and lights flicker and filter the pit of fond nostalgia. These memories cannot wait! He knew, and he was right, along with his followers, but those lost in fact and tact grow without head linked memories. Why do we need what we lack? A croissant with butter, and slightly heated.

A broken thought of uncomfortable interpretation with a comfortable response, and the world wilts within a tearful response. Republics fall, politicians die of heart disease, dogs chase cats, and common truth is overlooked with sensationalism left in the hands of personal decision. Smoke another cigarette, swig back black water. Puerile fool, I do the same. Death is certain, and rebirth is undecided, but useless banter is a mandatory release for comfort, peace, and balance. I may be right, and I may be wrong, but overall the decision is up to you. Bon appetite!

Explanation is the same, sharp goose bumps forged in the fires of Hell. Now how we burn like sticks upon disdaining flames of twists and cracks of blazing, worldly slumber. The darkness shines as dancing shadows perform a golden cascade of wormful judgment. A ride from departure is another tedious adventure, and turbulence sways confusion with quenchable thirst and hunger. Desire.

For L.

Memories saunter nightshade in the middle of the night
Dreams afloat in slumber within the duration of the flight
Weapons bare unsought flesh, the elixir in the light
We witness shades of somnolent streams and wear the wrath of God
But blame the unfelt finery of all these fields of sod
The testimony of our dreams replanted in the single nod
Of all these wishes, lists, and hitches
The body brings to plight.

The formula is simple avoid the eccentrics. Blood remains blood, a necessity to triangulate reason. Wisdom flourishes nourishment, and all things remain the same under question excerpt for that which sparks the question. If an answer exists it rises, and if not pessimistic tranquility remains the anecdote.

Time slows, and the banter becomes transparent, and the transcended translucence of dignity dines on the choice of reason. Meaning holds truth, reason enacts conviction, and the self imposes the notion that all these things are under inspection. Questions beget further questions.

A frying pan splinters thought because we swear to ridden deceit. Disintegrated thought is a gray top hat that bears its vigil proudly, and she thinks, "I, it, and her?"

"Fuck." Various anonymous.

Mental stops of programming, pockets of time, audible fixations, and upcoming destiny flash in the headlights of re-thought conviction. The act of virulent intervention and murderous revenge touch the body with a flailing grip, and loosens its hold.

"Harvey? Samantha? Who are these others like me? Rhonda?"

A prince was well for twenty days, six more moved on, and the illness festered. Upon the twenty-seventh, lifeless hair was found, and even his chair would prefer some life. Not a lot, but some.

It is either it or I that is the family we are to why? Ideals and time made acerbic because goodness pivots pounding rage with ramming, severed legs. The doctor is a doctor, and an alien physician affixing spasms to embody death. Which hellish void is this? Four thousand, five hundred, and sixty one. Dial seven, two, five, eight, three, four, three to form a mathematical formulation. Lead the way that most men follow into hopeless hells like he. Such is the bar of our six foot hanging. So I am for her, and contain many parts fulfilled, but in a pixie's crate she cries for worms, and her left remains are unkempt. The world is the same, peaceful eye that passes other worlds, and looks up from these stirring bones of original intent. We are the dead, you are the dead, and everything is dead. Dead and buried, but resurrected. Fear, caution, and fear again. Accustomed to and designated for all circumstantial evidence on the want and need of our featured fathers. A rise of decline surfaces once more to revel within uproarious ups and downs. The sun shines blue repose from the deepest grey. Nineteen forty six is the appropriate year. I have had a clandestine vision, and a scrambled fragment of reinvented time. This place, this plane levels out, and brings about a fragile, stationed tone. A phone is ringing, and the ring encircles an earlier arrival. Upon destiny, and its turning to the richest peaks of descending oblivion, we are reborn.

Have you noticed how clowns occupy their time with frowns? Wonder if you will the escapade that is the circus. Tents, elephants, the ring master's call, and the clowns without frowns discovering topsy turvey downs. The gift of laughter on a flying trapeze. The whimsy and wonder, the falls and the blunders, the circus.

"Have you seen my legs, I cannot see at all. Where am I? Where are my legs? Is this some sort of joke? Is anybody there?"

Closer.

Hello? This radio is receiving at x37, which is I repeat x37. Do you accept this parcel governor? End report. A question listeners, and are you receiving?

Her chapter is the third one coming, and is the most uncomfortable kind. Publication grinds in the teeth wanting mothers. Pretty mothers to recognize their feet will not grow planted around this dangerous sunset. Mothers to pet the stench of evil that lingers amongst the unified, urban loneliness, and follow justice to double the distance to peaceful death. Mothers to snarl another dab along this saucy bowl, and barb the muffled, trifled color. Mothers to scatter feelings, form will, and engulf life once more. Four without two is the struggle of these strangers, and upward creatures meet with nothing. There is no hope in these subconscious caverns, and one falls down again.

"Is pepper eight dollars and thirty cents exactly? Well call ahead in case these vamps drive cars!"

Boiled despair are we, and feeling eyes more than facing cheek, we feel these sensations in repeat.

"Am I the liar for having fashion to rest, while standing short of popularity, and with our strident home bashed in obscurity? Am I defeated with a faithful would that mates the faces of the swaying fates, and this righteous bottom happens before her guessing could states thought confused as concern consumed. The surrounded want of complex insanity is left laughing again. Even though everything remains forgotten, and age lands this speaking wilderness. I am dead. I am dead."

This visage does launder objects left alive, but a harpy still waits to rid the system's hive of marshaled footsteps babied beneath this black. The spectacle leaves, and curls without calling, golden brown. Rounded with cooking spite, and once cleansed away, the world he keeps surpasses the recoil of living memory in the threshold of our spillage. Our detached heads are upon this willful fall, and campaign a run for self withdrawal. You and I are lifeless action, yellow backs and wounded bellies, robots. All is random process, and now we preach one name with one dimension, God.

A tree is seen within the distance, and mighty like the mind of man, it is a place for conveying strength, but our complete and total submission takes back might with cold volition. The two with two build four, and file the blooming leaf we pour in the library of the sore. She is a bad penny, and recognizance slinks its way amongst the herd that are her dead. We suppose, and we slash the homage of her breaking row, and although three do hear her rising soul, only one has called for swift patrol.

We are the drawing stains that table this alter of our remains, and fucked we are the indecency that continues. God please bless these words cloaked in coloured crowns because it is with sentenced truth that town is shown. Upside down turned right side up, we speak. And were we able to stitch this absurd taste, than this darkest lounge would conflict with fear, and title death our chewing stroke. What lies beyond the squeaky killer is a man forging forgiveness from ignorance. So back we are against our youth, and up against our old, and under this road of directed secrets we leave a track of blood that squishes down to pack the dust behind us. We are hopeless animals unfit to derive from corrupt finality, and who without these teardrops keeps the heart at bay? What vast explanation can we scream so others may bear some bleak weakness in the rustled mind of secured trait? We part and spike a sanguine penny.

Something would have, and if we were to try we could, but we come to change this blurry hope without the knowledge grasped in mending heavenly music. Now everything is alone and desperate. The stars dash without eyes, and brood vicariously with language. Our free will is barbarous, and we are passengers on cruel intention. We attempt relief because of this temper to which a crypt grows cramped, and the fruit of déjà vu is in the dirt like sullen twigs.

"Allow us the white that roams the testes, and let us dock and plot attained degree in the sling and slump of voices. We created this suddenly, and to be the caprice of a pencil with old generality false amidst this conflict. We are the greatest good of a magical God. Carving a pumpkin, and poking the talking pavement with appearance we discuss the passing lead. Her body boasts mankind's music in a crusade of the Crocksinford movement, and a yellow breeze amends this even change. Men arise from not the beginning, but the transition it rarely flaws. Philosophy in the narrow deliberation of inheritance claims nothing. Individuality is not in swing with a world old and pocketed by its inhabitants. After the lies it adds and binds, it tells the royal records of faith ways to exist in his righteous slumber like silver, maggot polka dots. Picking aviation over the fat his sword devises, confusion devours the mind, God waits on charisma, and theory replaces man's denial with spiny, poisonous collaboration. Hypocritical and ineffectual sections of domain that are branded as coercion and read as wicked mockery. The deposit of numbered wails soothes out this life by way of a second child. What head do you consider, and remember time is now?"

Lost balance.

The world has been killed, or heads are speared, and restraint passes the foggy dew of this anguish sandwich wrapped in wonder bread. Heavy motions stick against the roof of the mouth, and head south into a trap for crap. Remember nothing from this fall, but in a thin bounce recapture what matters because the rest cannot be had.

"I for my master hand this out as black and white, and black and white alone. To find myself I must lose you in a country no longer than time, whether in her or maybe in him this transitory month conceives the why. Why?"

She should with gold construct his corridor a tapestry. Lament follows glorious demise in an industrious shard of barriers. The thoughts we have come to crave, and this bed bound for rest flees from everything. This last and ironic task is a wasted road which literally no feet will travel. A brief and timid trail of disbelief glances obliquely in Adams' boys to give birth to Christmas and Eve's smallest wishes. The final idea is another figment of this fall, but each one is sure of the other's established belief. That if to fall we are to tumble one by one. Specters.

Here to be reality, perhaps there to, but for now it shall be here as well we are. Once again a brief flicker of sense has been dipped into the picture. The answer is this, validity is found where certain truths do linger, and behind the surfaces under question. As humans we cling to dead faiths and self-perpetuating notions, and memory is transparent with radiance, but leaks into streaks amongst the things we consider real. Reason is the downside, and logic encompasses loss. Lost possibility in the realm of the living, and a loss of options on the strip of human death. We seem to destroy that which we do not understand, bury what we believe to lack truth, and grasp onto hope through the use of a dead God. Pray for forgiveness, but wonder what cross bearing building you throw yourself with indignant responsibility. Why? Habit perhaps.

We barely come up for air, suffocating from the lies we throw toward any visible neighbour. We eat, shit out the leftovers, and throw them into the garbage like an abashed ape waiting for death to stop the waiting. We do not like society, but do nothing to cause change, and wait, wanting someone else to alleviate the problem. We wait while we shop with our hands in the workings of money and comfort. We accomplish the task set up for, but could we not aspire for more than self-reliant purpose?

The underside grows in the inhale of permeating breath, and releases its influence slowly to destroy minds, homes, and the legislature. We question the handouts conceived as societal bliss, but we do what seems to be done. The repetition of generations stuck to the floor, and the glue on our bellies was pressed by us. Options in the world of the foul? The stench of castrated death thrown into the barn and hidden away. Filth stowaways forever because we have obliterated the exit thinking we did not need one. Television is somewhat distracting.

His response, well I have already mentioned that part.

"Splat!"

Swaggering, they rolled around, literally, and strange, quiet things devolved to complete orgasm to the power of ten.

"That was great!"

Off of Cape Sex, the ravens mingle beyond the cliffs and crags. Need is confused in the happy sheath of modern man, and its diseases question the rejection, the beguiled saran wrap, and celibacy. Potent yes, but ethical to any term of acceptance, no. Nothing has changed.

She danced around the coffee table topless, and undulating audible traces of passion, she slurred in swoon with the music as glasses clink with a brush of her leg. She stubbed the table with care, her long, dark hair bouncing in rhythm to her step. The style of her choice was long, loose, and free on her low planted head. The carpet entrusted her toes as her movement strode the room. The walls brandished beige in an abode adorned in grey, but at this point her hair held all the attention so particulars roam and idle. She pauses with the song change, but then her motions regain their stride. She jives her hands, and her legs move to and fro with the dancing tone of temperament. The lights are dim as the sound increases, and she resumes her similar clarity. She breaks her groove with a moment's notice, and the recoil is in the glass. She swigs it slow, but tastes it right as droplets run between her breasts. She feels the warmth from deep inside her, and within the lines of drunken toll and crippled apathy she slumps within a breath. Revamping the sound with a better record, she re-administers a drinking plea for honesty.

How little jumps twinge behind respect for the reigning foe. No prayer and no faith because we never originally received them. No was the answer, and salvation was stolen. Dead I must take you with me, to repeat… and to repeat… and to repeat… and to repeat…

"I am a restless man suffering addiction. The sun glares in my eyes, and yet I still look on. Jubilation is in my addiction, and my squandered life of ambition does hold its grasp, but without a snivel, a sob, or a scream. With happiness I give my addiction power, and let it grow for tidal waves of passion hide within its hold. I question not the impurity of body, nor cry the loss of mind, but instead regret the stolen time upon accepted crime. My power is my fault, and addiction gives my pleasure flowers built with the sand of towers that rock did crumble to construct. These crimes abate my hearty platter of disgrace and pedigree. The grimy chains of temper's rumor fill the tracks of ventured sorrow with accepted plight, and cry no second chance because upon the first, it was thrown away, and lost beneath the waves. Yelling vespers to tell the truth, but gone within the sound I wander this blunder until I die. I seek not the thrill of yesterday, but the re-caught glimpse of tomorrow, and these mirrored tales of sober wishing equals nothing more than tears. The sadness of a broken heart, a stolen child, and a wounded man in hiding. Motionless with old age trembling in the ideal dreams of wasted notions I am among the seams of vacuous tedium evoked by the re-cast shadows of these terms."

Me.

"I am hot, shucked, and itchy. Scratches on my flesh, and hair wriggling above my chest. Pellets in the furrow of my brow, and my upper lip is dry within the crinkling dew of perspiration. What now?"

Man waiting for death because his friends are dead, and home rents Hell a sight to see.

"I am myself bloody."

Hearing home wore well, humanity is back, but of his comportment rather than their body. Does this frightened door mean anything to you? Escape stands for dusty revenge. Life has been pulled to plains, and swept to the season behind the pen. To the open page, the type which death unleashed upon the sitting hordes, and on for great, old England to move the destruction up the table downward. Hollow evil is at our doing. The more time races on film, we do regain November. All the bodies are silent in a habitat of dye. We are odor until the stars claim their limits, and these horrors fall forever. A blue flame veils our ship of ignition, and a musty figure calls away the inward blaze to purify it. Is this the beginning to some better day?

"No."

When it was with dismal honesty upon her, it missed with slight exception. Afraid through Hell she is, and out of shedding skin is pumping through. It is this storm in reading, and the when and where of a small continued would. I am he, and he is our father in a living glance. He and I are this as one, and in our taking, righteous and just is this guest of hers that would be between the floors and stuck as yours forever. It is full away. She, he, and this. Convalescent, but ebbing deterioration. If this is a beginning then let it begin.

Usually the first question that all artists answer would be setting. This enables the viewer, listener, estranged to occupy the documentation laid before them. The setting is simple, basic, and personal. Most are, however, this place in which we sit is definitely ours, and conveying it is indulgent, but it further establishes a beginning. The view consists of one of the grittiest, most degraded corners in the city, and we see everything. It is concocted and performed before our eyes. Most of which is not recognized by those involved. That is to say they do not know we watch, and if they do, paranoia has just inflamed. Streetlights brighten the room after dark, and as we face east the sun enlightens it during the day. The walls are white, the ceiling is high, and everything outside is turbid and nebulous within flashbacks of dirty acid bliss. Basic, minimal, and ours. It is clean, and the news is on, something federal because the government controls the airwaves now. There are quotes scattered with stuttering newscasters, and we suppose the censors sit right there prodding whenever something is askew. We do not really listen, but jazz replaces the news, although the censors still sit in. They are everywhere, what can we do and say that the censors will take away? An ambulance echoes from outside, sound and not vision, and we wonder who overdosed this time? The censors will cover it up so we guess it really does not matter.

"I cannot do this non-existent potential of human life, I give up! Nothing is better than something, why? No compromise, rejection, anxiety, need, damnation, and judgment. No repetitious decay. I do not want this lack of foundation and meaningless shell of life. I do not need this need for acceptance, this desire for forgiveness, or this condition of dreary inheritance. I have no want for any of this. I am afraid, and that is what has kept me for so long. Not of what I lose, but what I find. Hell is a reality of mine, and I have seen images brushing the windowpane. My apologies for this and the past which created it. I know not what I do, and this is my excuse. I have no sense of anything real because I am already callous. This final blow simply brings along the conclusion, and although I fear it, I shall carry it with me. The finale is in my hand, and there is no longer any audience of captivated interest, not even my own. I am finished, and there is no turning back. Thank you for what you offered, appreciation may not have been lay bare, but love will be with you always. I will miss you, but hopefully not forget the time we interjected. You will be my living proof, a burden I regretfully imply, but this ride has gone too far and I really must get off. I have no strength, will or self not formed of ungrateful memories and my perpetual senility. I am as dry as a leaf in the fall, and tossing in the wind I am decrepit, suspended, and bound. This is all there is, and this is all I have. My thoughts are dark and tired as I am sure yours are, but keep on the fight, and bear your fists up in honor because warmth constrains goodbyes."

Having thrown up, and lying down again, could not return to sleep. Shivering, sweaty flashes of waiting, waiting, waiting. Nothing, but nausea and slanted coordination. Standing is difficult and focus upon the keys is blurry. Feeling sick, shaking with the jitters, but happily digesting the boggled sickness.

There was blood on the street, a spray of red stain across the sidewalk below. Dance around it, continue the walk home passed the vomit and garbage within every footstep. Hungry and haggard, sleep comes down.

"What will you do when the party is over?"

A slogan on an invitation to come and experience the love and power of God.

"There sure are a lot of rats down here."

Hell of a business, propagating freedom, structure, and brotherly love. It gives a warm, spring chill as hair stands up eager. Stressful trauma is the end. Feet and heads buried in mountains of dirt, and even in coffins a mission permeates from us. A mystical language passed on as response. Through a door we have turned, and this tour way has made a powerful date with the devil himself.

Lost with patterned phrases picked, and over. Angelic, but aloof, existence gives man mortality as this indignant reasoning. Attacked, blue faced, and worked over. These crates were unwanted, but when we looked down and found at glamourous best, mangled hollows, they became our destiny. Here for those who would have noticed, but now they could, would, should, not. Man is a book of freshened ideas, senses do try to bind them, but they cannot. Man's clotting skin is as gruesome as the abominations we have become, saying, "Get up and taste the planet."

We trip through a maze of contemptuous sea, upon chirping destruction because a beast is killing us! We were fresh, and now we are found reborn. Children receiving words in their mouths, and beginning the avalanche of man. Life has ended, and we are spirits inside space, exploring secrets, and falling down slopes. The seas have all been drank, and without pumping sprit gives way to the hollow body, which is left as unsolved. This drowning has ended, and the dead tide the years ahead with designated slots built as personal experience. An apocalyptic symphony, person to person, and orchestra to orchestra. The finale is the same, but the remains mean something different. Life is that same bouncing ball that pulls us unto demise, and onto this cryptic, symphonic delight. It is the passage that leads the road to the clearing after the tempest. The trek that reveals our deaths, passages, clearings, treks, and tempests, and now reborn it is spat up, all lived through in one sense or all. Personal occurrence on a worldwide level, the bread and butter, and combinations of maestro's finest work. There are many stories, lands, and legends. Answers no, but gossip. Hesitant reader, beggar of truth, the brush under the unthinkable grows peerless and powerful, even distinct if you lack belief, and it is urgent far beyond any reason. Silently controlled, not taking us, but us taking it, and there is no survival for a promised being.

"I am sitting in a Chinese restaurant, one is the same as the next so the model name will suffice. I sit alone, and classical music banters above minimal table noise. A new table has arrived with ten guests, two or three families. Caucasian. I have committed eye contact with one of the women, she was the first to arrive with two small boys. Then another couple with two young boys, followed by the first's husband with yet another older, but young boy. Who wants what? Who wants this many men in their life?" An unknown, woman.

"I cannot remember what happened. Forget about it. I was drunk, and there were seven of us. Move your legs. Now they are moving. Let us go over there? Careful, you know you do not have very good balance. I do not know!"

"I had a dream, the most beautiful dream of burgeoning plants, and crimson defiled walls. I walk down a mezzanine, and twilight circumvents me. Inconsistent noise engulfs me. I turn a fork, and then another, and then the noise is gone, and music replaces it. Nothing known, but a song with a violin factor. A mushroom grows in my hand, and then at a leisurely pace dehydrates. I boost my heading, and massage my brow to look forward into the iniquity of oblivion within orange illumination. I squint and squawk with the music dwindling as soon as it came. Noise resounds as nameless faces rebel within the shadows, and suddenly then I am gone. I no longer exist, live, or feel. I hear nothing, see doleful silhouettes, and feel numb to all vibration except for the taste of salt water taffy. I awaken in a poppy filled field that turns to marsh and mush. I live in a bowl of mushroom soup, not Campbell's, but some cheap imitation that tastes like water, and smells like scalding, thick milk. I sink in the murky substance, and submerge with darkness caressing me once more. Then my body spasms, my eyes open, and I lie motionless atop my bed with a tear on my pillow, and my throat swollen shut."

"I have claimed to hold a philosophy without teachings, manifest, or textbook. How then do I hold a philosophy? What do I believe in? I believe in expression, faith, and thought." Jim.

I like sinking here, and thinking about goodbyes. We did not meet, anticipation strains flashback strangers falsified as the web of all this blasphemy, wait a moment.

"I love you."

Level out these tendencies, grab control with capricious hands to delicately pace out petulant ground. Another new work with self on the page, and a new machine, perhaps with cryptic stereotype? Sitting on the sea with fresh ideals, and the tired memories of the bereft. Speculation and tribulation. The water from the buzzing cooler, and the whispered whim of sequenced dreams to disorder focus closely. Pursuit is drawing pursuit. True, shaken nausea pinched in movements of maestro's purest work, lost on a vibrating machine, humming and hawing. The volume increases.

"I love you."

I remember the days of my innocent youth
Purified time fulfilled with exposure
The table was set, and the kettle did boil
For it was tea time at my place, twelve o'clock sharp.

My friends were in line, supportive yet lifeless
Their banter was pointless, consistent and loud
Although not a one made a solitary sound
I winced at the sight of loose stuffing or straw
For that was their life force, their power, and flaw
I sat and watched, and they did the same
For it was tea time at my place, twelve o'clock sharp.

I remember their names like yesterday's date
Various in structure, stamina, and fate
Mrs. Twigs was the one who sat in the corner
She winced and she whined, she cried, and she bribed
Like my sister before her, she hated my pride
Scrunch the dog, and my lifelong companion
Sat in style with his hind legs half missing
So his body was present crumpled and guessing
While his legs in the backyard set up a lesson
For it was tea time at my place, twelve o'clock sharp!

I once cracked an egg named sequester, even though her real name was Ester. She followed a quack on a roll and a jiggle, "Yeah, you Mack, got a dollar mister?" Greenish and sinister bore this mentor's dumb waiter because it was tea time at my place, twelve o'clock sharp.

I thought I saw a light above, but I did not. No crushing planetary collapse, and no space saucer of any kind. Did they miss us? Are they making us wait? Do they really have ulterior motives?

Lesson.

"Inescapable as a killer, I kill even, and have even made a killing. We died together. The grass vanished into burnt remnants of the plateau on death's hill. We are gone, and life is another quiet peak."
Dalton.
Intelligence is important! As a front of humanistic ideals swagger outward over the puritan motives of preservation, humanity carries the millennium with ravaged guile and disease. In order to survive, cut backs are inevitable. Intelligence is important! The party.
Introduction, "Is it necessary?"
Conservative, literary views say, "Yes."
I say, "No, but I will abide."
The following is something, and contains some hard and drenching stuff. I have persisted, and have endured to come up ahead. Breath comes easier now, my mind no longer hurts, and my body no longer yearns. Thought seems less mumbled. Perhaps I have crossed closure, "Who knows?"
Seven days of time, bad luck, and most of all thought. Knowledge. Growth. Glad to have found a way of venting it. Take what you take, open your mind, and enjoy.

It was 1974, and a pre-disco, industrial gutter. Freedom was found, and banned as amiable formality. Adolescence into childhood was a façade of self-deliverance. A year of mumbled uproar.

It is endless and senseless, holding power and flaw, but resides within one's own paw. We hold it within us or are we within it? A paradox designed with design's intent on the tread of weathered footsteps. Blank, warm, and lying still. Blowing bubbles to the faint hearted, ill tempered, primitive dwellers of today. The pervasive prose mashed into a mangled pulp that is the banter of fellow suitors. Disclaimed and removed words are over used, and meaning was never held between them.

A song to see the seashore, a twig to feel the earth's floor, a sigh with no remorse, a tear with no consent, and a babble with no brook to concede the vibrant motion wandering town with swift hubbub. Spreading adventure to bud a delicate intake in the amounting dew. Fantasy mirrors the themes of gloom, and hangs in the propositions of grand demise, the illusion of conviction, and the toll of bearing value. Too little time with too much activity. A writer writes, a reader reads, and tales of nuance assemble the vacant text. The trivial encounter of a misused utensil left as an antiquity to someone else. The fervent stride coaxes the brambles of mind to tax the burdened body with the articulation of a grunting donkey mounting some peak with the loss for its reason.

"NEXT!"

The line progresses and the axle breaks the persistent call of suspended grief. The clear, tabulated cause of belief enforces this diction, and this crude, sloppy estate absolves the living realm. We are one, and one is many. The end.

Credits running verbatim, and the service calls clients to fill the scrolling names with being. Click, tick, rickety rick. Reeling the train forgoes the track, and to say the least suspicious thing has left point and conception as the standard of service unto self.

Death is loose, free, and substantial. Regret, ignorance, apathy, these things provide stagnation, but breathe, heart, and function are the act of God's intention. Pure society. Progress stems from clear, clean character and the dichotomy it provides, but belligerent time creates complication with awareness starting at the beginning, ending when finished, and assembling logical thought, practicality, and the instincts we have in the concrete, material world.

It is Sunday. The non-day. The senses, expansion, flexibility, and tolerance. Learning thus we are a hard act to follow, and our fans gnaw teeth, rip mouths, and grapple claws. Two spaces would have been preferred, but the reference to intent is in the message of one. Transfixed by more than a conclusion of emptiness and its intermission, the words extend to drift in memory's comfort, and washed, and rinsed of residue they straddle sweet conception with the wisdom of swooned sensation. We step in awe and welcome the want.

Beached on ivory shores and misanthropic virtue, we still wash our backs with soiled debris. To breach these unclean wipes of objectionable boredom, we fall away, and the years rest with us. Dead, we slay our dragons well.

An orb flavors translucent markings hanging lowly in the sky, and the predators are coming, and they see us in their scope. Displeasure and pain induced by their gain. Maintained for labor and coerced with the wand of their plea. We granted these travellers a safe house, and they impregnated our plans with disease. The dying race of their overtaking, and we rise to higher occasions, but not on this day of reckoning.

"It was strange, twisted, and disgusting, but you can only shove something up so far for so long. After the surgery life did not return to normal, no matter how much reassurance I have welcomed over the years. The scars are here with me, and every breath makes me shudder in remorse."

One.

"It was strange, twisted, and disgusting. You see it had been torn right off, but with modern technology a new one was remodeled through the use of DNA. Everything returned to normal after the last fitting, and we just thank the lord for this formulated gift."

Two.

"It was strange, twisted, and disgusting. The way it laid in incubation, and produced such an odor. You would not believe how bad it smelled. It was as if it was fermenting, or worse. What amazed me was how you could just grab onto it, and swing it around for hours. It was handy in the bedroom as you have guessed. It really opens you up, and makes you scream thank God for the metric system."

Three.

"It was strange, twisted, and disgusting, and rolled through town like there was no tomorrow. It tore through the trailer park, and little Tommy Rogers lost his parents. Doesn't have anybody now, poor kid, all because that thing came down and messed with the livestock."

Four.

Is Rose sick? Directions. Is decision easy with direction? Does it fade away with withered age? Do the questions here get answered or do they span the space with quiet lips? Memories encourage choice, thoughts distinguish depth, and voices curb the distance. Lost and warm with blank diction and humble pride. Words unseen are bleeding in an incessant blur of spokes. They seem to be sweet, random sweeps of poise and character, but a binge of stricken luxury on vowels, consonants, and cursed control also. They do add up these fates with definition, but they multiply and lose control with steadfast admiration, and when sopped in whirling irony, introspection loses sight. Calming words keep coming to lead us clear away. Misspent in the dolorous confines of the stylus. Subject to the ink, and inside the lines, postured print becomes a mate of paper.

What kind of desolate articulation is this? What garbled sense does limit this lie to kill the test of time? These rhymes of reason plague me, and I do declare I like the tone of their whistling, romantic rhetoric. To speak the wells of English brevity and maintain appalled conformity, and I wish upon these words.

A panoramic view of madness, frolicking marshals of age and time, and a dialect of white tiled waiting. Fluorescent depths of sterile improvement. The irradiated sunshine blurs faces as aid and discourse ride a nauseous, cramped gurney. Women holding children, men loving women, and people alone tending themselves. Curiosity brings case in case to the stale forced air of stirs and echoes reeling sentiment. Bleached dissonance instructs calm patients in the wake of the quake. Derailed, bereaved, and delivered, we are on our health, and in this room we are stalled with tags and forms. The instructions require security.

Jim,

In correspondence to your letter I am well.
Culture fabricates itself without regret. Tension perks my brother, and discussion is broken with distance heightened. Wrists sweat profusely, uncontrolled, and propelled by a stance toward victory. This realm is ours brother, ours for the taking. Please enter with a response. A factory built atop this sight would widely grow with prevailing Mother Nature

taken with the loss of all green pasture. Rise to the occasion, be pleasant to the experience, and the experience will return the descending favor.

Abelard.

Jim,

In regard to the dementia of my frowning mediocrity, my boredom has fallen to neurotic impulse and outrageous abundance, and these insane aspirations are tilting forward, but I am fine. As these keys fall and spring this has begun!
Before all else we should discuss positioning. That is the direction of progress. Be patient. I send reassurance to clarify reality, and check in with the world out there. For you it solidifies the vague conception that I have given you. What the Hell are you doing? Foreshadowing aside, discovery has pickled my state. My mind is functioning enough to type this letter, which is to record our communication, and the knowledge of the other. Remember brother intelligence is pure and right. The party is with you brother, and the party does not forget. No bias and no mercy, kill the world, but foremost the species. All things! Death is our answer brother, and death is our escape.

Abelard.

Jimmy, they call him the retard, and they being his familiars. They frequent the scum of the earth, the tribal and the purloined. He does not mind, and neither do they, for if they did they would not be known as his familiars. They know him as a man of passion, a follower of truth and honor, and a man of emission. They like him, trust him, and follow his righteousness. They express spirit, faith, and compromise his favor. Paranoia sweeps in at seven, and the children become restless as Jimmy sits on the leather sofa, and regurgitates culture in circles of light that illuminates the lamplight. Glowing rays of positioned, green light jumping through the perfumed air. His eyes are red and circled, and they dance in his head like marbles loose on the floor. They draw the room's attention, and bodies scatter corners with shadow and vision. The room is tense, mildly, but Jimmy is comfortable. This induced state was steadily marching, and his succession was following after. The beginning. Today we stomp tomorrow with nocturnal atrophy.

"Where are we?"

"We are here in forever."

Back is Dalton, the ruin of John, and the cause of her sharpened screams. She hit him, and he dragged her across the wall. John just lied there bleeding, and rested in a fetal position similar to hers. She cringed, afraid of her outcome, and she blacked out. Dalton raised the club that grew from his fisted hand, and hit the top of her already bleeding head. He did not even seem to mind, aha! She heaved belly down as consciousness came back again. Her mouth was muffled by plush, purple shag. She did not move, but relaxed easily, motionless. He clubbed her back heavily, and a twitch, jump, spasm, and replant was the only reaction.

"BASH!"

"John watched me first kill Peter Johnson, constable for the police force. Then there was that poor Nancy, but she deserved my temper. Then Sue who was named a whore, and then skilled as one. Little old Miss Widgeons, the expression on her face as she bled upon my knife. Bleed so thy heart bewilders this bereft confusion."

Dalton.

"Life and the playground it spans is ruined." ABPoe (1969)

Life had always been blue polyester spreading the universe, Macdonald. This lapse of motive has departed as soon as it arrives, and a question of design hides vocation with an unlovable quotation. Leading nowhere, visions of morbid antagonism find societal refuge.

"I thought you were so tall, lumbering over strangers, but now I see you are shorter than I. Your conscious is leaving Macdonald. Your darkness is slipping back into the deep end. Do not worry everything is going to be just fine. Come on now go up to bed. Sleep, rest, and dream of travesty no more. Well goodness no Macdonald, death's pursuit is not murder's intent."

Here rests Revelation Macdonald, and the man they call Poe. Thug!

The lizards have come home, and a daughter diffused from the shades of murder has to search down without dissolution opening guard. In her soul is courtesy, and the problems of the outside world curse in sedate seclusion. Death in thought, and thought in this kingdom leads down, backwards, and towards her. This sideshow tastes delectable addictions as men stand free of production, and through yesterday's breeding all is complete except conclusion. Apocalypse has come, God is sentenced, and no soul shall rise from the stench of pungent pate. The diminished, the dissolved, and the rot within the walls; this world is raping bliss. Lost to saunter within the dreams and nightmares of a population. This needs to be said and heard! Your sins are your offence, and I hereby ask that motions be made to charge this man with perjury. You are obviously lying sir! You know what I am talking about.

"Difference equals difference."

Love stings cold and sweet as the church bells ring. Rice scatters at the groom's feet causing him to fall and break his neck. Crimson stains her white satin and lace trim, and she cries for her babies to see the light of day, and for moans of pleasure to be heard amidst the honeymoon sheets. Beyond the churchyard hangs this swing from an iron bar. Children no longer play there, but she cries for comfort in this children's dead lair of joy. Gravel sits below the sinking swing as sand castles wilt in vacant contingence. She cries and thinks, holding his head within her bosom, and her warmth trembles in her thoughts. Cornmeal muffins cooling in the pantry, while cereal decays in its unopened box. Mice hunting for cheese, cats searching for mice, and dogs wandering for cats. Man craves his best friend, and women feel for men. Children long for their mother, and children steal other children. And so on. What a silly game of useless nonsense. No head or tails, but a faceless coin sitting in the stomach of a gumball machine. A dog barks, but is never seen. A woman screams, but no one sees the deed. No real conclusion, but evidence to support it.

The world shatters at a pin's prick. Arms are left as flesh and bone, and mind reduced to a bowl of jelly. Jiggle, jiggle, stop the ride I am going to be sick!

Draining logic, insanity swallows the pointless questioning, and assurance brings outdated trivia. Pigs in the slaughter with growling indigestion, and purgatory waits burning sulfur based air, and ground desecrated by the feces of man. Reflection looking back at you through the eyes of shadows because sight no longer sees. The grasp takes hold of the forearms, and the bitter taste backs up the throat. Noise filters upward, and smell uses the exit door when the heroin dies.

Lyrical speech from mighty taste. Poe like a sniveled conviction, claims false meaning as we fearful gorillas reach with burning ends left long ago. Our eyes open, and Armageddon! Slowly go further, and we are the instinctive, dark light, and the will of mercy makes another attempt at an asking plea. They with nameless being open actions within this hollow encyclopedia set, and everyone here in the milky glances of distortion falls down. Decide, escape up, and beget what? One needs falsehood as a customary sail across the virtual sewer of exploitation. Funny how our time concerns the soul, and the pounding wood against our death is the head of this key full of evil.

"Are the leaves really my resting place?"

A man in black and blue, black from the waist down, and blue from the waist up, sits corresponding with two under-aged prostitutes, and their correlation is based on footwear. They sit, converge over coffee at expensive rates, and uphold a weird, direct view. Behind us sits who knows who? All we hear is what we hear, a slurping straw, the noise of children, and Alanis Morrissette.

"He mentioned it to me yesterday."

"No I probably wouldn't know."

"Shove over Louise."

"Push a pedal, pull a lover, and rock a rocker Tina!"

"Fuck!"

"Fuck!"

"Must you girls always curse?"

"Come on Ellen."

"I told you not to call me that!" The mother smacking the father.

"Ouch!"

"That was weird." Everybody at one time or another.

"Repeat what you just said."

"That was weird."

The memories of yesterday atop arrogant tales, and conversation from the tired, broken dead. Over and over.

"Shut up!"

"Give me some honey."

"You arrogant son of an ape!" Again the mother slaps the father.

"Slap!"

"Ouch."

"How many times do I have to tell you to wash your hands boohoo?"

"Mental abortion."

"Me too! It is kind of awkward how the blonde guy walked into the door first. The look on his face!"

Junior finishes it.

"Is he living with his mother?"

"He was, but I don't know"

"Get over there and sit down!"

"Ouch."

Over spoken or overheard conversation. A greeting of twitchy existence, and you know the truth behind purpose. The possibility of waste or reasoned destiny. Cycles question behavioral science. We have finished, are done and gone. Running mad with fright. Being watched without end. The culprit is a fairly attractive, young man. He maintains dreads, and facial hair triangulates on his chin. He too is finished, done and gone, but we have all arrived.

A few days later in the realm of the strange, things are happening. The robust world of insanity has devoured our feeble souls, and our simple beings. We surrender to the institution of bizarre tendencies for escape. A peak of refuge reached in the new heights of the game called life. Manmade contraptions of growing, uncomfortable realization. Soul hanging combat, and our hands are the cast to which a mountain grows, and there stands Alexander.

"I have control."

Time slows bearing ordeal to the paced arithmetic of God. He holds his righteous toll with hardened glee as the facsimile for proxy, and the fresh, stout enclosure for physical being condemns all facets unfelt to bewilder the moment unseen. Floundering tribulation onto the self, the physical being continues carefree and full of fancy. Up to the brim with orthodox procedure, the being erects self suited trial, conveys its flagrant tolerance, and binds the mass confusion with his own. The people to the people. The endless embodiment of failure, the processing and decline of each unto themselves, and the recruitment of false intention forecasts false security. The anchored mention of solicited bias and the incriminating sentence for our misplaced heart. Refunds are not withstanding, and records settle in the living proof of sacrifice, but within the false pretension sacrifice does not exist because it is forgotten with re-established standards of fallacy, and this too is false. The self that flaws this biased screening is unkempt, faithful, and worshipped through the support of ideals. The standards of temperance, patience, and purity. God is not left with his mathematics.

Introspection deserts us with disbelief enforcing thought to question not one's self or process, but instead the plastic world of childlessness forced around the self. The self has no hold in a place where the realization of possibility translates continuity into a reproached barb of fighting slogans. It becomes bereft and catches calamity with the insidious query of approach. As false as surrender it engages crisp reality with acceptance or doubt, and either way delusion or self biased conclusion creates and influences the effect. Dictation proves as toxic as the concerned quotients involved, and the removal of self and the belief in action remain the same thing.

Questions shine brilliance lowly on the hills, although removal is accepted, and transcends the impending reality with the creation of one's own. This is the conclusion, the contaminated propriety of proper order and ordeal that leaves one with oneself, and this egotistical approach should be condemned or propagated further.

Progress seems articulate and tangible in the horizon of tomorrow, yet extends passed the congealing state of affairs that deliver tomorrow. Stories told and fables old are the unending, misinterpreted direction of those abstract, but solid states of being that propose more than just the being itself. Progression defines reason, qualifies time, and confesses trial with a wager formed in the cold remembrance of yesterday. It builds activity into the effects of tomorrow, and balances the silent sway of motion to hold out a firm reply to those who question why. Simple and concrete, poured and molded with the tidings of celestial bindings, and even the most common of men are lost in the flirtation with glory never held and debate never sold.

Remember the scribble to scribe and recite. Remember to remember, and avoid the apparent deceit and its hold on the present predicament. Deceit is self-contained, and holds no grasp in God's equation. So we wander, saunter, and encounter this ordeal, and thus we remember patience.

Percolating possibility procrastinates proletariats. I do well to do.

Terminology is read, the italics have been dropped, and manipulation of a desired meaning delivers something else besides the destined outcome. I am my own allusion, the discombobulated artifact of some grand design, and the asylum for the affiliated progress of prose. Doubt and fear sleep in the storm, and attach themselves to the bobbing ship that I do sail, but the message of life, loneliness, and love rekindles the contrast. Sailing in the waves, off the brazen shores, derelict in the bubbling brine of stolen time, and crashing upon the rocks, deterrent toils decision. We cascade dividing waters. Crystalline motion in refurbished clarity matching the point in hand. Down to the task of enlightenment, the interest of fundamental basis, and the incriminating choice that proposes both. Life, love, and loss with a snub of an ideal victimizes the well departed. Further down in the depths of the soul, the layers peel back and let go. They drop in the absorbent solution of person to lose the position of self.

Luster is in the approach of choice, and irate nature claims the slanted view. This leaking mixture of fault is the tradition of misused hearts that seethe to coax volition. Our secret is the positive caution that sets the alarm for distress in the excavated wreckage. We are sloppy in the intention of citation because the prolific attendance of beckoning tragedy is in the daily routine. Stuck in the mud, sinking in the sand, and choking on the exhaust. We are sloppy, tentative districts of raging vindication in the fields of logic, reason, and self. The perpetual notion of solidified motion ripples, and tones the brisk flesh with hard nipples and feudal sex. Naked, writhing erections and unchanged sensations. We are biased secretions of ebbing solution. Plot has difficulty reasoning point. We do not know what we have jotted down here, transcribed there, and now to contort this page before us we have a new feeling formed. Self-discovery. Psychosis baffles, and astonishing introspection has found reinstating the above a relief from the turmoil on our plate.

Have you removed yourself to forget the past and the present? Have you fondled the world to prepare for the future? You are reading, and what you see is based on that. Why choose this to begin with, and is it making you think or feel? At the same time are these questions logical based on the current situation? Our relationship of teller and taker, it remains my assumption that I am failing the request miserably. You shall receive calm waves of serenity as momentary escape. Wait a moment, why need rest, here and now? We do not need it. If we did would we be here? We would be atop a shelf or a bench collecting dust, fallen skin, and mites. This for the moment would be unknown and unsound. Dead words scattered in a binding. So why then is rest necessary or is it?

Silence reverberates back. No answers, no replies, nothing said, and nothing heard. Are you there? Maybe I am not asking the right questions, are you there? The visualization of reality is here, but perhaps we should grasp something more influential? What is your reality? The moment of place and perspective that is now? What do your senses feel? Bare your soul for a change, and tell me everything. Allow me to be the reader, and you paint the picture that I reflect. How? Communication is null in void. A new discovery, writing, although involving audience and lecturer is very one sided.

Escape is not necessary. No one needs to get off the ride and wash their shoes of their vomit. Sit here, and fill heads with dreams. It is not tiresome or weary from speaking, and escape is not necessary. The end of the dissuasion. We will continue to tell, and continue to take, and if either needs rest they shall do so by closing the book. Agreed.

A man screams, "Set change!"

Lights up, and three men enter to remove the tree, the bench, and the body. A man wearing a hat and glasses enters and watches vicariously. A chorus line runs across the back of the stage, and it is a big, Hollywood rush of people and mania. Fast, continuous, and stretched out. The rush slows, and you hear.

"Scene two, let's go ladies!"

The three men return the bench with the body still on it, and place it center stage. They exit.

Marriage is the utopia for choice, but is misconstrued due to the rash pursuit of the choice. Comfort, affection, and love; these things establish choice, however reason and haste delivers the arrangement with compulsion. Messed up or is everything else messed up. We are fine, but we seem out of place when really everything is around us. God, almighty father, let it be. Amen.

The passing time brings confusion with the distraught trials of life. Fear and guilt. Stuck without parole like a roach in its hotel of sentenced, random structure. Not knowing very much, what we do, we trust. The things we teach we trust, and the things we do not, we do not understand. The things in-between do not really relate to either. Blame is on mixed communication, denial, blasphemy, and pain. Exposure makes Jack a happy boy, but Jill a jealous freak. Weak legs, and the only sensation is the groping blasé of maggots and worms scattering this way and that in our skeletal home.

The bathtub fills with anticipation, and the water then empties through the drain. Feeling clean means feeling better, but when we are drying in dirt, stolen by death, nothing means everything. Relief? Do not pass go, do not collect two hundred dollars, and go directly to jail!

Rich, thick, creamy sauce is delicious like mayonnaise. Recognition of death provides disgust with a clean, red sheen that beacons into brown a recital for the impression of fake wood. Fingerprints form the bottom of the smear, brown fingerprints that examine existence, but there is no answer. It came and went with us. Listen and absorb because we already know the answer, and instead forget and invade elsewhere. It will come again, and the voice shall say,

"The thing you ask is logical, but there is no answer."

Demands and commands bounce like rubber. Lies and bullshit fit like gloves, and maybe that is what that smell is as life holds no discreditable objection. The moment on hand is the purest, most tangible direction of personalized time. It holds no disadvantage. Action is immense, powerful, and assertive stance and stature. It emanates purpose, and from that notion of purpose comes infinite possibility. This is the meaning of life, or at least is accustomed to our liking, and therefore holds truth. Present it openly, certain that it will be conceptualized as a blessing, and not forbidden because it lacks apathetic styling. Choice regards time, and not vice versa. The present represents the past and evokes the future, and the range of circumstance is personal opportunity. Examine purpose, and progress through self with the responsive attitude that guides our largest quality, love. Represent tactical realization and their possibilities, but devolve them. Think about it.

Moment one.

A child lies in a chair with his feet on the floor, and his body reclines into a deep position. His head is enabled to rest down, and looks up. He is not moving, but complains.

"I cannot eat anymore daddy."

He reasons with himself for a moment, and a fuss crinkles within his face as his father watches earnestly. His wife sits next to him also with an eye on her son, and another on a small girl with an auburn pony tail. They are of the forties persuasion, and the children range from nine to eleven for the pony tail, and six to ten for him.

She is reading a magazine briskly, but her head is slanted to the left in a boring expression of desperate pre-activity. She wears shorts, sneakers, and a tight, generic long sleeved shirt. She is plain, but crosses her legs in hope of some sense of sexual captivity, but there is none. She sits, flipping pages, and wasting time.

The father and son leave, and the girls are left alone, safe and sound, comfortable and wasted, enjoying the afternoon romp, and the pleasures of womanhood in the solicitude from men. More freedom is to come. Material prosperity unravels mediocre stagnation. Tear loose, enjoy, and run rampant. Intoxicate your sense, and your living wealth shall be worshipped. Run free to trample unfit measures, evoke unclaimed footsteps, and discover the possibility and wonder.

Transformation brings process, and in process comes change, and within the change is substance. Substance equals meaning, happiness, joy, and real love. This step of mortality is a monumental step forward, and evolutionary process on a minimal scale. We are already eradicating rational impulse! All reactions are to be physical and felt, and not broken and eliminated because of the state of mind and thought. Natural reflexes are muted, and the specimens lack the thought to leave the physical body in an unknown state. To step back mentally by removing the world.

The human race is drained of all use, is non-existent time, and is plundered of all function. It is left to die on scientific obtrusion. Silent collapse is to follow, but this tight ended catastrophe is not demanding. It brings truth demolition, and escapes power to stoke embers of stolen home. The transmission is denied.

"The mutable jelly bean is white, followed by pink, purple, orange, red, green, yellow, and finally black. Cancerous jelly beans are the worst. Eat them first!"

No actual intervention is required, and no actual living is involved either. So then what is living, what is life? Like everyone else who lacks the answer behind that, I think there is no sly solution, and so continuance is evident. What was said, and what were we getting to? That point we touch so briefly, and avoid harshly. I have no idea, none. Let us come to some insightful fancy. As probably mentioned, or maybe it should be, rules are meant to be followed, but are only issued as guidelines to keep on track.

"They lie," as a respected friend once said, and in a simple, tip of the tongue explanation.

Nothing really matters because today we see through the eyes of a madman, and now and forever. Amen. Now it starts although this is all that remains. The light flickered.

"I can be seen inside by Belgium. The giant head given unusual filth, me."

Strange, more so.

"From the mouth of new and into a time to see was a creature bare and waiting there. I do not talk because my answer breaks the room you have remorse about. A flaming bet, forceful and bloodless. The summons is less when all the eyes meet, and follow conclusion, including Macdonald."

That is you. That is Macdonald is you. The smear of direction has unlocked tribulation, and has grabbed thought to look closer, longer.

"Macdonald used houses and apartments, and then cemeteries. Pets were utilized over the years as well as a few heads they shipped to their enemies. During the age of Bardo Poe, that is Macdonald, and that is you."

"That is what?" You.

"Red anguish to open the pit with yellow daylight hiding in the corner, and smelling of the orange, morning flame, seasons end while a beast comes forth in all."

There is a string, and a line based back to her. Further along than us, these chains are down and through.

"ONE... LAUGHING FORTITUDE BESET BY FILTH AND MEMORY. DISCOVERY AND SUSTENANCE."

"I will destroy the world, and carry on with streams of godliness. Ocular demonstrations of death upholding injustice declares no homage for the living. Ghastly fate is a sight of hellish malediction. A raw draft comes from across the room, is open to diminish the heat, but now the wind limits the warmth, and will not extend this shivering defeat. Death? The temperature of unsolicited scruple drudges this tale, and encourages response to be more than apathetic detail. I should state that I am not dead. I am alive and well, living with existence as my own. Young with the visualization of today, tomorrow I die literally, and this shall be my testimony. The heat returns, and I cease to claim this seething broil. Tranquil, but sweltering, the stale air rustles in juxtaposition to the figments of coagulated death. Life is in the written region of lucidity. Black light is the only light, and noise is everywhere."

"Bounce, bounce."

Pool games create incessant, sinking balls. A crack whore yodels over one of the tables.

"Colin Clive is watching me!"

We feel a hallucination coming on with senility sitting on the lap of a saint. Circles to nowhere. All is repetition, and unflavored, fluent waste of tone and person. Time, space, and self are sucked in with no return to sender. Red light allows man with response, but respect and restitution are repulsed by the hierarchy of clarity. Woe vomits enough to cough and spittle, but perhaps to the disadvantage of undying youth. Memories of childhood are spotless as they flounder on and out without rhythm and order. Splashing imagery with corrosion as the blame for heart seeped emotion.

Special and frivolous are each moment that recollection forces upon us, and we hit against the unknown holding a frightened face to the opening of today. Answers are saturated all over the walls like vivid blurs of stopped time and ended life. We call out for help, screaming mainly, and glance through the brilliant light as carnival music sways high above any auditory boundary. We stand here numb with a dwarf at our feet explaining,

"This suffering is mounted upon you, and thus is accepted."

We ate the meat with flaring teeth, and gel stained our chests as it slid down our chins. Tapping our appendixes, the dwarf swaggered back and forth in a drunken swirl. He was short, and very short at that.

"Crooooooooooooooo..."

The reverberated syllable swam into identification by side-stepping the ears because the bellow was without traceable life. She was wailing, sobbing, trying to pry our fractured legs from the fallen obstruction. A heavy enclosure held us back, and this little man left us with distraction. Given that weird is mystery twice, wandering there is a terrifying thing. Gasping and surrounded with horror. There were pricks, few, but painful pricks. Our legs were torn apart with spiking jerks of relapsed spasm, and smell consumed the air as it tingled our nostrils. Her body was tugging hard, and it was well worked, but we fell into the abyss we feel, but we did not fall at all. BAM! Square in the head, and our heads. We were shaken, our flesh parted, and seasoned the walls about us. Darkness ate darkness, and black engulfed black. No sparks and no flame, but wreckage from the wasteland.

"Please God, come on baby."

Her tears outweighed her voice, and we were gone without her and within her, and she was lost with us.

"I FACE YOU NOW."

Fiend, fornicator, and filth, he who hath taken voyage, and who is close to this affectation of knowledge that contains this dead humanity by way of choice and reassigned props. Dead, extinct memories of dead ideas and sound. Crocksinford, the living realm is your treasure, and have you saved it from this spicy piracy? A thread which might interest the blind mass, when death drops perplexity to wrap the ground and garbage violently, she, Crocksinford shall rise, and she will awaken delivery. This prolonged depression inevitably creates chronic exhaustion, and without energy we cannot support our health.

Power is at the root of the human experience, and our attitudes and belief patterns, whether positive or negative, are all extensions of how we define, use or do not use power. The choices we make each moment are expressions and symbols of our personal power, and we have to make choices. We are meant to draw on our inner resources to find the material strength needed to leave behind our outmoded beliefs and behaviors. To see ourselves in new, healthy ways. Healing is an active and internal process that includes investigating one's attitudes, memories, and belief with the desire to release all negative patterns that prevent one's full emotional and spiritual recovery.

The necessity of change makes healing a terrifying experience for many people, but healing requires taking action, and is not a passive event. Faith is able to do whatever is required to maintain the balance of body, mind, and soul even when our minds compete without emotional needs. Still emotional needs and the mind remain nonsensical clamor.

"WHERE ARE YOU? I WAIT FOR YOU. NO BIRTHDAY, NO JOURNEY, NO SALVATION. IT BEGINS WITH YOU; WHERE YOU MAY BE SEEN. SPEAK! RISE FROM SLUMBER TO RECOVER DARKNESS FROM THE DEPTHS, DRIFTING, TURNING, SHE WAKES? NO."

Minus life, and the meeting of survivors, they do not return, and this is over.

"RAGE OF HATRED. DEFEAT COMES TO PASS. YOU THE OVERCOME, THE WORLD IS MINE. DEAD AND ALIVE. APPEAR IN ASHES AND MAKE YOUR PRESENCE KNOWN. SPEAK!"

All is dark and rotten until she steps. She is humanity's saving grace and irrevocable reprieve. We are to swim in this vortex, and sink in its depravity wanting her. Sinful contrition, and the lack of pity is the wading pool in the center of grotesque nature and the punitive way of life. There is nothing, except this space before us, and we must eat to be merry. Realize the failure and pray no more for mercy does not exist. Eat the meat and be merry for we are here for the rest of acknowledgment.

"REDEMPTION ABSENT STILL? CONCEPTION BOASTS AUTHENTIC POWER. REASON IS ABSOLUTE. WORSHIP ME THE DELIVERER OF PAIN."

No hope for a savior, and no revelation of succor to dine at the table. To suffer and catch the corpses, the ripped flesh amounts to a statuette. The mortal world is destroyed, the human spirit is enslaved, and the crash of all was experienced. School graduations, anniversaries, and childhood nicknames. Car races, nuclear testing, books, movies made for television, after school specials, cigarettes, and coffee. There is nothing left that is normal and known, after all there is nothing.

"BLAZING AND BURNING."

Lacking function with reveling reflection, compulsively back cataloguing, memories are very mortal and clinging thus seems inherent by nature. Imagine reiterated bursts of fiery haze like razor sharp gunshots of personal remembrance. The living consequence of the dreadful course of everlasting time. Reborn. Hovering amidst glimmering color, light and sound, to return as a lapse of an emotional breakdown. The reoccurring pictures end and the sound corrodes.

"I am blurting out insanity. Please let this end, gagging, spitting." A dead man.

The disclosure of our lament is based on false Gods, menial truth, and our unimaginative temperament. We are filtering energies as superfluous discovery, and useless rubbish limits a fitting existence. We are dung piles compiling uncelebrated disgust.

An orange sunset vigorously writhes in its agenda, and composes pictures into words. A plan of action transforms into a cramped wrist.

Tentatively speaking, writer's cramp, and a pre-pose menstrual cycle system. Give it a reason, and it will give a tale of correspondence.

Build a temple from those who know you, and translate their talents into a portion of ideal control. Utilize the acknowledgement and understanding of the truth to travel to all things conscious. Awareness will control the motion of personalized truth, and accept the more euphoric experience. Pulpits will be the intelligence that is perception, and the appreciation of translation as the physical form is collected, living data. It is not accepted, and instead pursues its original state of derivation. Preaching tackles thought and the corporeal conquest of intelligence, but the regulated standards thereof are the extenuation of the real and not the imposed.

What society terms as reality is separate from the personal identity. The self should comply destruction with an awakened spirit. It is an actual, concrete change toward a moral world because change is slow, difficult, and confident to breed safety in the truth. We have to absolve competition, ego, filth, and sin from activity. Persecute truth, trivialize endurance, and revolutionize belief.

Exist with temptation, but argue with failure, deceit, and obliteration. Disclose life, death, and this whim of execution. Question all logic, and stumble upon discovery with sunlit success. We are on the threshold of frenzy, and rebirth is in our fingers, but we must apply correctly.

"The mind is left with nothing more than itself." Someone I knew once.

"He was a dot we noticed with a web around him like a kingdom spun of golden thread. Glowing foam incarnating holy power that stood there upon the hill. The shadow cast this frivolous encounter."

This being is a shining urchin of a god-like mask draped over the land like an extended arm of greedy omnipotence. It is he, and this is his shoe for an answer. He is kind, and feels life as it is at home in the eating lines of self-deceit. Ensnared, entangled, and insecure in the manifestations based on the spider and the fly. The fly in which the spider eats has fatty flesh yawing and punctured. Devoured and reborn as the moment of defeat, the sorry state of losing, and the end. It has come with substantial purification, although with tearing skin and tugging gristle. We sweat, and plead for decency. The volume is loud and overwhelming. Yelps are heard, edited, and played back. Cut and paste.

The reels wind tight as the screen projects our bloody death, and the soundtrack continues with tumultuous delirium. Control? There is none. Retreat? We have come too far, and pins, needles, and fangs bear tasty morsels of clinging mass, and we are eaten. It is a distasteful survey of sausage formed from a meaty pulp of fat and muscle. Slipping down the esophagus onto the stomach, and squeezing through the intestines to erupt from the rectum. A tremor of tender meat with the stench of disorder farting from a gastro-intestinal tube as what remains of the feast is digested. The worm eaten rot of dinnertime. Are you hungry? We feel, we think an appetite comes. Stirring and splashing the reddish clumps lump to the wall that is attached to the plumbing that links to the toilet. Throw up bags from the wash of a thousand flushes, and the putrescence of gnawing joints, pinching tissue, and bending a meal.

"Bliss, wine, and ecstasy. The unknown."

Collage.
"To forget is to forge a partnership with oblivion. In order to triumph over loss and death one must remember. In an informative age, forgetfulness is a vehicle for weakness and debility, it is taken as incompetence, and a sign of losing one's grip." Abelard.

Our present engagement is lost again in a horrible trek of mental labor. It is a foggy airport state, upside down and flying backwards. Beasts are screaming on this crack of warning, and laugh out these gargantuan restraints, and like the travelled few within this we are dealt the same, thick theory of shrieking answers.

"And one. It is ok."

In the water his feet submerge alone. His breath is deep and silent as voyage spreads its declaration in reply to the flailing why, and it rejoices in our thanking voices.

PART ONE

A MAN STEPS lightly atop the fragile, framed foot of a woman standing close. He rashly blusters out his sympathetic apology, and she simply smiles and responds.

"We are all sorry are we not?"

Recognize both viewpoints, and their interaction seems almost staged. Put on with artistic perfection to stress and acknowledge our subdued personalities, but they are not. One reacts to the other within the lines of appropriate public activity. Society has surely developed irrational standards. If nothing else it has trivialized and minimized any sense of personal correctness. This of course falls unacceptable as opinion is slightly slandered.

We shall continue, however, the topic shall change as that deems itself a saving grace from social disclaim. Observe and take notes to change the regulated levels of social obedience/disobedience and justice/injustice. Interrupted by a woman coughing, our glance became raised, and froze in orbit. Starring motionless toward our backyard, full of delusion. Time stopped, had been broken by a woman's hack, and lies diluted upon a monotone hum. Immediately erased, we are back squabbling. Time has moved on, and started again, and this is entirely over.

"I am the what in which is I. Something heard to sit in with Luxembourg." Jim.

Abundant sleep is an answer. Triumphant she is now! An evergreen race with spectators smiling on for a second installment. The discouraged commit to memory the deposition like a pack of wolves malnourished with increasing hunger coercing the strong to eat the feeble. Gathered into the hands of this ridden road with villages burned, and life extinguished like a beetle squirming for a place to hide. All is up, hit with a single shot, and exists now as meat set out to feed upon.

Power slips and tears apart the town called home. Support is out back fighting, but with fists down, and faces weeping.

"Crocksinford discern our sloppy hope, and guide indefinite rebuilding."

Kept down by body, the morning saw his sword to hers, and far beyond the cat tails resides this dame's decree for her children's refuge. It holds her glee, and she like them falls too. Ambiguous leaves to gather on this settled plot.

I as I are it. Raised to her, but obliged to him. We were worked out within one asking, left to her, and right to him in order to contrive the library that describes defining me. Scripture picked as king, and the likes it seems was momentary. He is it, and it is this. A prize? A lick unlocked by mortal charm. He is behind our throats, and heads bow about him like the inherent days of months. You like I are him. Regretful as we, but time turns howling men, and thus we do receive.

"Are we there yet?"

Pain is a great fear. Engrossing, physical pain. Broken bones, pierced skin, and gory wounds. Walking down an anonymous street with fairly steady traffic, probably midday walking down an aisle, and BLAM! Crossfire. Bleeding all over the street, the side of a building, and no one pays mind. Junkies stand around blind. Wincing a roar, begging, but nothing. Bubbling there to curl up and die. Bereavement opens to the black beyond, and the devil cuts off the head in a single, solitary swipe. Fear it because what we fear usually comes looking for us.

The party is a newly based conglomerate of artistic revolutionaries that asks you to join them into the next millennium. Raise fists in approval, and swallow the pride. Walk with us brother because the fight has now begun.

You as a human being lead a pathetic existence. Procreation is meaning, and down a path of destruction our species has evolved. Over population drains resources that are needed to provide worldwide longevity, and the path of the twenty-first century prods self-knowledge, discovery, and fate. It is a time of confusion, and a passage paved with neglect instead of preservation. A healthy tomorrow requires provision for a healthy today. Be intelligent, and face the truths of tomorrow with the facts of today. The distribution of wealth, media hypocrisy, liquidated reliance, and ideals submerged in evolution. Avoid the red herring. Take your reflections bravely. Breathe deep and bear these facets of future, and the truth of tomorrow. Be intelligent because intelligence is important. Be resourceful, reach the world's potential, and not just your own. We must act now before our lazy routines rise up! Call it in the name of your brother, and call it in the name of the party! Intelligence is important.

Genocide is a practical approach to extinguish human life so that the preservation of the world may be enforced. Control the population, and prepare to designate the future. This will enable self-promotion through artistic endeavor. The end is the underlying force holding political, financial, and cultural power. Intelligence is important and shall be promoted to reveal socially misleading and incorrect worldwide structures. Change thought through the use of extreme measures to guarantee success.

Welcome to desperate times, a place of confusion, a path paved with the destructive age we live in, and the facts of tomorrow and today. Intelligence is important, and a means of process to the problem at hand. The human species is unimportant, and we ourselves must make drastic change to look beyond it. We are many, and longevity will not supply our growing number with suggestion. Decrease demand, increase supply, and improve the chance of progress to solve the future problems we will encounter. Who after all in an unbiased manner is fit to survive? No one. Absolute strangers are still absolute strangers. Execute all the worldwide prisoners. No matter what the crime, immediate execution. Get rid of hate groups, drug addicts, alcoholics, and sex fiends. Free the world of the elderly, sooner than later. The deformed or the crippled. The whistlers from construction sites and gay bashers. Religious fanatics and atheists. Witches and hags. The neighbour upstairs and that girl down the hall.

The reason behind our filth is decay, but the decision one makes with the coming of apocalypse is the practical approach. Think clearly because I know you will make the right decision for your country, and for tomorrow. Uncle Sam.

"All life, no exclusion, and no bias. Even I acknowledge my extermination within the process of worldly destruction." ABPoe.

One passage. One.

Hide hill, yesterday. A silent and special murder today. Understand the proposition, and the tale of Armageddon. The death of you and your world as well as my own.

"A drastic attitude, another case of loving too much." The sheriff.

"The tongues then were especially tasty? Tell me sheriff, what makes an eighteen year old die like mushy cake?" The deputy.

"Nothing more than built up fate. A natural juice to brook from application. Dwell too long and you may get lost." The sheriff.

"And what a meaty piece of man he was!" The deputy.

Another passage. Two.

"When old enough anything is possible and within grasp. The world can be yours!"

Raised in the hopes of dreams, and the apprehension of nightmares, we are unaware of the essence of reality. This is our mother's gift to us.

"I heard the circus was in town, and walked straight up to the ringmaster and bluntly said, I can juggle three bowling balls blindfolded."

"Give my hands yours then, and come see my monkey."

This was the ringmaster's response. We went, and I saw as it slicked its way through my palm. Back and forth, and in and out. His breathing was heavy from the growling indigestion that lurked inside him. His monkey caused a sickened reaction. His hips pumped heavily, and my hand became covered with the moisture grinding. He finished with his slimy erection sticking to my pant leg. White, sticky, and dripping downward.

A man's desire for sexual intercourse is perverse. His drive for gratification and sensual temptation is a great part of the mortal world. For example, when intercourse cannot be attained, self-release or masturbation is used. Reptiles scaling depths in the art of getting laid.

"So slight prostitution made me a member of the Little Brother Family Circus. Working for a man whose monkey was limitless made me a deviant addicted to so-called, shared monkey love, and as a circus member and a homosexual in the forties I was somewhat taboo."

These sick men forging perversion with innocence and forgiveness. They control themselves with addictions. Gyrating flesh with bodily fluid to corrode morality in naked trembles of disarray.

"It would seem I could do nothing more than juggle three bowling balls blindfolded."

Unneeded details of over exaggerated, degrading smut. Sex is sex, under rated, but over practiced, indignant, pungent gratification.

"He wanted me, he wanted to be inside, and he wanted the facial shot. His jealousy overpowered his thinking, and he burst from his cover, and stood there hovering over the two of us. We were preoccupied, and neither of us took note of him."

A shot travelled across the room.

"Sludge slapped my face, and Carl hung limply on top, pinning me to the bed tighter than before. I screamed as I probably should have, and there he was holding the steaming barrel. The gun protruded from his grasp, and his temple flared. He was enflamed with passionate carnage, and I suspect his finding me was not expected or invited. He stood still for eternity, and it happened, he spoke, 'you filthy cheating whore!'

I asked if one could cheat if one was truly a whore.

'What the hell are you doing?' He was yelling.

He shot once more, and the wall's enamel chipped where it took impact. I needed something as far as an explanation would go, although I did not get one. Rigamortis was swelling in my ass, and he shot once more causing a chest wound. This is all I can remember as I lay bare staring at him staring back, and Carl just hung there stiff and bleeding. Far away, and even further away from this was the outcome. Two deaths and the lifelong agony of lost obsession. The irony is he caused his loss, and cuffed it to the headboard railing. He hung Carl in the closet after he cleaned and groomed him, and then he proceeded to rape my corpse as I hung from the iron pole attached to me. He walked to the window, shed a single tear, and blew a hole straight through his head. BANG! The gunshot. And BANG! His body whacking the floor. We died upon the temper of a monkey at least that is how it goes this time told."

The deranged world of sexual intercourse is not a horny revelation.

One more passage. Three.

Paced out. So that he sits in.

"The air was foggy as life, and jumped through flashing sex with squirming mechanisms. The attack was unpleasant as I sat there struggling in a bedroom glowing with sexual delight. I hid behind the closet door. Watching, overlooking eyes without obstruction building animal malevolence. I waited my love for this pausing distraction to take control of perception with its present appeal. We fall into it, and it binds us with a good feeling that everything is perfect, but delves into something abnormally different. That was when I questioned it. Why are we here spilling, body, mind, and soul for such a sleazy audience?"

These people, these violent, evil people. Voices to call echoes of unending thunder. Please release us, please let us go.

"Why?"

"Please just let us go, we did not do a thing. No. No! Stop it! NO!"

"Strengthen my legs so they may rise from the implanted carpet, away from this white, dead space of biased pride and fluid contempt. Speaking frankly of the negative downslide amplifies nature's deceit. These thoughts, this escape, all frothy deception in this unmoving state. Staring, nerves dead, reactions erased, and reflexes unmotivated. There is this wall, the white death of all my father's tears in wrathful thievery, and revenge accelerates decay. A monotone discussion is left unspoken. No feeling of hunger or thirst, no sense of reason, no craving of any kind. Perfection. This wall covers my feet with concrete boredom to be measured as resilient, sponge toffee. Push and it caves away, and stretches. Pull and it follows tug. Stretching the boundaries of existential cliché. Blink. Stare, stare, and stare. Blink. Concentrating black shadows are very seldom seen as this wall stares back with gleaming familiarity. Mine, not its. We space out, and glimpse at revamped memories of carpet lined flashbacks that question meaning, but not instinctively. Lost from yesterday we are staring, and the wall waits as we remember stolen laughter in the souvenirs of the pasts golden moments. Stare, stare, stare, and blink. Selfish removal from the present acquaintance leaves the carpet clean, the wall unseen, and a chair with slouchy pillows. We are lonely, crying over life's passing happiness, and shall remain barren forever. It parts without reason, resurrects when noteworthy, and jostles in and out. Fading when neglected, and arriving unexpected when happiness rolls away, and tumbles toward the sea. Nourish me with happiness, real enchantment, and not these pictures of pre-used felicity. Wreckage and cataclysm. Heap after heap compiling into a party of blood culture. Spastic fits and uncontrolled corollary splinters discussion with the refusal for choice. You are welcome. Everything is all right!"

Peculiar and tantalizing temptation crowds the streets nowhere near China, but the Chinese are high in abundance. I see balding, old men with canes fighting over fish. Position yourself properly, directly, and without fail. Tiny Tom Thumb shall prevail, although lacking substance, quality, and sheer reason. No explanation, the worst film this year, and two thumbs down, all the way down.

There was someone at the door. She did not knock, but entered cordially, and resisted any uncomfortable feeling that may have derived in doing so. She was small, not midget-like, but smaller than I, and she wore various formations of blue which hung in such a fashion as to swirl across and around her tiny figure. She stood there with a look of confused certainty, she was comfortable and certain, but confused as to why. I simply sat with response being a look of aspirated joy. She responded with a similar gesture that concluded with her sitting down. We briefly glanced at each other as if in some daze of unnoticed belief and assurance. We together were comfortable. Calm distraction took us over and she was gone. No longer sitting or standing, but back out the way in which she came. I sighed with her leaving, and anticipated her return, but for now she is unseen, unheard, and gone. I do not miss her because I will see her again in a dream of life that is a dream.

Dead superintendents and everything is a grey brume of misfortune, but did she speak blissful shelter from the battle to come? Where does one hide? In the frames of general colouring, the images replay across the blackness of glacial energy, and the shadows of dead memories. Thoughts victimizing thought. Perception unraveling misconception. It locks on target with assimilated advantage, but in doing so articulates an unconscious standard of something completely conscious. The unconscious setting of personality attracts, reproaches, and upholds conscious decision and the rationale for the being itself. Thus any programming on a conscious level is distorted by the setting of the personality's unconscious attachment. This simply means one cannot reprogram or alter the conscious classification of being without removing or abating the unconscious fabrication.

"TRIBULATION. NURSE THE INFLICTED SCAR HATEFUL COVER. SHOW YOUR FACE. BODY. VISION. TAIL SQUALOR,

ALLOW PLEASURE GREETING. RELEASE THIS THORN! HELP ME HELP YOU HELP THEM. AMPUTATE THEM."

Contemptible waiting sprinkling down in slow motion caterwauling.

"That my guts splash the backdrop of this crossing comes as no surprise. Torrid, loose, piping hot ends. A gelatin-like glaze on stony cement, crackling under odoriferous heat. I know I have tried and challenged. Someone shoot me in the head so that this can end. Tired and challenged, failing only through cowardice. Altitude perches in a tree, and plummets toward the rocky soil. A nice splotch. Form ran around my thrombus, and blandly detected asphalt leaving a quantity of squirming jam to clutch the grass, and strand the vegetation that it lays upon. I crackle under fragrant ignition."

"Examine the hole, shoot again until the spasms coincide. Let my glare burst with a gunshot to spill layers of skin, bone, and goo. Blow away my head!"

"LET IT BEGIN, EARTH AND WRITHING BOUNTY STRIKE. SLICE MALIGNANT STUPIDITY."

Playback distortion comes with remembrance, and with this remembrance comes a superficial form that is this so-called obesity. Complex circular cycles become principles inflected. Aching pressure manipulates our numbing sensations. Destroyed posterity is our extinguished drop into unprofitable breeding, and productive use is ravaged into procreative waste. Our ancestors are all dead, our offspring is swept away, and these are the ways of nonproduction. A blasting stupor, flat, heavy, dead, and dull. Crossing descent, calm, smooth, and moderated; pestilence and fornication unequal volcanic force. Weight is gaining and the pressure is building, SNAP and SLICE!

Paradoxical rhapsody. This fertility is now whimsical frenzy. Enthusiastic phantoms made from figments of fiction. The absence of meaning scores sounds of gibbered delirium, dizzy vertigo, and the complete capture of the brain. Disordered impressions of our fabricated past. This mania recalls derangement, inconsistent acts of foul absurdity, and our senseless hallucination is ungrounded. Stories and novels of captured thought. A deceptive conjuration of worldly spirits and artificial sightings of God. A fraudulent retelling splitting asylum banter.

These are the steps and stages for guile imposters, and charlatans of mental reservation and false subterfuge forge moments of predetermined routine to hold no bearing. Habit has become followed and accustomed to addiction as one's self is almost premeditated nature. This is our compulsive contortion, our bending accommodation, and out stable answer.

A reason is bound to happen because elastic truth supports the collapsing civilization and its desperate congregation. Parents, children, and relatives ruined as extendible debris. We have washed ourselves well away clean. A random mumble of dislocated words, and statements juxtaposed and spliced together with finishing nails. These excuses are the slaughter of a rebellious mule. Slice! The existing fragments of motion and time pause the air and the wind with the essence of flowing rhythm. The stop to apprehension alleviates tension, freezes linear percentage, and receives free for calling a set of twelve, stay sharp, steak knives.

Play back.

Play back H.G. Wells and C.S. Lewis, Robert Louis Stevenson, and Arthur Miller. Play back school dances, first time kisses, and virginal loss. The wars, the trials, and the political bonanza. Play back birth, life, and death, reason, and falsified explanation. Reversed discussion to build this programmed feedback as the past, present, and future. Play it back. Play back Groucho Marx and Buster Keaton. Capture creative expression and play it back. Destroy thinking, the scientific method, and Murphy's Law. Annihilate discovery, originality, and personality. Subvert religion, abort faith, and the imperial hypocrisy. Play it all back. Puns and slogans, international planning, punishment and pain, fornication and cocaine. Play back colds and flues, whale extinction, and flowers in bloom. The quilt on the bed, the picture on the wall, and that chair by the desk. The cat by your feet while the whore is giving head. Her slobbered delight, and his hardened petting. The spasm of passion in her garbled suction. Play it back. The landscape of profound perception, and vague representation. The artistic endeavor, and the ritualistic distemper. Carnivorous observation and wrath swoop at freedom to release calm, clamping irons that clasp our ankles. Distorted plains of mystified genius, torn moments in time and place, stories told for humor and horror, continuation or in part or in full, play back.

Things minced together, and frying in the pot. Sizzle, sizzle, and sizzle. Look closer, listen carefully, and be very, very quiet. Observe this mass of mess and unconcluded pieces of fortune. Play it back. Our planet is gone, our species is not missed, but watch and listen for details because here they come. Take heart and play them back to be formed and played back. Utopian states mend these stitches of meshed scenario, grave dispositions of celestial progression, and fact, and fiction. Play back.

"SHHHHH... THE TREES QUAKE AS EARTH RUMBLES ERUPTION. MOMENTS LAST A LIFETIME."

Evidence and time ended in syndication, and will never be forgotten above buzzing everything else.

"Prepare her, and us for this battle calls. Rise now with her for she will prosper, and through her Macdonald shall rise to victory. Cherish our saving, and protect this new found child because she will bring salvation." Shelly Crocksinford

"Push Gregory push and let your heathen body rise with birth." Unknown.

Question. Where am I going? Answer? Good answer. One must appreciate the answer when asking a question. We shall conquer, preserve, and overcome all obstacles, and do not forget to ask about the free, upcoming seminar.

"Rigatoni in a sparrow's mouth."

Back to the original question, where am I going? Freedom. Exploration. Hobbies. More! Initial steps. Explore possibilities, stuff, and news. Change. Victory, it is July. In retrospect the previous conversation took place in questionable ego, and so on. I have once again proven no matter where you are there you are. Questionable to perspective, but losing my thought, my life is as it is right now. Sitting, scribbling conscience gone, theory diminished, and distortion heckling promotion. A table top and a turned chair. Basic introduction, you see not the setting, but a shop with coffee on a patio. Patios are a public place full of wonderful eavesdropping. Public transport topped it, best entertainment in a large city, but now and here patios are happening! Drink coffee, but a low amount, and smoke in distasteful pride because all of this and more are within a realm of passersby.

"Oh my."

A baby cries. Asian children talk to their mother. Boring tid-bits of human conversation to sample vocabulary, opinion, thought and concept, but above all else the mundane choice of topic. Strange as conversation is predictability strangles every corner. Anyway here is content with one thought,

"Where will I end up?"

Raise the cup, and take a swig in hope of golden dreams, and pleasant days for ability and praise in the utilization and recognition of both. Walking down the street, now read it once more to the Monkees' theme, 'here I am walking down the street.' Jazzy.

Quotients are the crows of mercy, and cataclysm rides beneath their feathered franchise of ordained rhythm. They are thundering rocks sailing with sinking perspective, and they are crawling auspicious mercies across the gray turned blue waste as the sun shines with victory. The weak, bleak, black, slack tomorrow lays at our feet. Tender conformity cracking splotches in the impaling concrete below our strayed, dusty, and scarred footing. Interludes hold down the future with whimsical fancy for hope and delight, but memory pre-empts the end.

Imagine bleeding ears, and sound roaring through every sense ripping. Burning and buried onslaught, weary, tired, and happily dead. I apologize friend, family, stranger, but power lies reeling, and often conceptualizes fond acceptance, preferably deceit, but freedom constructs this criticism. There is only one conclusion blowing in mind, and that is to stop and pray we do not melt. To pause and hope that we never discover this. Fact or fiction, realize the proposition, and claim the fault because we disorient ourselves if we do not. Forget the technicalities, and dispose of the irrational. Tempt starvation, but with bounty. Prosper through courageous defeat, and acknowledge the power we hold. Self-worth and observation, practice and theory, all equal habit. Encourage difference, and supply this regal intercourse a duty of rest.

The rambling of a madman may not make sense, may not seem comprehensible or compatible with you. Think back to those ancient prophecies and those antiquities of modern thought, lost persuasion, and difficult digestion. Ponder for a moment a man screaming with his eyes transfixed on an unseen being. His hair strays and streams in chaotic discord, and an abysmal undertow carries his tune. He screams of his children being eaten by a cat. A large, fuzzy cat. A large, fuzzy, pink cat with a menacing polka dot trim. It makes no sense so people stare, and walk on towards their meetings, but he raises his voice, and continually speaks of his children, and of his cat.

Pink shades of twilight glisten in the moon's reflection.

Ten twenty seven vents from the black faced, white bodied clock that sits upon the night table. Resting atop and below cotton bedding as time radiates red light into the sheen of the wood floor. Flaring from the clock it reaches the wall opposite to the pen connected to paper, and the mind connects with body. Lucid apparitions walk in incoherent introspection and anarchy is becoming apparent with the written credentials here restocked as vengeance. The focal point is objectionable because morals are stolen. A tactful purpose is implied, but words, mechanical placement, and robotic timing have tainted the job. Cerebral tendencies are unclear and narrow.

"Buy, sell, buy sell!" Continual play from a television yelling for cheap rates from the next room.

This is a frequent myth that is transparent like glass, and a panel lowers from above as we fall with clear resemblance. Zealous episodes bask in the sexual sounds entwined in the decadence of usage. Come, and crawl as nausea breaks up into broken bowels. Fragments shake hands and sit together to drink mutant theory based on menial calculation. Intellectual stimulation glares from the corner screen as a game is playing, and old Polish men stand around watching. A splinter of a dream, which had vocabulary baffled and memory out of mind. A distinct and disjointed dream of auditory lunacy, and palpable phantoms tune this loss of bodily control to swim through a plastic formation of physical deformity.

"Do not enter!" A gunshot and a siren.

A mental current of confluence turns into a solid solitude. A proposition? To one extreme and then the other, and back again. A solution to the intricate puzzle before us is simplicity. This is explainable, but lacking the voice to come to terms with the exposition, we are forfeited, wounded, and begging with blood to hamper cotton bedding. There is inspiration, confirmation, witchery, and sensations of pressure. Joints flex, muscles ache, and a dwarf guides a red, transparent light. This is a moment of beauty and tyranny afloat on inexpressible, indescribable, boisterous gratification. Text had left, and rational complexity has stopped bewildered. The red turns to white, and the white bleeds into black. An arrangement of jumping, splicing black as if the total spread of death's reality was lying there open. A single moment when the world crashed and this black blaze burnt with fiendish height the vindication of Hell. Blood splattering, nerve crunching pain, gore flinging and swinging in the shades of black as colored eyes shudder shut for fear of greater fears. Devils and Gods, demon shapes erupting from the lugubrious iniquity.

"Why do I not remember?" You.

Penetration blurry with disciplinarian growths of gripping collaboration, and with independence fleeing, dependence on these inflicted colors increases. All that is mustered is melting with the particular visualization of specters and ghouls as these exclusive shades of color dissolve. Variety in purest white caught beneath the passion of black. Running and colliding with trembling aggravation, and spiraling forward with precision and focus. Perception had pin pointed the distortion. Yes! Fuzz on fuzz, buzz on buzz, and a slow drip to a quick shower onto the framework of uneasiness.

"Help me."

Blinded light is escorted by the spectacle of fabled memory. Smudges of squalor overflow the ravine that is the mind. Words and only words. Words and only these words, but they are like all things equal. Yin and Yang, up and down, the beginning and the end. Lost to saunter the dreams and nightmares of a population. This is it? There is nothing, but fluid, sticky rays of color. Roaming color through a jelly of black. Swirls of color rolling over each other, and having extraterrestrial sex. There is only perception within color, and each folds a new interjection of conception. Capacity is nil, there is no physical form, and this planet was never born, but there was a basic form of one-celled organisms based on the effect. Wavelengths of energy meet and divorce with a formation to the necessity of interaction. One is death, and two is life. Repetition, persecution, and silence in colossal abandon. The reflections of the present state, and the voices that speak with unsound clarity. They clutter sight, and dance in vision. They crumble, the crumbs unfold vast space, and the space extends to where we have this transfixed, fragrant desolation.

"Tell me a tale."

Descend and reissue the state of flickering past. Permeate a sigh, a whimper, a moan. Create a moment out of living proof, and snip it out to tell these capsized feelings of a stolen breath fenced in with time and ascension. Perception is swindled, and freedom is dead with still cells and broken wills pierced beyond repair. Blisters are battered and oozing recognition. An awareness with crystallized time unleashed upon somber cadavers, and fitting by pure association with a customized elaboration. Now steaming, and spread out across the floor, a gooey substance tumbles and smears streaks to eat all clean aspiration with its thickening density. Death.

The devil turns the spit as flesh chars, and clots into a rampant abyss that wanders the ash and coal. Sizzling and screaming an audible sensation, it is hot, stings, and is gone. Boiling and peeling skin smoldered. Sprit is grappled and falling, the body is buried, and the mind is red from shrieking. Being is rotting in blackness, and the red, vibrant clock leads the direction of home. Here we are, here at last. The dice have fallen, and we are stuck, being swallowed, and consumed to all new lengths. Unforgotten, forgiven burden. It is immaculate pressure, and an optional time to buy. A bizarre exchange, sense or no sense. Lessons in forgotten temples and forbidding production. Pitter pattered frequencies of cosmic zest, and the next logical step to enforced, galactic despair.

Nothing, but absolute silence. Nothing, and more silence.

Ranting, anonymous voices, but perhaps only sanity would say so.

Insanity is nothing more than a societal condition. To the crazy person the normal one is insane. Nothing more than a precedent erected with personal translation. First rate with sickness and departure, innards rumble, stomachs stumble, and we are caught in resounding violins. The forgotten beginning has recovered the end. Sweltering waste in a composition of assembled pieces of fruit. Cherries, pears, and peaches. Grapes mixed with apples and blackberries.

Form is not found spelling around in bloating perspective, but in the minimalist charm of a world of unfathomable propriety. It is the next logical step toward demise, and for progress it is necessary. For growth and strength it is right. Let it be for all to see, the diminishing persecution of mismatched words, falsely adopted prose, and diction that eliminates a product to split perspective. Focus on tons of concrete lunacy and fabricated abstraction.

Religion is what exactly? Hopeless attempts at hope, relentless struggles for forgiveness, or guilt ridden hypocritical bull dung. You decide.

Resounding anger because the evidence is guaranteed to be played with, and these influences upon perception will differ every time. Radical thought is conceptual, and leaves reality as a victim based on present, personal states. Now ask to whom? To you, you know not. To me it is known, but with vague consequence I hide it. I know the answer, and you do not because I in reality have questioned it. Do you understand or does this stand as fleeting fiction?

The partition of form is found in everyday life, sparks the truth, and inflicts drooling mentality in its interludes. Fallen dizziness looks at malevolence with projected ambiguity. Parents dance, their fingers clasped between our hands, and we dance through the marigolds once more. A burst of order takes control, cutting off any form that is not of its creation, and blocks any form that does not encourage it as reality. A retorted hold has struck our sorrow's trail. We probably watch as forced delinquents, but the sun shatters visions of lime figments with words beneath the rocks as blood, and we do not notice the yelping figments we eat. Warm decay hovers behind tears and fears that place and pace reaction, and the crowds may live as men, but within the strife of witnessed wonder. These are the dice, and we live amongst their rolls to give doors depth, build guilt, and guise space as a room for recognition within this world. We have the talent to string a coffin to personal expression with plenty of plump wrinkles to affirm the dancing lies. Entering with nothing except for the ample hours sopped in bloody tinges of turning black. Conception stems a sturdy stature to carry redemption, and the apathy is never dissuaded to live with the difference kept amongst us. Things seem mixed with the clean figure of death against the rocks, and it is he; the regulation of a great scream, but no soul. October sears the scalpel of the world, and humanity is engrossed with tyrannical philanthropy. At least for those who subscribe to prosper in vacant, post-modern foolishness? Death lasts with the homage of a chronicled corpse. We will hang from the neck, and saliva will hang from our open mouths as this kink in the neck breaks the wind pipe with a gurgled twist of falling to the floor. This discovery holds nothing also because we as convicted men and women propel scaffolds of memory. We direct the flagrant ego by self, and deliver no appropriate level of positive or negative expression to the awareness of experience. God is the right of every man's psyche, and the devil roams somewhere left of there. The gargoyles of sobriety endanger purpose from both jets of genius.

Revelation Macdonald

A swaggering jewel in a pocket of space. Revvy Macdonald.

"My parents were born again Christian, and with disturbing malady that is my name. These channels in an affable way remind me of them, and Samantha my wife."

Sprinkle existence with the dreadful unhappiness of our species, and form no escape. Like life there is no hope.

"I recall this place from a struggling dream of my acceptance. Doors were shut, walls imploded, and all the parts were a vacuous explosion. We had no children due to a low amount of sperm. I lost her then, and even though she had stolen me. When I died my family gate was closed, and although exposed it was definitely impenetrable. Danger reclines in my skull as a conception called time. Sticky steps of mischievous duty on a scandalous affair with the devil himself, but I prepared for this consequence. The beast that brings neither flood nor desert works north through the hollow forest of life. She which we have written of..."

Life continues on in ignorant bliss.

"Doctor? You did make all the boys that were present, did you not? Crate after crate of belly and blood." Toluene.

Five more now lie behind wooden concealment, and an icy wind blows these murders to hang where reason slams our explanation.

"I feel like I am hanging upside down under about thirty pounds of wood. Chaffed and furry, it even sounds almost kinky. I stick up my thumb, and wane away in the washing of her youth as dice swing and jingle in her cushioned pocket. We fade and the race continues."

Life resumes loose from the fabric of excuse. Gone. The people and voices link together by place and memory. They play like the film, perhaps a dream sequence from a film that resurrects a dream. Freedom talks with advice as if it was a bartender.

"I have searched inside, gone down the hallway of oblivion, and found the facts of life. The message that followed death, and the horizon drew behind it hammered frameworks of mapped, developed souls in a pit of limbo that swirls with all its undercurrents. When we gave feast, and purged turmoil from the plate of the Gods, we found consequence to be the moral of every story. I am one of many, and one part to the infinite structure of individual complexity."

Layer after layer of representation or symbolic persuasion. A questionable resin of decision, patriots!

"Mourning was extinguished, and left in blackness erupting in a fireworks of proportion. Racing, speeding through signal pools of human plea. Bending for sex, but nothing. Sturdy, but displeased. Darkness inhabits the trees outside with the surface of all inside. The figures stand on personal payment here, barren, desolate, and floating in the collected years. Improvement was slaughtered in the basement, and locked in the crate of its choice."

Trapped in the trunk of its choice, what a life? The mere wear of the skeletons we hold. Gates and shadows on fainted heartache.

"The house was big, my father was brutal, and my mother was Crocksinford, while myself, a small occurrence based on influence. Power bonded my father with his house, and that power keeps me here. Lust binds Samantha to me, and love disposes of my parents. A declaration of power is in position. They kept themselves in check, and we did the same. That was the inflicted punishment that passed on to me. A creature of Crocksinford, and a family plot of faithful generations. I should wish the grief onto the offspring of her loins like those before her. However, I cannot, and there is no case of alteration, but the constant struggle to the time of our leave. Waiting and waiting, amen."

Ripples

Envisage a fantastic sight this evening, and a gallant image of Mother Nature's finest splendor in hypnotic combinations of tranquil pre-occupation. Stormy clouds above a turquoise mass. Murky water crashing in on the beach caresses, and their malignant wash-up. Stand before this glorious reckoning with a sense of disbelief, and questions, more questions. An icy chill shoots trepidation through a collar torn to simple questions upon its simple question. Queer entrapment locks an overture of acoustics as a label of charismatic imagination, and emits blue, black, grey, and turquoise galore.

The power, fear, and eternal topic of a god-like force dancing, driven with the questions. This damned foreclosure of society's direction takes a step for curiosity, and pushes a multitude of designated answers. Recall this tale for future re-telling, and please allow for disbelief because these ripples of thought swoon reclusive safety, and surely, please come back to teach with drenching mystery. Please retain bountiful beauty with splashing recognizance. The salt to bias bruising.

Understand, and curiously corner man, the dead bodies taken to sanctuary, but still man. Children begotten of many shattered returns, caused excretion, and the seeping exception to these sleeping shadows. Try and relate. One what is yours, and the other what can be heard allotting these rotten bodies response.

Mixed lies, affordable friends, and eaten noise. Versions held within us, and the corner steps to the way of smoke and stone, wonderful monsters, and prophecies in this world of ours. Now from what to oh my God is the passing discussion between the dead. Who was first with the cheaper truth, and whose lips warn you of this dead end thirst? Mine? This way is gone, twenty-five typing words a minute, and this abstract absurdity is ending. The spider devours the butterfly, and everything is odd and turning with evil judgement. Pain's greatest language. One who is true and just returns sooner or later, and is hopeful in the world he smokes.

Does nothing we snarl and shake, taste and want not stink of dead worms, false interpretation, and stupid solution. As upright elements laughing at the wind, the thunder is as a God. The mosquito that squints at the many knots of oppression. Everything. The fangs that grow to an unknown end in order to exist with the burden of biting the bogeyman's sting. False identity being as the air comes closer with a dream of beauty and an informative nightmare. We have heard a low, cold rumble of something wonderful. Indecent benefits repressed with these personalities of ours as guilt ridden snow. December, unless the beast imitates gumdrops of flaky white truth to realize this case of propagation. Control files the cashiers as heads stain angular strangers exploding, scattered quotations.

"At one time lesbianism was highly fashionable, and opera was all the rave."

"I am the legs that robotic roads bond with heads searching a way for him. A spoke is caught upon reflection, and why is the question that answers me."

A small lagoon points itself at the beast, that is the head, and the metal death that oozes in the pooling slosh. Houses have fallen, and cities lie screaming, awaiting a holy battle that grows from death unfathomable, but as hope fades quickly, words calculate outcome as response comes to contact.

"Is it he who wants that ends humanity?"

There is no come back because we have died, but still the tale goes on, and the film progresses with visions of death and birth. A glimpse at our roots is in the backdrop of travesty and the back lapse of omission. Foreclosure through the epitaphs of obsolete destruction. Blood stains, bleeding wounds, and head damage. Physical contortion, mental breakdown, red herring, and lemon snapper. Tale after tale, motion after motion, and here we are, although here is under question. Pure mania as a madman's distinction reverberates through parallel degeneration. Wave after wave, and roll after roll tolling our call.

"We are here."

Having fortitude to use your own reason constitutes freedom to make public use of one's reason at every point. In freedom there is the least cause for concern about peace and security because we gradually remove kamikaze impulse from intentional artifact. Enlightenment fruits from the intellectual cultivation of the practical. Ways of thinking and being that form a relationship with what exists and what one knows and does. A critical attitude would be specific to modern civilization. Civil freedom provides the mind with room, and permits humanity to extend itself to its full potential. It is a function subordinated by what it constitutes. Whatever compensations accompany enlightenment they are supported by a common imperative. Simple virtue. Various tours illuminate the history of idea, and each individual whatever the age or status, from the beginning to the end of every action has to be governed toward salvation. This is an operation of obedience that has to be made into a threesome, to include truth. Truth as the degree of direction for the conscience.

This is linked relatively to the practiced limits of life. The displacement of relation to the religious center, and the methods of doing it. The proliferation of how. How to raise a family, a house, and nurture the children. How to build cities, erect states, and foster one's own body and mind. How to lead an army, and help the poor beggars. How to search the way in the name of principles.

To accord movement with society and the individual, culture forms both political and moral attitude, spiritual or religious practice, and the prescription to the teaching of God. To find authenticity by questioning the truth put forth by universal rights to every person. In order to solve a problem with natural law respond to the acceptance of truth. There is a problematic certainty amidst the relationship of phenomena that develops reflection. The tie of relationships bundle truth, the subject, and power. The subject gives the questioned truth the effects of power, and questioned power the discourse of truth. Leiten which would be the religious meaning of direction.

Religion, law, and knowledge maintain humanity consequently as a point of critique to uplift men. The primordial responsibility is to know knowledge. Justify reason to rationalize procedure.

A stroll down memory lane for everyone on the city block deals unfortunate time a reunited scale of detail. Moment is moment, relived, re-glued mitigation and mirth. We are the whim of a god, and the freak accident of a holocaust unraveling an assimilated and denied legion as a revolving part of a pulsating force. Vivid, blue light flickering, shot through human discovery, and now replanted time itself skips the sparking drive, ricochets into momentum, and speeds through space in the maintenance of memory. Spliced in a world of tragic, daily experience and detail. Devastation in the minuscule period of decay. Opened and closed like accounts of therapy bleeding through the countryside home like a chicken with its head chopped. The cards of choice plead and filter us through what exists. Vulgar nonsense.

Stories, true and false in wreckage, spite driven havoc swelling above the swine that is our stench, and breaking flinches of hostile takeover escape momentary grace in the captivity of repulsion. Nothing is left except filth and death. One is the next. Perversion eroding decision in the fecal matter of the worldly population. Piles upon piles, brown upon brown until not even brown exists in the blackened dementia. Here we are grasping these terms of degradation to the breaking point. Torn from multiple, fleshy distractions we are controlled because fabricated propaganda has replaced logic. Stung by paralyzed slobbering, masturbating, jabbering, spinning, and spinning controlled. This is what we have to show for our time here. Leftovers.

The staircase bends forward, but we in all directions are thrown unbalanced. Tripping to scrape reality back together with the dull edge of a spatula. Flows of conscious thought, and personal retraction refract and reflect. Assembling images, picture copying picture. Delivery rings in our memory for it is over, and this is all of it. Now only forward, sloppy motion toward a deeper growth of woods, further reaches, bending factors, forward without a choice to mention. One by one, one after the other in universal lines, writhing with pain, and caught with riveting desire.

Stolen dreams replay meditation, and the song in reverse plans blasphemous flashbacks of decadent living. Torture following torture, souls ripped and seeping. Death is what remains. Spittle and secretions of pitiful resistance. Fractured essence in a backward spin toward the center of this trance, and the middle of the void. All is left here within the displayed memories of occurrence, and the questionable state of mangled no escape. Woeful cries enslave numbers, tears for the dead, and whispers for the living. Thirst, hunger, and passages toward revival. A lost cause for these victims lay weary. Broken vows, and forgotten rituals. Succulent loss for the dearly departed, and the raging Hell of all existence. A tempest's refuge of dismal regret is a witless haven, the human race, and this fiendish planet. Drained dry, sucked, broken, and dead.

A fevered heat of spastic terror, and bizarre monstrosity takes on this concentrated massacre. Feasting orgies of howling shivers to infiltrate the sensuous extremity of fear's subscription to sense failure. Bursting shots of adrenaline with jagged pounces of impulse as mental allusion crawls and creeps. A completely shaking, foaming, lobotomy. Fantasies of nausea fuck up experience, and blow away the fierce blast of revolting death. Strung out and up, backs torn with gashing wounds, blisters, and blood. A reconstructed stain against the rear view mirror of an overflow of twisted gore from the ceiling, the walls, and the floor. Handprints fester on dirty smeared glass.

Sketchy fidgeting, bodily reaction, and mental frustration. A state sputtering contagious disease, and all ways are torn, and all directions steer torment and the loss of recognition. The serum of a jelly creates an ocean of tangy oasis. Unconcealed drainage thawing, submerged in muddiness. Open, moving, and distilled. To measure evidence is potentially achievable. What is possible to witness is vague certainty, improbable practice, attainable degrees of possibility, and fractured impressions of circumstantial scripture. Fact. Matter of fact rests as reasonable perplexity and uncertain intuition because the circumstance determines the interpretation. Undefined puzzles combine to expose inauthentic proof through demonstration, and not to follow conviction onto process, but to counter the evidence.

On one hand this, and on the other that. Perception. Our madcap sobriety in a tumbling path of instinctual heresy labeled as a token of remembrance. The art of memory, to blot out and forget is deranged contemplation and escapist guarantee, but memory has no warrantee. In anticipation we fail expectations. Abruptly startled vain calculation, and personal digestion are the philosophical conditions of personality. They are biased and steep, leaning crooked with undiscovered support as fastened posts to frame pillars of contortion. Symmetrical crunches of angular diversion into a complex shape, common and uniform. Built in knobs that bulge the dials to control a population. Singles of revenge to tourist temptation, and reap the reapers of psychosis.

"SHE SPEAKS, NO. WORDS, LIMBS, AND MIND EXTEND TOLL."

Have fun and do not let your head squash in.

"Sit down and remember how to read. Get more Canada!" A new country slogan.

A smoking stall smokes. One, two, three, four, five, six, seven, eight, nine, ten. Eleven, twelve, thirteen, fourteen, fifteen, sixteen, seventeen, eighteen, nineteen, and twenty. Twenty-one, twenty-two, twenty-three, twenty-four, twenty-five, and twenty six. Fornicating with demonstrations of penetration. Foreskin is optional, and self-lubricating, but menstrual canals are clogged. Please overt attention away broken and unspoken.

Mumbled and jumbled, fertile surrealists of neural implication. Perception is flapping, ripe and delicious. Standing and awaiting sentence. The judge beckons, and solemnly stares. His Whig is off kilt, and his eyes are wide. He gesticulates vigorously, and his fingers determine direction. He chortles out some higher values.

"You. Prepare for fate, and the pursuit of an end!"

A pursuit of an end trivializes a beginning.

"Questions?" He asks, but solutions are vague.

Back to the beginning, if a starting point can be verified. It was the middle of winter, hope, and good cheer. Bittersweet upon reflection, the perfection of an apathetic sweetness. Numb and cold with darkness entombing city walkers, street passersby, and the steps of complacency. There we stand cold and white, and shadowed with the testimony of the shadows themselves. It was January, but February was close. It was dull, and dry with snow white darkness. We remain waiting with no means to any end.

Sitting in a room with nothing hanging on the walls. The window is open as light cascades into a space beyond infinite television. A breeze blows faintly, but the fresh air blisters below the old and stale. The stench of smoking smells apparent, even though any sense of smell has been suppressed. Here one day, and gone the next. Spectacles are talking now.

"So here I begin."

What? Illusion presents thought youth.

"Twelve imaginary boys lick coffee cans for composure, but swallow the grinds."

Tongues wag hallucinations of broken items and assaulted response. So there, the end.

"Something had to take advantage, and control of the weaker. Manipulation of the mortals is an illusion led by the wise, following, forever sworn to secrecy, and forging purpose in those lacking it, we have laced the living lives of men. We gave you meaning, and you swallowed it." The Gods.

Spending moment after moment, story after story, for what?

The dining of bestial pronunciation surrounds Adam strolling, biding time, and building strength. The very nothingness that lurks, lies there within Eve's feminine womb, walking poisoned steps on the legs of a beautiful landscape. We cannot, however common it is in practice. Conception raised, and broke the flooding tension of her landing gush! Why as we breathe she breathes, as I tremble she shivers, and with this intention her presence is known. She has arrived on our timely occasion. It is the wonderful plight of harsh, small language.

Spiritual instruction teaches us to keep our focus on ourselves, not in an egocentric way, but as a way of consciously managing our energy and power. Do not waste time by thinking, acting, or praying because the point is to actually make the commitment and dedication that healing requires. Heaven is not a complicated realm, and seek to believe only what Heaven has issued as essential. All circumstances can be changed in a moment. All illness can be healed. In all likelihood we have made our lives more difficult than they have to be. Achieving health, happiness, and an energy balance comes down to deciding to focus more on a positive than a negative, and to live in a manner spiritually congruent with what we know is the truth. Live what you believe because change is constant. Happiness is an internal, personal attitude and responsibility because life is essentially a learning experience. Every situation, challenge, and relationship contains some message worth learning or teaching. Positive energy works more effectively than negative energy in each and every case. We live in the present moment to practice forgiveness of others. Heaven thinks in simple and eternal truths.

A spiritual glitch in the assumption that bases human perception.

The ambulance is now going backwards, and chickens dance in a cryptic balloon. Thought darkness. Murder, ransom, and half a banner reading evil is at the core. A fashionable contest, but separate spikes please. The drugs Jim, give him the drugs!

"Irony doctor?"

We are the masters of justice in our tomb, and are as slow as the animals we represent. Take note, we have entered this booth termed forever. How is it here? Tangles of vocal adoptions titillating traces of vagrant scenery. Quickly return and give thought to what was first presented, information as with life, death, and rebirth. Existence after bloating and crates covered with dirt. The time before and after the entrance here, and the exit there. The whole is the hard way down, but now here, we control escape, and will do best to follow instruction. Sure of minutes in the mental frame of death's adversity, mind germs, darkness and light filled with stains.

"Govern Crocksinford Bernard, for jeopardy has soaked the earth, and a head has claimed the guilt."

Blinding the wicked is the easy part, but making them take notice is more complex.

"Lips cracked and parched from dust. Sentences have lost objective because the working model is dysfunctional. The living become the dead, and the dead the living. Change and reversal. Here entering there, and returning back. Do you really follow camels to a eucalyptus tree?"

Somewhere in the desert dying of thirst. Are fear's henchmen calling for blood?

Her body was small, fearful, and with each breathing instant came closer to the rending glint of oblivion. It was something she instantly noticed in this palace of vague impressions unlocked with thoughtful intent. There is no regret or doubt, but matter of fact and state of mind fade to walk passed darkness, skip the underside, and catch a bus onto better things. Shards of sensory sediment settle smoothly. Perception dilutes positioning, but there is point and rational text, although we request obligatory evidence crucially. Moot point.

Whose reception is with standing? You, come to understanding, and frolic in this abundant sarcasm. A simple lesson. Reality is yours, it is simple human nature to perceive, react, and adapt. Perception and bias are yours, and can be played with, manipulated, and mangled. Testify to this opposition of thought because reform burns hard and crisp with stirring belief. Discover reality, manage it, and destroy it for its conformity with caution or ignorance. This place blocks reality, and now build it from interpretation. Eureka!

The forces here, which murder there, are almost there! They are the test of blended thoughts, and holdings for a mortician's phrasing. Upon a closer look, up close, get up real close, these fates are seen tripping through whimsy as noisome, signs of life. Human beings. By head and by beast, the milieu is swallowed by rampage, news at five thirty. Solipsism crossed sense, the stream of rational became irrational. Battles were fought, death was taught, and destiny was locked with marked punishment on the universe sucking in reverse. Infinity to the minuscule compact with time and space.

The world has become a box of the smallest size, and is held in the hand of a God. Slaves and victims are we to resonate the unlocked secrets of convicted sin and dreadful wisdom. Dreams and nightmares wavering and compiling this sweeping holocaust. The story told, and this performance rest easy to forget what persuades it. Nothing has happened, and nothing can be done. Nothing will discourage outcome so pain flows, and anger emits in every direction, allowing change to sweep over beckoning tragedy.

Prepare yourself for a bumpy ride is sure to follow. Relax, and enjoy the feature presentation. This irreversible horror that brought us here, good and evil.

Both are always present, ever there, and existing in the darkness claimed by the spirits of the dead the living bend to fulfill need. Captured in angst until used and discarded, then one reaches the final destination. Hell does coincide with evil, and the good are free in the power of being. Both catch the beyond without limit, and fly above a heaven unsought, but Hell reflects our judgment. A trial surpasses the territory of supernatural engineering. Designed and distributed with the intent purpose for good or evil, and the amusement of higher beings in a game played by Gods.

We are pawns in the caustic fiber of reality, mortality, and philosophy. The hypothesis is a modern conception proved by personal theory. Life evicts possibility, and to die with no more sense than when you began is stupidity. Beneath the trauma, life explodes below the static of rise and decline, and imprints space with its tail. Faces glow with their voices rambling reason and logic. Perpetually stuck with no choice forever, we are fused with the depths of our impulse.

Once chosen for duty and accredited with one's higher purpose, we are played in the world by balanced forces. Evil swings at good, and good swings back at evil, which causes evil to swing back harder. Fabricated space to claim your place in the systemized Heaven of Hell, to flourish immensely or corrode painfully, beyond delusional fate is the basis for negotiation.

Apathy applies no action. Silent, we are always yearning with no intelligent level of plentiful opportunity or the morality of existence. A world where nothing happens except delusions of grandeur. Born free to shit, eat, and fuck the best of high standards. The contemplation of paths never taken, and desires never fulfilled holding back purity for all eternity. Many facets of atrocity appear a golden yellow shade in an individual's head, and to put into words the horror passing, searches the tub of scattered customs in this ordered cruelty. Now into quiet November, the entrance of this village strikes the hour of our calling with a killing banquet.

"You seek a head, a beast containing many names. He, it shall prevail to cleanse the population. He and it will seek the willing. He and it will deliver the estranged. He and it will persecute the deviant with the death of mankind eating the souls of our persistence." Jim.

Spit the stew pieces back into the pot to brew infinity. Annihilation continuing forever. Prophecy has now been written, and replaces the death of what we know as truth. The prophecy continues.

The strange usually rings truth because life mesmerizes and permits delusion. Naïve creatures of yesterday's memories, and the tales of the dead condemning fabrication of days drowned in the crippled, the deceased, and the damned. Moments are dead, and they are played for yesterday's living. Broken, but unending, over and over. Caught like the groove of this verbal record. Subliminal messages dilute the forgotten control. The frail mental induction fragments any previous existence. Immobile corruption takes place easily with soul control, and leads to spasms and twitches. Blood stains coagulate with the sleeve, within the pores of flesh as the pin pricks toward the pin. A cut, rip, piecing push that ends with blissful tears. Substance enters, exits, and re-enters. Ripples course and shake against the flesh with waves of moving shapes. Pictures blur within black and white borders, and smell disdains the truth. Everything is uncensored. Breathing falls heavy, and perspiration leaks into vision and guilt. The gods look down with omnipotent glee as the propositions wander passed discreet omission. The bastard son whistles and walks with a stick in his hand. The ferns even wilt in his gaze as he looks for the suspicion of youth, and the bugs that scatter from his mighty path. Life is the quintessential paradox, subtlety and the occupation of self.

"IN ORDER TO ILLICIT SENSE OR PURPOSE FROM THE ENTROPHY ONE ENLISTS, ONE SHOULD NEGOTIATE HIGHER MODES OF BEING BASED ON ESSENTIAL NEED. ONE SHOULD PRACTICE PROPER CONDUCT THAT ENTAILS ERADICATION OF SUPERFLUOUS WANT, PERSISTENT NOTHING, AND THE EMPATHY OF ACTION THAT CONSTRUCTS THE BEING ITSELF. ONE SHOULD CONVICT DIRECTION AS A PATHWAY UNTO GOD, AND THUS ENLIGHTENMENT, ACHIEVEMENT, LOVE, AND CONTENTMENT SUCCEED AND SURMOUNT DAILY LIVING.

ONE CAN ABSOLVE ONE'S WANT AND DISTRACT ONE'S NEED TO WHAT IS READILY AVAILABLE, AND TO NOT DO SO RETRACTS FUTURE STEPS FROM THE BOUNTY

OF ENRICHMENT. BLESSINGS ARE ENDLESS, ALTHOUGH UNRECOGNIZABLE, AND ARE DISSOLVED UNDER THE CITATION OF SELF, SURROUNDINGS, AND PURPOSE. ALL OF WHICH IN THEMSELVES ARE BLESSINGS.

WE AS HUMAN BEINGS TRAIN A CULTURE AND CIVILIZATION THAT IS DERELICT BECAUSE IT PROPAGATES THE ILLUSION OF A LACK OF CHOICE. THIS IS NOT THE CASE. FUNDAMENTALLY WE ARE TRAPPED IN OUR BOX, LOOK OUT FOR COMPASSION, AND LOSE SIGHT OF REAL EXPECTATIONS THAT ARE NOT CONTAINED WITHIN OUR PERSONAL ABYSS. THIS RESEMBLES A FREE WORLD OF LOGIC AND TRUTH, BUT IS A SNARE THAT STEALS IDEALS, INTENT, AND INTEREST BASED ON POSITIVE HARMONICS. CHOOSING THIS WHEN GRANTED A HIGHER CONNOTATION OF PURPOSE MEANS WE ARE LOST. WE ARE WAITING FOR SOMETHING TO HAPPEN WHEN SOMETHING IS HAPPENING. LIFE.

THE UPKEEP AND PERSUASION OF FALSEHOOD IS ISSUED AND REALIZED AS TRUTH, BUT THE PERPETUAL NOTION THAT EXISTENCE IS WHAT WE MAKE IT IS MISGUIDED. WE HAVE ALLOCATED REMOVAL TO RESPONSIBILITY, AND HAVE ASSIGNED TASKS AND THOUGHTS TO FURTHER INSTRUCT OUR WORLD WITH FATALISTIC CALAMITY. POVERTY, MISUSED INFORMATION, AND MALNOURISHED CHOICE ARE A BREEDING GROUND FOR CONTINUANCE. BY LIVING WE CREATE THE LIVING ORDEAL, MAKE EXAMPLES AND EXPECTATIONS OF THE RIGHT AND WRONG, AND HOPE TO REMOVE THE SLANTED VIEW OF OUR PACIFIED PROCRASTINATION AND PESSIMISM.

WE DECIDE THE OUTCOME, CONTROL THE IDEAL, AND PATERNAL LIFE IS BUT A CONSTANT STRUGGLE WITH WHAT THERE IS WITHIN US. OUR LIVES EVOKE A PROMISE. OUR BEING CONTAINS THE CHOICE. ALL WE NEED TO SEE AND DO IS KNOWN AMIDST US ALL. IT IS NO SECRET, AND THERE IS NO TRADING NUANCE THAT OPPOSES INHERENT REASON. WE CREATE THE POWER,

ENLIST THE SENSE AND STRUCTURE, AND GOD AGGREES WITH WHAT IS TRUE AND NOT WITH WHAT WE THINK."

Swinging pictures are necessary. Arizona patterned with an orange coat of fur. The Navajo's print deters victims from the mercy of the white man. Calypso starving on a navy boat with boisterous and belligerent disruption. Black dye. False impromptu. Slavery a savory agony, smacks lips on a coconut's bosom. A tease of tempting flesh, deliberates conscious aptitude to the reality of any objection to point. Being without form feeds devils and gods with a lapse of ego. To those regular listeners we have illness and boredom. Called to order every suspected sin, and built decapitated life to create the world. We are its inhabitants. Suicide is reform, but you probably would not be able to read it.

Anyway, banality is questioned when only self, without ego, introduces positive being to the moment of reality. What responds to assault and interacts with physical deterrents are not worth words, but also require mention with the query of reality.

Weenie loved his dog. He would pet it every day after school, and the dog would drool as he sat on the stool to sit in his quieting pool. Horrendous, linear vocabulary runs a spread of thick sauce across the bagels and cream cheese.

We sit under a bridge with a shivering coat pulled tight to warm the neck. We pull it tighter as the cold bites harder. Murky with the sky very grey, and the dancing water as thick as rain presents the density with circles. The influence of self dictates and dilutes reality. Centering oblivion to prescribe therapy, we live through these words. Audience merely transgresses the attention to solitary impulse. Intended critique is everywhere, and with one man's attention, opposition or agreement would be presented. If interest is bestowed in writing, then response to those words would be construed and ingrained into habit by way of assumption.

Table hopping with arrogant noise. Christ is shaking a Formica table with a typewriter. Vociferation trembles with the possibility of collapse, but hearts and bodies climb on the choice of today. This choice enriches the sanctity of living, and disillusion farts trivial today. That is valid. Validity having legal efficacy or force. Value is fair return or equivalent in goods, services, or money for something exchanged. The stance is an intellectual or emotional attitude is valid except bread. Tepid, dear departure, defunct or languid origin remarks.

Tobacco gets caught in your teeth, but remember and understand patience and wisdom. Language is beyond a virus, and language envelopes society's joie de vivre. Everything! The self of curiosity. Liberty, choice, want, and need. Loss and gain, and developed pain. Words are freedom, and although revealing action afield, the craft, standard, and study of this anomaly of idiocy lounges in the memory. The classic, surfing waves of hope and gravity are low on the rocks eating death live.

When in America words mean what they say, and vote various parades of static logic as the angles of prospect. Throw woman overboard, and men undertow. Thinking, feeling being is certain of things that lines do not weigh or measure. So why give up the meticulous, Sunday best for dirty thrills? No more windows on Mars. Unions of mice. Fish tanks and dance floors. Acres of snow, a trio of three, and the incarceration of nostalgia. Poetry for the perverted, but perverts never hold a grudge, and do not even bulge when all is but a simple nudge. Prescriptions for the underdog are frisky because losing is simple minded. Humility, health, and harbor. Forward.

Talk only of the interactions we actually experience, and perceive reality or existential realities to involve the self. They are however relative only to the observer. Fluctuating and evolving, capable of being magnified and amplified, and moving from low resolution to hi fi.

"They do not fit together," says temptation.

We have squabbled deceit, failure, and complete obliteration. We have persecuted truth, ridiculed endurance, and revolutionized thought. We linger now only to a quotation. Tender moments of cascading motion. We are free! God bless, we are free!

The theme of Alberta is lost in a ball of confusion. Born in the seventies, raised in the eighties, and now living in the zeros. Life surrounds the gods of youth, and new wave gizmos smudged with feminine masculinity moved from the supportive web. The bizarre and freakish wave of mutilation in a triangle of love and confusion. A world where belt buckles and cowboy hats pace surreal images of stampeding rodeos instead of earrings in both ears. Cows and studs. Recognition is gone, and no one understands these messages or songs any longer. Contrast is bearing its toll. Place is stuck with the compromise it once was, and down go the memories of time almost done. Stares and slogans, offensive labels, and all is said in a thank you.

Nov 18 1996

I saw her for the first time naked. Enshrouded fully in fanciful flesh, and uncovered tapestries of skin. I saw her for the second time embodied with the same fluent ambiguity. As with the third, fourth, and tenth consecutive time, she remained naked. Full. When we met for the first time, cloth choked around her reclusive, but un-shy morsels of muscle and skin. She was wrapped with clothing, fully clothed, and all I could seem to derive was a question to her choice of apparel.

There is a bus stop, and presently there is a bus stopped. It pulls away, and we have eight people standing from left to right. Two, bingo playing, stretch pants and sweatshirt wearing women, both are Native American. A singly guy wearing a baseball cap, a jean jacket, green shorts, and his white legs. Then stand five various Asians, probably all Chinese. They huddle under the enclosed waiting area, some have bags, and some do not. Another bus comes, and moves on.

Left to right again. Two Chinese grandparents, and their daughter's daughter. He carries two, small plastic bags. White with no writing. Then stands an Asian woman wearing a bright purple coat. Make that two women wearing different coats, but colored the same lush purple. Then we have our native, bingo players standing behind them all smoking. We have a single, Asian man wearing jeans and a light, blue coat. A woman stops and begins to talk to him, and a new bus comes to halt the view.

Left to right. A solitary woman, Asian, and looking very stern. She stands with her arms crossed, and a grimace rears her face. She looks very happy. A man in jeans stands behind the pole, and he is somewhat fat, white, and has a shoulder bag. He looks anxious, but relaxed with his hands in his pockets. A small Asian woman wearing sunglasses, and a large hairstyle walks up and crosses behind him. She stands there holding white bags with red emblems etched into the sides. She looks awkward and funny. Another bus arrives and displaces the assortment, and so it goes, over and over.

From day break to dusk is a run around gag of unknown derivation. Some come and some go, some move and some stay, but all uphold themselves equally. They possess reason and logic, and hold the view with vibrant interest, and intense intrusion on personal space. After all we all have some place to go, and are coming from somewhere completely different. So it goes.

"There is no life, there is no irony, and here does lie my youth, may it rot in peace lest this remembrance comes too quickly." Abelard.

There was a weird buzz emitted from the water cooler. An icy chill presence that makes hair stand on end, and nerves jumble forward. Samson knew what it was, and he continued down toward the large bottle of water and its holder. He positioned himself well, sticking to the walls as if they were totally solid, and protected himself through the use of a mop that he clenched in his hand. Forward he went to meet his fate, and suspicion spurred insanity.

It came up from behind him, and tapped him on the shoulder. The mop landed against the floor with the sound of clanking wood, and was followed by the slight rustle of figures shifting, which was killed by the thud of Samson's weight smacking the floor. He found balance, and turned to see his assailant, and there stood a spectacular sight that evoked such fear and upheaval that all was lost indefinitely. Samson fell once more under the burdensome weight, and hit the waxed floor with inconceivable ease, BANG! He lied sedentary on the drying wax as the smell stung his discarded nostrils. He was dead.

The coroner said, "It was a heart attack, cut and dried."

Technically that is truth, but as far as the cause, only one knows the truth, and he lies out of proportion in a large, plastic bag. Past fear, death, and even sanity traveled Samson, the only man to know, and the only man to die.

They said, "Man's demise."

She told back this false support.

"Things are constructed by our nervous systems, and realities are better described as systems of bundles of energy functions. Reality flows, and meanders like a serpent. The notion that reality is singular or one block-like entity is pervasive. Deriving from the evolutionary fact that our nervous systems normally organise the dance of energy into block-like things. Think clearly. You have to think clearly."

"I hate it when you are all fogged up, and going nowhere. I hate you and your mother, her husband, and their pet."

"So you are saying we are done?"

"Flip us over we are done."

"You are an uncle!"

A slap across the face.

Thirty three decades later. The gap symbolizes it has been a long time spent before reaching the sight. We closed in, and expected what was to be or was. Nonetheless, the ideal behind the persistence is important. We went with dedication to complete the vital task. Us two, let us say the hump and the funny hat. Two of the same, twins. The hump and the funny hat came unto the graveyard, and a sight that was expected long ago. They moved in knowing what was to be done. The funny hat carried the hoe head up, and went up to Poe. They had to see for sure.

They rode up to his grave, broke through the wooden doors, and there they found him. Fear is what came next, complete and utter fear. Bone shaking, nerve breaking, mind splintering headache fear.

"We tried to get away, but the hump died in the fire caused by the adjoining drop of his lantern. And I the funny hat ran, skirted through the thirty three years of mud, back to the gravel, and straight on to the cobbled streets of home."

This begins with bad ink, but it will get better with time. That is the way of the rolling pen. Lines of sleepy stupor defined. This is the centre of the world, and this is where we sit, scribe, and condense the living data into phrases of ritual. This is life, the inevitable death, and the sty of snaring observation. Sense, scripture, and ideals of ability.

A day like any other day has progressed to its center margin, and now cradles tumultuous clouds of faint blue obstacles. Motion enables placement, direction, and stature. Keep afloat by vivid motion because cement blocks stand free to hold the body out of bounty. These blocks of granite fountain beauty, and keep persona baffled with clear oblivion. A picturesque spectacle of expulsion creates a mangled oasis for this tour of duty. A portrait of a sturdy block upholds ourselves for memory. A curious attempt at remembering this vacant spell of collected time and self. Spellbound upon liquid structure that one thinks of as water.

"So you are saying we are done?"

"Flip us over we are done."

"You are a bastard's uncle!" A slap across the face.

"Bastard's uncle!" Another slap across the face. Smack two. Women are finicky.

This length of road before us. The cobbles click beneath our heels, and heads bubble lowly upon necks. We are scum, and we are filthy.

Gravel. The loosened gravel slowly becomes mud, and the mud becomes continuous. In our arms combined we carry a fire lighted lantern with glass causing illumination, and a very long stick, also a shovel and a hoe. We throttle down the muddy street almost dancing, and we are getting closer, almost hearing it. The taller of us two wears a funny hat, and carries the stick and the hoe. I as the hump carry the lantern and the shovel. Perhaps we are brothers? It looks as if we are talking, however what we say is not heard.

This man they call Poe?

"Passion and obsession took my path aimlessly until I reached here. I landed in the opaque abyss because my placement was previously adjusted based on murder. I killed three people during the tune of my strand of reality, and this pushed me here without retreat. Am I stuck in innate vision as sounds race over eternity? Have I recaptured happiness and joy, or have I relived deliberate, elaborate affliction? My body is gone, and I flow in and out of consciousness as nothing more than energy. Gas, wind, or air. I have no visible dimension except mist unraveling sanity. I am what dreams are made from, and my enthralled behavior with a famous, dead, well written man has always been. My name is Abelard Bardo Poe, and I am dead within the trials of life, and here we shall meet for the final time. My name is Abelard Poe, and here is where forgiveness finds punishment as granted reverie. Here the dead return and the living die, and I shall wait for you. My arms will be open because you shall lead yourself here in a stumble of timing.

Obsession relies on this place, but waits for return. My mother died giving birth, and being the alcoholic she was, threw my father away briskly before, and this caused my adoption into the Poe family. They raised me, and that was more than I could have hoped for, but with my troubled past our parting was foreseen. I flew the coop before my twelfth birthday, and rode the rails as they called it then. Holding childhood I was coerced into a white trash smelting pot of sex, booze, and ether. I think I was in Idaho, although maybe it was Utah. The story goes that I was taken under the tutelage of one, Baxter Murphy, middle name Bardo. He taught me numerous things about various things, and as his pupil I was glad to receive what he was giving, although in retrospect all that was truly learned from this man was the art.

He was balding, middle aged, and his laugh jutted outward as most ringmasters' do. He stood well above me, although by the time of his death, our eyes were of equal status. He was silent, and an over bearing man with a feel for the drink, most of the time too much, but he also held the art of taxidermy as a high regard hobby. My respect for him still soars, but without his influence my present state could have been avoided. We were together for a mere twenty years, but our overall clout rings in the world even today. Thank you Baxter, if for nothing else the middle name.

He was the first man I truly respected, loved, and aspired to become, shamefully many have filled his footsteps as my love affairs have since been many. My friendships have been minimal, and my admirations have been even less, but among them all one thing has always sufficed, men. They were all men, every one of them. Perhaps females never interested me, or perhaps my homosexual tendencies were too convincing to ignore, nonetheless my companions were men, all of course except one."

Now that sounds stereotypical.

"Fatherhood. She too like me was lost in a world based on loss, solitude, and degradation. Our meeting, and placement within each other's lives was almost an opportunity, however, my meddling caused catastrophe. The way of my childhood ran from me and moved into her. I made the trauma of my youth hers, and I still ask for forgiveness to free my spirit.

Let my bearing enter the Kingdom of Heaven, and sanctify my fouling in order to strip this sinful past. Erase this need, allow this growth, and take me into your arms. Caress my soul with undying forgiveness for my duty is served, and my penance here is done. Now, amongst everything, I wish to return. Go back through life, and correct these wrongs of modern love. Free me from your love, and this obsession"

Eternity with floundering memories of inscription drowning in strokes of anguish.

"Tragedy was my life in this violated reminder of yesterday. Things taught, now learned, again, and fights when fought now fighting take life. Gargantuan fragments of hellish recall in recreated sense. Always, evermore, and aye forever."

Whether by incessant damnation or heavenly creation the pain turns to swooning sentimentality, and suffering becomes living love. Cringing control breeds freedom absolute, and travels with the darkness as a temporary energy, and electrical waves control mental psyche and physical device. We are energy, electrical waves of kinetic energy built upon distorted memories to create reality. Are these shadows encoding our cell? No physical description has transpired before, and no pre-thought direction toward the attributes of vision. We do not exist, and yet imagination holds the parlor open.

"Ready or not here I come!"

Dreamscapes treacherous and true. Refreshing horror screaming the plea of insanity. The weightless, ambiguous being caught within fixtures is trapped in this crystal web of structural achievement. The reader engulfs the catacombs of boredom. Anguish deceives anguish, and you are caught within it. You are with us as misconception. Down here with jurisdiction on the pastime of the human generation, both living and dead. Entering without payment, and existing with nauseous scorn, spiraling deceit, and vengeful repetition. Repulsive salvation starves below destruction upon these brief pages of glued together past, and tomorrow's vindication does combat with yesterday's reflection.

Body, spirit, and mind shape outcome out of a revolutionary breach in evolutionary disturbance. Throw backs, regenerated swine, and hellions pure with marveled insight for the world's decay toward the infinite! Chaos breeding chaos, darkness spewing darkness, and confusion inspiring confusion. Freedom from the dominion of human thought recoils in the center of the maze to corner safety. Screw morality for mortality. The forgotten memorabilia of postcards from the edge of humanity. News at eleven.

"Heinous, unending contemplation toward fate, stars, and the journey to my end. Forbidden dwelling in psychotic examination. Bewildered, delving overwhelmed, and swooping down like a rapturous bird my thoughts have crossed revenge, and revenge has hatched reaction. The slaying of a kindred brother, a beloved lost friend, and a fallen hero for whom worship is no longer convincing. My love, and my obsession, have I fallen? Contempt ridden mentality." ABPoe

"I'm back in baby's arms..."

Reaction regurgitates this wheezing darkness with a leave of sanity. Persecution is growing, and feels the blood thoughts winding. Simple, singular thoughts winding up in reach of him. Simple static grips reality's final straw tight and strong. Slowly down a slope of soon to play antagonistic conversion, we are fulfilled in an available, bursting retort.

"Prepare me! Abed me! Recreate ability with full strength. No backing down, and no reproach, but constant action to visualized death."

Fall upon his face, this wretched display distorted, and contort this weapons end. Aimed with affection, we leap, and hope that we have the power, BANG!

Death. The end.

This state rises at an alley of the subconscious without which nothing would exist. Where that is, my senses tell me, I do not know. We are in rows, paralyzed, and the others look less awake. They look cramped, dead, and deflated. He watches minds tensing, and laying with them he attaches wires to cause this immobilization. Belch and feel sick as he comes close. Lie there dry heaving, and vomiting as a head bobbing fluently. He stands beside us laughing, and is ugly looking reptilian. We have not moved, we have no movement, and we have no mind amongst us. SPLAT!

This was first intended as the book, however, due to change it is coming to you via the use of this medium. I prey film does not ruin the message, the imagery, and the undying statement. Who knows except for you the viewer? Your opinion counts, your outlook, and your response. Open up and consume, taking what you take. Some will be repulsed, some shocked, and some entertained, but all I hope will be altered. Years have gone into writing this, and I once again pray it is not simply a waste of achievement. Understand and move on. Consume what you want or may need, and remember change in query is necessary. Again, open up and consume, and take what you take.

Thought darkness. The land beyond the looking glass sinks in death's terrain. See churning stomachs dissolve our fiber, and any desire for change has been chewed from assimilation. We are dead, we are eaten with a final gulp, and there is no more coming back, but here is where the symphony comes in passionately, but they stop, why?

Why? Why choose to take this pilgrimage? Why inveigle yourself with subjugation?

The devious keep roving temptation and the devil will gobble down their souls with laden and resonant sleep. He molds us, and makes us waste away into non-being. It will all come back as effulgent as numbers, and as memorable as streets, but nothing will give you warning.

"I am a man. Six foot three and three quarters. No hair, but a faint growth of beard takes its time, and over a month grows to about an inch and a half. Brown eyes, and no distinguishing marks, but flashbacks come to pass every morning after breakfast. Wit is my primary drive, cynicism packaged in upright idiosyncrasy intrigued by the bizarre and the benign. The generic terms of daily experience are riveting! People say I am eccentric, but no one testifies that I am truly crazy. Never underestimate the power of denial, the haste of self-indulgence, and the basic drive for amusement. In society's terms I am a degenerate and a deviant, and one hot topic. Anonymous dark encounters infatuate me. I love conversation, but people are restrictive. I am not bragging, but stating simple truths as arrogance does not behold me because my experience is largely compressed.

I think of myself as a writer. Is it Armageddon? Various forms of it journey through the inner turmoil of the human spirit. Good, evil, and the finale stages of mankind. I have seen evil hold fear somewhere collected. Hell is human nature. I hold no education, but personal experience. I would die, but I do not want to die. I have always fancied love, but cannot pass the application. I have generally avoided politics, although I do like to know what is going on. I have concern for myself, instability progresses into instability. I have a concern for my mother, will she ever know me? I feel regret for the patterns I have attained, and the indulgences I have followed. I have seen stupidity rabble in our streets, and I have grown up with the bomb that is us. I am not the only man to propel this am I? I see it on every corner and street, from one coast to the next the world is blooming, but the world is dead."

This is an optical illusion scourging these words on paper for kaleidoscopic dimension, but perhaps even more. Lights coruscate, a drink has been poured, it is not the first, but let it not be the last. Lights, noise, and sensation!

"Old men mingle with the young that squeeze the old, and I write."

"The time we prepare in the underside of humanity is a permanent pause. Chosen as the watchers of the world, we have curled as the waiters of apocalypse. We may never be needed, but we will be here for your convenience." Shelly Crocksinford

The titanic as well. Remember man's shoes instead of his wants. Want is syrup, shit in comparison to footwear. On day one if sandals were worn then callouses did cease. Protection is a simple, acquired taste. How these floating trials upon your feet feel if not protected by the simplest of runners. Nothing feels worse than a filling in the mouth except a juicy blister taxing your ankle. Walking over, and round, and through constant pain.

To a bed in the lower east. The john was Carl, but the killer disguised the closet with jealousy. He skulked while they slipped on satin sheets, moaning as he watched, engrossed by the sight before him. Of course at the time, they knew nothing of this, but he watched with envy and spite.

"Love moved on, and now I crumple and discard it. Fabulous creatures. A head bobbing until finally all that is left is a dripping organ and a jolly romp. They continue as I wait, and the gun was already aimed in their direction. I was ready were they?"

Happiness a jubilee since last we met, but nothing has changed except for the discretion of plot. Over exaggerations of sex as repetitive storytelling. One day becomes the next, and soon this year is over. It is our birthday in two months, and the dog gets fixed next week. The routine goes on without us, and change will follow in the steps of our forefathers. Everything is the same, and you have not missed a thing. This room appears green in the screams of infinite reaction to affliction. Resources persisting diluted honor in a peculiar word formation. The discovery of an axiom of home burnt down, and fields turned sour as a mandatory repercussion. Memory is a constant buzzing, buzzing constantly. Unabated buzzing of passed events, and matters relevant to the recent emotional response. A quotation?

"You win some, and you lose some. Some get rained out, but you suit up for them all."

Top of the page, and writing seems appropriate. Formality bewilders sensation, but physical imprints feel workable, and the dying machine scenario is a bit thick. Three machines, one thrown out the attic window in a whimsical want of angry frustration. The other two are aliens of restraint, and so the written word propels us here. Almost twenty days have passed, and now with another machine I seem to be working well. Love is sacred, boundless entity, thriving comfort, subtle bliss, and astonishing happiness. It is a gift from God, ourselves, or the world with endless servitude. I give thee love, and the sacrifice of all our fathers.

God, almighty father, and container of love and propriety of strength, allow salvation. The positive belief and inaction of all blessed activity. God has faith in everything. Bad habits encourage bad habits. A good person is encouraged, but a life's work. Need is ideally, God the father, but the world evokes survival, and society dissuades with money, wrong choices, and the physical ideal. Bad habits still encourage bad habits.

Focus. Meditation is a hard, mandatory outlet. To peel away the ideals and transgressions of self to associate with the ideals and transgressions of the world is a large ordeal. However, the spirit, God, and the world provide nurturing nature in which to relate. Sinful activity forms retraction, extraction, and distraction as the way of the world. The world, the self, and the spirit are wrapped in sinful nature. Still lost asunder. The preservation of faith and hope are definitive dreams of God. Actions warrant forgiveness so religious interpretation would say, and destined to deliverance is the stupidity and ignorance to favor failure. Change the broken record! Restraint of self's design is managed by the margin. Comfort. Change is apparent, and tenderness is gratitude. Onto things, and this yard to which we have been mounted. These moments are paused and extending. An endless enclosure of blathering equals is the world's summit of direction. A cranky, simple car on big tires that screeches.

"Fuck the world before it fucks you!"

Tortured realms to hallucinate happiness in suffering.

"This is not a dream!"

Depths of dissected pleasure, and pain, and concentration on self-destruction shall be born to follow. Have you ever wondered what death feels like? Why not find out, self-suicide is the way to go! A trap has taken hold, claws and whacks, tears and cuts. One takes after another, one delivered pitch equalling the next, there to here, and back again. Wrapped within the grasp of this pitfall's gnawing, grinding hold. It is tightening its flex of dental edifice while we lie down yelping.

Days are crimson halls, and their tables rattle and rasp enough words to be a frail witness to everything. Especially I. Protection is made from the dying swirls of drunken moans with one's own tone. The old, used smells of you and I, and even the calm, long talk of her and him. The waiter is serving behind the fairground gates, and coming to appease you and me, he creeps so no in or out could open to see our moon. Pounds of blackened bliss crackle here as we do. You are the wood, and I am the fire.

Matter lives ever trying, and walks about dim springs with him when moments sigh. Air returns when not from there, and belief for doubt would live our time to his. Then twelve evils for the just, carried by the bus, hunt and track heckles of hellish us! Go around, each and every one of you, and find the caves are empty.

Can a death just die? Shut in the howl, and trial the stories that we may call as he. A judgment of the invalid instinct and absurd demolition of the argument. Value is estimated, but futile, dogmatic deduction eludes and dissipates price. A moral verdict of one sided bigotry. Preconception warped on public opinion and popular belief. The general assessment of a skeptical descent into scrupulous puzzles of general hesitation. Consumption leads to a massive overflow of exhaust. Tantrums store copious forms of liberty, a collage of fertility rich through mediocrity, and moderation results in showers of relented sustenance. An empty abundance starving is full again with the flush of spring. A grudge renders the holster of emptiness to slip into something more accustomed to volition's machinery. Into capable, precious super excellence.

Adapt to and agree with, and consort, tally, accord to conformity. There is a capacity to produce good, and there is the same for producing evil, depravity, malignant injury, and virulent bane. This village is despicable, ruthless, and scathing harm. A molestation of brilliance as primal perfection causes scurvy and pestilence ranked and over run. Two hundred and forty six million taste buds, but relentless difference binds us together, forever and ever, amen.

"Who is burning that sulfur?"

Unforgettable. Belgium. The giant head given from unseen filth, me. Strange, more so. From the mouth of new into a time to see, the creatures bare, white, and large there quietly waiting. I do not talk quickly for this answer breaks the room we have remorse about. A flaring bet, powerful, bloodless. The call is less when all the eyes meet, and follow this conclusion, including Macdonald, you.

This red anguish suddenly opened the pit. Remember we are taking a strange, but difficult secret. The unknown twenty disguises, it, the monster, me. Any of one. A waiting spider, and a sea monster of great proportions. It has begun.

"If this Bardo Poe prayed every installment would this door echo in?"

His parts reside here with it, me, this creature, and this monster biting questioning decay. Evil has recognized evil, and this deceased father has paved this deposit. He has been nailed to a cross as a treat of drastic change. He is limp, and dripping blood. From drenched insides falls sharpness, light and terrifying, and now he is left as great and sinister. The head, the dragon, and the father of ill-tempered thought. An interesting dedication of mind and change that swats layer after layer, city after city, and house after house. These so-called animals guarding accurate reality.

"THE DEAD, HORROR."

We depart with longing. Fierce creatures still waiting in the corner, laughing and laughing. Forget who looked about, and realize the sight. This viscous contempt struggles and dies amongst us dressed in gray bones, and caverns our way here. There that is here.

"Die creatures die!"

Twas the night before Christmas as told by ABPoe

Twas the night before Christmas, when all through the mouse, not a creature was stirring, not even a louse. The mocking all strung by the whimsy with flare, in ropes that faint piccolos swoon could not bear! The build thin fear wrestled all fate in their heads while visions of burger buns pranced in their beds. And Tom in her purchase and I in my nap, had dust pedaled town for a long hitter's rap. Then stout on the pawn there appeased much a stutter, I bring rum my head to be what was the butter! Away to the window I grew like a clash, lore hoping the ladders land few up the lash! The noon won the test of the dew sullen foe, wave the cluster of today to subject hello! Then what to my sauntering lies would appear, but a miniature day and late shiny John Deere. With a riddle of liver low timely and thick, I flew in a moment tit bust see saint dick! Soar rapid ten beagles whiz force say lame, as we sizzled and doubted and mauled them by name: now bash her, now cancer, now chance her, now wicks in, on vomit, on stupid, on fodder and blitz in. To the top of the torch to the hop of the call, now cash away, bash away, flash away all! As dry heaves we wore the mild fury lane high, then lay meet with an obstacle count to the pie. Low, cup flew the stove top the courses say chew, with a gay pull of boys and faint piccolos too! And when sin is sprinkling, I stirred on the hoof, the dancing and cawing of each little pouf. As I spew in my bed and was burning a bound, down the whimsy faint piccolos fame with a hound. He was stressed call in sir sum his dead to his soot, and his loathes lure tall varnish said with lashes of loot! A sun dial of ploys we had sung on his slack, and we looked like a peddler rust opening his track! His lies wow they wrinkled, his pimples vow sherry, and his leaks were like hoses, his pose like a fairy. His scrawl diddle south was drawn up like a cow, and the herd of his win was a sight like a sow. The lump of his type we weld right in his sheath, and the poke lit encircled his bed like our teeth. He had a cod piece and a sound little deli that took when we waft like a mole full of tele! He was hubby and rump, a right pulley told self, I daft when I saw him in light of thyself! A blink of this eye and a list of his dead, tune wave me to grow I said nothing to wed! He woke taught a word but lent weight to this Turk and willed all the locking, then burned with a lurk! An' fraying a linger along tide his doze, an' living a God, up the rim see he blows! He rang to this day, to this seam save a thistle, an' gave way they maul too like the frown of a chisel. What I cured whim explain as we drove out of light, "Sappy Christmas to call, and call a goodnight."

    The serpent waits upon wood. Mathematics watch the living film, and the point is feces falling to the ground like a covering quilt. The school of numerous sitting tales spins even sleep as it waits. The sinking throats of winded life learn to catch the flying refuge. If defeat is now, and slowly grows up the pipes, then the wrathful could of our father's know how is upon this sudden urge of judgment and rage. Paroled twice, our closure filed the wood and all its theory in the mind no city shows. A radio is good when music means everything, but aspects in mysterious endeavors are the same.
    We are left where the wood floors husk us, and there is a cab we can catch to ride the shipments even. We are persistent to run down the unsure feat of knowledge that this knocking fate makes harsh, but now shoes submerge in the downfall of runny traction. It said it was tranquil, and that great things were never better, but then the present tune for a mind full of hurdles screeched metal and torturous repetition.
    "VENGEANCE ANNOUNCE BANISHMENT OF MY SON IN DARKNESS. PULL, CLOSER, CLOSER. CONFISCATE JUDGMENT. AGONY. ELIMINATE THE UNDERSTRICKEN BY

DESTROYING ALL. ANNIHILATE THE WORLD? COWARDS, I DETROYED IT ALL!"

The villain.

"VIGILANTE, VAGRANT DISEASE AND FORNICATING LAMBS BEGOTTEN OF A SON WHO TORE WELCOME WELL. IMITATIONS OF WALKING ON WATER, UNCLEAN PROPHECY. DIABOLICAL TREATY, PREPARATION THROUGH SIMULATION. IN THEE, BEHIND EYES, THOUGHT, BENDING TRUST, RULING YOU. YOU ARE MIND! STAND AS INTRODUCTION BECAUSE THE STRINGS ARE ATTACHED."

The devil.

Nothing, absolute silence.

Warning, this is not a drug picture. It was not conceived on drugs nor was it produced on drugs. However, if you want to consume it on drugs be my delighted guest. Screen, credit one, white on black.

"WATCHING. SHE ROASTS ABOVE COAL, BURNS WITH HER CHILDREN. SLASHED PALM UPON HOME, AND THE CORE OF PERSISTENCE IS DEAD."

Waves spray against the window as the rain collects and pours. Hope thought, "Make sure your umbrella doesn't get blown inside out or you might get blown away behind it, or you might just get wet."

We are all reconciled difference, substantiated ordeal, and righteous vengeance. We are all solidified thought warped in the mind of God, and this wondrous, marveled plight forms the left and the right. The left and right are intangible modes of quantum physics. They are expressed by every sense, possibility, occurrence, and thought. All life is thought, and articulate consciousness bereaves betrayal as the self brings thought to action. We are clumsy, but unyielding. Manageable inconvenience and the objectionable, crackling fault. We are being pushed, pulled, and thrown out to be perfect, but slip into something more comfortable. The wrong cream of a delectable masterpiece. We Immaculate Conception. We abuse, bruise, scratch, scourge, and maul. We blunder and plunder beneficial application, and cause the good to discover the bad. We destroy the victory, rip resistance to shreds, and forfeit any further devastation. Obnoxious beasts.

We are dots on charts, but if we explore the chart, and find the other dots, we change the system, and revolve to a heightened length of life. Failure is death, remember failure is death. Failure while living is mere recollection, and a reminder to live and remember. We are junkies craving satisfaction, creating and stimulating formations of activity that transport the embodiment of our strung out state. We have chosen desire as if it was the daily feed, and this indulgence has achieved the high of our choice. Squandering quality and quantity we are hasty for the desire of euphoria. For example, comedians become hooked on the desire for laughter.

To be a junkie, one must possess solicitude and anxiety for that desire, and nothing more. Our desire is for life and creation. We have not a soul, but desire, and this desire is no longer available. We are left, strung out and screaming with humor as the only way out. For example if a man sneezes into a handkerchief, and soils it to the point of contamination, he becomes rather upset to the lack of a white sale at JC Penny. This is taking into account the number of persons condensed as Americans. Laughter? Relatively, a man seeping soot from his chimney should sweep. He should bolster right up there, and call for inspection of the problem with his purpose up the chute. A man has no way, but the up way. Exultation? We wonder jubilation.

Quotations are the point, the object, and the rationale. Dead voices sing, and all we need to do is hear them speak. Teasing their wishing memories with the evidence of life. Heaven and Hell have exploded together to blend images, sensation, memory, and magic. The trail of dead matches the living, and the wreckage inspires this telling tale of total calamity. Purchases on personalized credit are the living, at least for those who apply, pacify, and qualify. The world revolves as it has done for too many years to count. Humanity climbs a hill of its own filth, to trip over its stupidity, and fall right back in. Fertile creatures that we be, can we not detain chosen destruction? The end comes in the arms of timing.

"Buy now, and sell later! Sell now, but buy later!"

Death is world renowned, priceless and penniless, and no longer contains suspense. Back with the tale of a threatened rage, and there is nothing behind us. This is the hang-up.

"Please try your call again or dial zero for assistance."

Think first. Walk for fifty steps, and stop with comfort as false composure. We are the meat on the table, and the gods, chosen and not, shall feast upon this fetid flesh with gnawing fingers, and teeth slipping through juicy pulp. They will devour us, and spit us into the world we have eaten to pull the plug from the drain of oblivion. The ways we conceal our ignorance we will never see, and blow up the ability to do so. In these bright depths baffled, but gradually progressing, room is open, and we are slowly catching the pace.

"A SCORPION STINGS WEEPING HANDS TO INFLICT INTOLERABLE PAIN."

Perilous is the way we age in memory based routine. Sensing, reaching beasts, and friends. Local tunnels appear, and then close, same as whence they came.

Nancy thought, "This is odd?"

The pieces of pure, past-made atrocity makes monstrosities of us all. Affliction and prediction from trying ends of this coming, modern dream. This is now in swing with daily bonuses. We are things inanimate, and untaught rot. We are the deconstruction, and the placed and sorted inauguration of dispersing ambition and astonished suspicion. An exuberant, lavish enigma that is us.

Men and women are a contagious, parasitic blood belonging to the pull of shedding fangs and torn, bare skin. We as the flock of the world wander to the slaughter, blindly and without opposition to time collecting the waste. Hopelessly falling, we are groping ourselves with ignorance. The planet we have killed, and the universe we have forgotten while digging the graves we shall possess, blind and quick. It is already done, and sits here waiting for the definitive answer of final conclusion.

Thrown away with the possibilities of truth and existence itself, we have locked the door to happiness, and this single purpose leaves meaning as flimsy collapse. Death to everything we know and see, and we are now pushing the button, do you not remember? Recall this digested suicide of brother and self. The last fading moment of bending light bright, brighter, and then brighter still. Masculine levels of solid white, shrouding belief with the growing soul of this surrounding. The moment of light beyond imagining, and you do not remember? That moment when the light evaporates into bubbles of seizing decay, and the white forges black in a blaze of death's vitality, and you hold no recollection?

The black forms this pit and the energy in that single moment when the world crashes burns a black blaze of fiery heights. Blood splatters, nerves crunch, pain and gore fling against the shades of black, and eyes close for fear of greater fears. Fear of devils, gods, demon shapes erupting from blackness, and you do not remember dying? We due to language think that behind the flowing, meandering, interacting universe created by perception is one solid, monolithic reality as a platonic iron bar. We are wrong.

"We shall see, we shall see." A carpenter.

We trip down brazen corridors hardening. Welcome her with love, affection, and prominent worship. Bow and cry forth, our savior, our mother of all promise. She is ours, and she is here. Our born blessing of menstruating flesh is a specimen of procreation, and a potential secretary to be. Macdonald by ancestry, and Crocksinford by destiny. She is a cross breed with maximum potential. This was what surfaced in my teachings, and my childhood studies.

We hid with building force, raising incentive we grew from the barren earth strong and free. Promises of purest thought led our way amongst the darkened shadow of our backyard. We concentrate to full extent, driving toward our destiny within this fragile web and whim of his. Have we prepared for reckoning?

"What?"

A small boy within his boyish dimples looking inward with a whine to the hip of his mother. A swooning need for reconstruction of ideals, and opportunities are vastly required. He gulps for comfort. A yellow dress strokes his back, and then her own. She comforts the boy at her hip.

"Joe, back in the room again."

She waves her hand at a nearby child, and Joe is asked to return. She once again strokes her back. Her hair is blonde, but absorbs the straining shower from above, and slowly wanes to red. Joe's dimples implode, his head bursts from nervous tension, and clumps to the bosom of the yellow dress. She pushes his lumpy-headed body with riveting capacity, and jumps back with full force into a gutter of fleshy debris. Joe's appendages gurgle from a connection break, no forearms, and no legs below the pelvis. Torn and gushing with his head face down some twenty feet behind her. Bumbling from filth she runs to shelter. Up the stairs, across the porch, and through the door. She closes it behind her, and runs down the final stretch. Finding the end of the hallway after sometime enshrouded in light failure darkness, the building falls between cracking slabs of earthen failure. It is over, and there is nothing left. The course of destiny is the reflection of futuristic voyage. The future extends from the present, and destruction populates the decades done and gone.

What does one do if one knows not what one is, and has no fabric to sew explanation within oneself? Normality is designed to structure society, and is cultivated by social injustice to incriminate and weaken the mass. Those who control mass appeal control the mass, but within this plan there is the human error, and the only flaw to this conceivable red herring. Our personalities dissuade complete control, and in order for total control to take place the mass must be either diminished or flat out destroyed. It is your basic conspiracy theory. They are trying to control us! They being the conspirators, plan downfall through the design of society, and in doing so tell us where to shop, what to consume, and what is right and wrong. Those who follow society either in bliss or ignorance play the majority. Those who oppose anything are the minority. You are to blame possibly by reading this, although this is only a hypothesis. In truth only I can be accused of subversion, but chances are?

"Tis close. The barriers are breaking down, and we are upon the brink. Hold pathos and understanding, but fold my cards in hopes of sweeter days, and in praise of something smaller. Myself. Grand enough, but inner guidance is essential and impertinent. There are no travel plans, and only tickets back and forth. I hereby fold, and stop this ponderous action because death is more than I call it, and better than I feel it is. I hope heaven exists, and hell is not vicious reasoning. Please, let the devil not exist in hopes of my head, heart and remorse." Unknown, but beheaded.

What matters? What reason do we have to stress consciousness? Death? The onslaught of the future is between strokes of genius. A repugnant man with no morals to conclude provision subscribes to the reverie of pointless words. We lack remission and control. We deem inadequate waste as the memories of life. Pointless, we are nothing. Dirt scattered across the globe of a junkyard. Trash. Men carry coffins, and women carry signs. We arrive safely, warm and relaxed, clean and profitable. We sense, we wish, we blow away into the impressions of sound. Maestro's finest work, everywhere, everything, radio. Welcome.

Sounds are sensations produced by vibrations that travel through the air and are detectable by the ear. A soundtrack is the sound itself. Sparks create bursts of genius, wit, and energy. Silence becomes the absence of sound, while speech contains sounds spoken, and music arranges the sounds, words, or instruments into a pleasing sequence. Whereas loud, aggressive, and undesired sound describes noise. Pop is a fizzy drink, and soup is liquid food made from boiling food. Mute button. Sound broadcasting, melting, melting, gone. Screaming, breaking glass, and pornography.

Rhythm produces stressed syllables in words, or emphasis and length in music. To beat is to hit repeatedly, especially with a stick. It is a regulated, repeated stroke. Tunefulness or melody builds this sweet sensation. An exception brings the throat, burning, taxing bile. Arrival in the dirt writes our wilting palette in the incarcerated, intoxicating delight of disclosure.

"Preposterous!"

Again our lives transcend this turning agenda through the planning of someone else's actions. Bumps to wave farewell transpose the next involvement. Change squishes evolution down to a stump of relief, and refreshes the catch of this forbidden preference. Perception talks, wound in bias, and brings home comfort.

"Bingo!" Granny.

What would you say if I was the devil?

"Laugh."

Exactly.

When Haddensville commanded Macdonald, "This to that!"

He said, you said, "Stupid," over and over.

He began once more with eyes animated by a key payment of fear, and anticipated argument. Days flew, and they flew more not making August, but days standing short. Fiction spanned out, the professor continued to ponder, and we kept in stride vigorously.

"Bardo Poe prattles over prayer, and pays every installment so this door travels in. When unversed smudges return, we escape."

Shopping for buttons with Bardo Poe, that is you, and that is Macdonald. That is these parts that do reside here.

"Evil recognizes evil. This is why a monster hilts the investigation of moral protection and thought. Beginning a language to notice the clatters and knocks. He gives way to interest, ability, and form. This is in my house. Use he, and receive she, but through me."

When the dice fall, they close on judgment. Falling as a pair, and sliding across the floor. Kings have fallen, fate has sprouted, and we are fictional. Chaos spun the top, and now there is no stop.

The white I have seen is the whitest white of whites. Texture upon texture, white. Maintaining the area of my vision is benevolent white. Solid, fluid-like in shape, and consistent to all persuasion, white. Thought, sense, and perception is flat, bare, and white. The white smear of a backdrop that lies on every side. Darkest at the center, and fading into shades of grey. Grey upon gray until white, pure white. Black is the heart of this wondrous spectrum, blackest black within the whitest white. Forced opposition in a tactful position of celestial bliss mixed on a stroke of gaze. Constant and unchanged. Recognize this foreground, and notice the difference of similarity in their combination. Black and white merging with the bond of love long separated, and rekindled hate penetrating the disabled shades of independent tension. The two are one with trembling aggravation and we are blinded by the light of remembrance passed.

"White slacks, and a salad seeps oil and vinegar, but we do not feel the gooey slop plunking down slackened polyester. The seeping edge goes down this logic until a day marked time shall turn. Overwhelming danger is this ostracizing evil. You, it, or thee, where are you? Creamy youth was once my pointless life. Yes." Abelard confined to himself.

Who? A woman in a red dress carries a canoe. Her lips mouthed sex, and her hips swayed whips of slapping reeds. Uncomfortable pricks of warm nostalgia. Tears for a mother's virginity. A fifty year old woman with her garters supporting dependence.

Who needs a word, a wisdom, or a wish of wretched mistakes? Who needs seldom sacrifice, scrambled sense, and senseless wonder? Who welcomes hatred, pride, shame, and the self? Who warrants acknowledgement, appreciation, and award?

The blessing is in the breath, and the verified reason is felt in the understanding of the individual. The universal truth and state are alive within us. The tactile approach to God is within us. The devil's entanglement also remains within us. We are the wrath of conscious conclusion, and our dislocated mass derives from us. We are the nightmarish dreamscape of reality and ourselves. And this is the telling tale of our existence. Our reasons, lesions and freedoms bear this ripping whole as the daring sun. The heat evaporates the skin. The nausea separates the sense, and the overall success of death is guaranteed. After all it comes to us all, and all of us create it, this enigmatic ordeal of conclusion and habit. The reason is in the life.

"Why are we alone?"

Strength comes from breaking hindered movement quickly. Might can come from nerves, and the aching mind binds it useless. Hands are consumed with rivaling pains, building acknowledged regression. Sleep falls into retrospect, and is crisp like over baked butter tarts. This dragged release is a time spread relapse.

"It is coming!"

It is hanging from a tree waiting to ripen, and once it falls, it has fallen. Surrounded, grade school leftovers, the dreams of demanding turnovers, and little theories of him, her, and me. Cookies, snacks, and treats. A bell is rang after the proposal is sang, and there before the crock of reality it rings. It came or always was, and holds high a new herd of heads. Demise is fear, and worshipping it with glances, we lust in the dark, and sink in insanity where these reeking blows make thoughts drip.

Wisdom is a tangent dissolved through action. The grand sensation of practical transcendence correlates time, person, and reason in order to describe the moment. It is the effect of contrivance and ideal, and its properties resume posterity, perpetual gain and loss, congealing appreciation because of the lack of growth. The limitless regime of created moments is limited to the cerebral tendencies that interpret and approach growth. Mental subscription to the pre-supposed estimation of character, chance, and ordeal. Everything therein will be again. No corpulent change can derail the completion of wavered circumstance. No subsequent perspective capitulates order, logic, and truth, and neither perspective nor circumstance form the reason of moment. Instinct develops all things in a lattice of glossy designs. Mortals prepare for the awakening of the moment, but without the awakening of the self, and entirely with surroundings, infinity, truth, or God, and therefore the encouragement of mankind. Retreat and entreat man upon his purpose, and end upon his outcome. Ideology, realism, sensory aesthetics, and passion build every waking moment, the living being, and the marginal casualty of both. Fabrication is allotted with the singular basis for example, and not the union of man in its entirety with which the desired approach is being.

A woman once asked me if I was writing my memoirs. My response was, "always."

Wonders of bewildered amusement. Wonders of uncontrolled topic, the everyday kind, small and insignificant, continuous achievement. It is good, go ahead, and enjoy.

Words rumble in his head, glistening, and fusing with the coming of time. He stares up into the sky, the blinding light of all apocalypse, and a shot blares out. His head slices forward, and the stick falls and smacks! He has found his death place finally. The voyage is over, and darkness lifts like the veil of a widow. Her eyes brazen and bleeding green whimpers, and nothing more. Inheritance disturbs her, but she makes do just like her brother. As does their mother and father. All lost and dead, bodies rotting in the burrow next to his. They existed to the entire world except for him the most prominent. The world perceived by our senses is not the real world, but the construct we create. Reality is always plural and mutable.

Wreckage from the Wasteland;

Time flows brother, erupts like whirling dervishes of isolated response. To pin down situations done to ego and self; time runs frantic like the planets in space. Evolution is our heaven sent solution of restitution. Rise up in praise of tomorrow, and hold high a figured grasp upon our descendants who are within this alleged web of self-deceit. Brother, we know who you are, what we want, what we get, and what we hold. Declaration is plain in all we say and do, and that is if lifetime memories are as they are, then they are mediocre and sublime. We present ourselves as that, mediocre and sublime. We are everywhere!

Abelard.

"The year of his coming shall fall in great November, and when the heart of man beats without a conscious mind to fall back on premature methods. When society collapses, brother kill brother, and faith in perseverance is destroyed. He shall come with the cleansing of purity gone sour, and the whimper of Heaven shall stir panic and neurosis as Christ's second coming. The ground will evaporate as the floods boom louder, and the quaking soil cooks in the flames of execution. When all is true and a blazing cornucopia of desolation, the world will die with all upon it."

We must be able and willing, and that is the exemption for prophecy. This is truth, and thus there is no planet for personal space, and there is no reality except for the perception of personal reality. There is little truth because everyone harbours lies and misfortune. There is no gain because we have already gone too far. We have to step back, look at what we have accomplished, decide what is worthy, and create that. Ignore the stages of society because they will eradicate themselves. Go for yourself, and go for those like you. So then, take logic as a plan of simple fact, and evidence therein is the truth. We will cross the threshold, and the only question is whether we will survive. Rather should we survive? Is it for our interest we do or for this planet that we slowly kill and dry up? Is it for the truth or is it for fact? Why then and how shall we evade the possibilities of decline? Can we? Should we?

I believe we should be swept back into the sea, thrown back and sworn to prosperity not self-reliance. We lose ourselves and what we have in order to question this truth. We must discover the possibilities that lie beyond our grasp, and take hold of what want needs, and not what is best for us. This is not for me. This is just for you. Listen and take note, and this truth will burn bright, but carry a new horizon to prepare ourselves for what is to come. Give undivided attention to things that are basic, and this introduction to a turning stomach begins to finish.

With that first step we fall, deeper still with the second, and the third, and the fourth buries the ground we walk on. Complacency digs us out, but under, and we stand still to watch the undertow curl up on the shore to wreak havoc with the rocks. We are the rocks, the sand, the pebbles on top and beneath; we are the mayhem of the sea and this mayhem is what brings us up and over. Buried deep with the trivial crags and nooks we try to convey, and the communication undermining the sea. We are the sea, the slope and scale of it, and we control the tide. The bliss and piss that swirls us round so we swish and wish for larger waves. A vicious plain was born some million years ago, and from this we rose. A bacterial ooze that propagates and fornicates and watches away the afterbirth, and so we are. We the definitive breach in exorbitant prestige. We the force that causes victory blows the burden of so-called life, and we the fathers and mothers of ordained decline rise and fall merely being witness to the push and tug of our excessive asylum.

"Black ash skips down my spine toward my ass, and then rams itself up there, burning the insides out."

ABPoe

Invocation for a tale of mercy. Heaven laughs at fate arrogantly, and says, "Where are the forceps?"

The patients are diluted with drugs, rest under fresh anesthetic, and droll onto oblivion. The rumors scare the tourists away or at least some of them.

"NURSE SEND IN THE SPECIALIST!" Heaven always yells.

He idles in on britches and a white smock that hangs open and rustles amidst his wandering chest hair. His shirt seems almost vacant.

"Hello, there now, how are you today?"

Just fine thank you.

"That's fine. Do you know why we are here?" His hair strings loose like ruffles or lace matted with the scent of a dog.

We are here to receive help.

"That is right. A few simple tests, and we will be through."

Fine, just fine.

Tom Freeman, the leader, "We shall know if this figure exists."

You can call time whatever you feel like, and any old time will do in any tone of voice. Pick up your whistle and blow.

PART FOUR

IMPOSITION CAN DISRUPT THE PAST

THE REGURGITATED BENDS, the commotion, the steam, the truth, but can you see only one. Beginnings are dark with the average, upright continuation. The miscellaneous age dwindles and dislocates the possibility for minuscule conversation. Does anything unyielding from circumstantial enforcement forge possibility with evidence? The visitors approached known reconciliation, but terms for an experience form days of daily nothing. The meaning debases feelings, and comfort dissuades the nutrients as steps increase and move round and round, swooning as words wait. The leaks with calm plumbing, and the awareness resonates a script. A forgotten, long voyage.

Yes presents irreplaceable traits of immaterial concentrate on endless signatures. What happens has to conceptualize peculiarity. Why do words, for not much else knows better, know what redemption remembers? That will and most of all its artifacts are different. Perhaps these passed down conclusions spin, but any dysfunction overlooking failure is potentially free and unobstructed. Really fundamental, resounding, weird music to bind to greed optimum footsteps, and the morning.

What is a person? Do you have paper? Maybe not.

Where does all the consequence die? Having scrutinized association to bring the vicious, snarled, and swollen thoughts the distance, congruent acceptance is replaced, and the future is such enjoyment. Complying with the loss of continuance, respectability requires the restraint of humanity. How wide is a man who has nothing more of nothing?

"Yes."

Tones hold the ideal of a systematic waiting, residing here, always greater, hovering with isolated proposals, and the hands did not hear of a telling life. The contagious always grows, and entertainment is crazy. The being that binds observation, design, and activity for something bearing triumph and review into the world. Which point is that? A burden bearing fortune. The predominate villains. How can language and fiction begin dissolving in questions without encoded dealings? However vengeful live life. Dead already, goodbye. Confusion, but think and swallow the loss in life. The terms cannot touch, and the only thing that is not interpretation is always losing hope. Action compiles traffic at eight fourteen in a churning flame. Definitions, disgust or consent do get through. Oh yes, the consequence occurs, and now like a mistake from above, the biased line the room. Something from suffering that impugns silence gloriously.

"My probation officer called earlier?"

The enlarged lack of reading contemplation, and scientific culture slide by for posterity. The meaning in tomorrow is an encyclopedia truly known. The apparent regard brings sentimental eternity and the monolithic waste basket below. The shadows tide resemblance of what has been with a soul and that is rightfully spirituality. The incoherent numbers of possession are the integral throw at what is successfully the footing on Tuesday. Destiny drastically working has not the dead, but the living resource to notice tears of a subordinate quickly, and it is only through their questioning brilliance that they huddle from the truth.

The right functions can never leave, and no is yes, and the power of calamity has left. Laughing life will not ever know the apprehension and exhorted eyes amidst the continuance dwindling into the future. The minuscule was to live to the decline, but instead we have awareness without the inside accidents. How can one living tempest matter that much?

Substandard noise that defines here with exactly the point. Perish for a part into life. Where can problematic posterity be given away? The light and disbelief disagree. Waver meddling feats, and hope. Can the truth ever really matter? The difference is reviewed far from home with unimportance, but looking forward a wriggling head bungles the understanding, and may never create the condensation. A bubble reserved and left respectably alive regarding employability in a picture attached to wishes. The decay of deceit, and debris that beats death perfectly closes in. How can a burden hold the love? When things go bad, describe acceptance the transmuted destination, and pleasure with walking not writing may very well coruscate through identification. Actions to live and the world.

The only thing in the world enthralls life, and collecting figures condemn an oozing wound out of control. With the loss of life, although the circumstance cannot reach out, the definition runs curious here to erudite land. Marked unknown due to under question penmanship is the meaning of a simple rendering once and a while. People justify promise to move on. Despising diplomatic poverty we in that moment present terrible discomfort. As to the self, complexity reverberates singular comfort. Told to do that, tomorrow forgets trespassing on suicidal thought, but can anyone remember? The only thing that rekindles the practises merrily goes round in life to carry purpose. The subsided submerge shrinking, whirling, wrong, but where meaning is ignored and left unsaid, the thing that stirs the sour state never knows the difference. Left with terrible burning the orange of Halloween, but even the burns said goodbye to living and crawling continuity, except for chaos standing in the smuggled construction of occurrence. An open awareness of debauchery that stifles the opportunity for sweating out the creepy and the systematic nothing.

Maintain the smooth, let creative consequence hatch forgiveness to the furthest cry of poverty. Arrive redundantly to a road as the unfathomable overflows room for the bewildered wilting of importance in something else. Go beyond problematic process, and deprave the future of hope, captivation, fortitude, and the usage of all the same, crumpled memories. Alone, the understanding has all been trivial notion, and precious vibes more than fluid breath from the behavior. Life is the ritual attitudes, and an encore other than definition of personality. The truth to finally reason a way of life distinguished quickly, and the betrayal that does carry the hard hope.

Prove One

What the grey left behind on the fidgeting self. The speculation of breath and behavior lost in the subconscious because death so long ago contaminated the proposition that has tomorrow. What can weary description have done? What can be done?

"Farewell."

The prescription of more than a wasting indifference should be the introspective life of nothing. Let it go, be, do not sit here and come above the land to crumble into society and become absorbed in vain. The box has given discrimination tranquil relation. Long gaps of tomorrow that run to the outcome ending temptation. Something enters, or did, and forgoing the other thing is quintessential of one choice. A cup of coffee recognizing reflection as desolate, and the closed standard of the mind, lost or gained is unbearably collapsing. Green grass bends easy, and a look around will not improve the strand of blossom. People think the choice has become clear, and swaying out to self allusion, capture purity and banter. Vegetables carefully going to service.

"No I am not alone."

Despising solitude, nothing pleas for more nothing with willing disbelief. The intermission met upon tomorrow with nothing and decline. Right now and tomorrow, for if they are identical judges are all alone, and the eyes know what invigorates the sense more than the future multiplying the notes of fiction. Most think not because worth does not fall with a long tug, and the foundation lifts up contemplation, planting chance, and letting love. Has it been tried? Change for a wish, but decline everything that presents bitter swooning and loss fidgeting it away. Time for what? Scrutiny and continuation as friends? To idle in the living room ignored, the stillness struggling, and the voice has yet to call earth the truth. The resonance of life indoctrinating representation, oppression, and freedom combined. Opinions can tread, can a soul on the ankle?

"I really need to rest."

A moment turns the whole, articulated chorus, and inspection resounding indignation of singular truth will counter definitive lines of difference, but if the singular masks the effect of trouble defined through a fumble it is the captivation to engorge today. The lying list within waiting curiosities. The lines shamefully plucked continue to understand, and the chaos of joyous variation in the lack of every progressing force curving creation can go against nothing, and the connections stir no proven ignorance once more. Clear the commodities with deep breaths blowing nowhere, and thinking corrodes, but complaints warmly blooming obtain life. The fantasy and depravity no one breaks is the infinite beauty that slags the fitted literature with punishment. Right now the love of tales can be trapped and enjoyed. The dust clouds of safety sanction time and the foundation of the fortunate aspects simply project the propositions. Today!

"What about the rebels growing up and the whining removal of the presence thus entrapped?"

The middle either secludes tomorrow or dies every day. What is important? To see the truth right or wrong. All the life just up the street. Instead the bends remain in the intertwined care, and flow here in the snare of exchange. Static goes forth indescribable, although the self has left the reason speaking one's own, awake emotions. The welcomed yesterday that cannot be the victory.

"Was that yesterday already?"

"Can I help you?"

The answer was futile, alone, and stumbling. Those that had sauntered the tribulation know where a fragrant memory fades trying to make today, and consequence once more met a moment upon a moment. Do not fear wonder, and understand the possibility of prospect. Writing the inherent remembrance of easy listening, the disillusioned reach out, but the soul is time. An old add for something already dead and sold. How can this be? No one has won. The logic is the history, but what of the life? General, vast understanding dies, and the causes seek people to live. Looking in, simply wanting life, and not possibility. There are actions, joy, and reason, but bridging contrast cannot be the truth. The postured memories of a demented mind ignored, and compassion scorns the parts. Steadfast repetition flying as murky crisscrossed thoughts present imbalance and conditioning.

The roots of the living avoiding meaning, yet the steps and the words very likely shall purify the echoes. The tasks with instinct intercede and the restoration of the past's expression is submitted to others. The experiences show the conviction, and together harbor dreams, but does the wish to compensate universally direct these words? The evidence knows of understanding without comparison, and although the hold is transfixed, perhaps one should question the stereotypes every once and a while. Tomorrow falls behind as do the explanations, but the matter becomes conscientious, and is labelled wrong. Even happiness shrugs the perplexity off, but with the popularized arguments of not knowing. What is in the possibility that is not decisive?

This choice proposes a distraction. A symbiotic form just will not give up. The water has already disintegrated in sunny waves and circumstance crashing the ultimate true redemption has now looked at further limits. The most important of prescribed propositions would be being too quiet. As the heart swoons wishing surpasses uncertainty, and many frowning heads pass the future. The articulate stripes never reason more. Why? The blessed on either side with bliss. A rhapsody that strikes sunshine, and a solution that looks away to outgrow the written whole. To see promise within the radiator although within the dirt is a dilemma resembling salvation. The lucid consolidate some time. Where is the resurrection of a choice? Known and wandering seems an endangered beginning because living for oneself is a confine from long ago.

Exhausting, chaotic emancipation. The same heads of submission become superior and the disadvantage that they should clearly state slowly slips away. There is some connection to the deficiency and more questions. The greatest eternity left above water is not plagiarism. The writer's path becomes the truth by reasoning exorbitant life. Disobedience and corruption welcome the possibility to praise radical conclusion, and even in opening the malicious, unknown walls lack scope, but propose the room. That is the point! The artist's way allocates programming by a choice. Trivial emotion with the probable restriction. Perhaps the reflections know better, but everything clusters, lost in light, and references can only maintain behavior. There needs to be a continuum of proposition. Truth should matter with the consequences. Does the melting pot stammer out sin and salvation? The rivers to the essence of pleasure, before the toss of perception will explain, and what can be the random, synthetic reason for the past? Can a stare down on years and positioning go even further?

"Who gave this stage oblivion?"

At present the repetition. To close free from control is not on the street, and happiness provides these travels of acceptance. Reason cannot practise the flight because the fleeting terminology could be changed. Regardless the weather is conquered with time, and not the self's decay. Strong men fractured completely, possibilities of miraculous right, and no correction into salvation. The past that lies down on the truth looks further at tomorrow. Well what do you think we should do? The intoxication becomes conclusion, the hand can write, and lose finality. If consequence seems nothing more than slapping fiction all is the heart's content. The answer comes easy. The explanation resulting with interest. Life is hope amidst the repetition.

"Do what thou will."

"Does anyone care anyway?"

"See the momentous importance of difference."

Standing here, what is not these days, but do you know why you are here? Broadcast almost every beginning, and what many question one accepts. Interpretation and reason are seen as one between the wonder and the crumbling, churning earth. Progression wilting from a decadent soul. Pass back the thirsting learning that forgets conviction and sadness to see the taxing aroma of disquieting reality. Who is first? Cold youth. The unclean bottom of choice, but what does that mean? What is acceptance that carried through age composed condemned conclusion? The dying reverence is built with fear, and from comfortable remnants of interpretation singular consciousness reduces tomorrow. Life is regulated performance, vanquished vindication, and irreversible exclamation. The perpetual percentage of a living treason as the branded minutes describe the pace. How can such inspiration be lost? Is there anyone you call?

Do words laugh with distinguished eyes or just by choice articulate memory? Are words inappropriate? Haunted souls standing behind time, but what does the disruption draw from the whole? The one resonant realization unto the next, invisible universe. People are the test of friendship.

"What can truly be lost with just my passing?"

The memories stand snarled and accessible with decay. How are you? The life is more prominent and purges the playing memories with favors. The greatest of children, the moon, the evening, and being. Houses not out of style, but loose from the option nonetheless. The gifts of growth like dreams could let the purpose understand until it all dissolves and rises to live. Momentous occasions, friendship galore, and all caught in the system of an eye.

The postulating parts of the difference cannot extenuate the hypothesis, but what about birthright? The influence of the predicament, the accumulation of the uncomfortable out over the assemblage, and the hold on both never changes, but glancing schemes count the actions. Figures of design with no place to go except somnolent declension. Do not forget, but remember. Not much, too little, and just the searching flux of the self. Nothing shudders when the illustrations interpret decrepit gains together because so much of it is the essence tried rather than merely choice for the hands. When nothing of potential struggles, and only the senses of resonance remain to touch, then we may ask.

"How can the top be the same?"

The rasping interpretation is the future. No comparison knows unexpected necessity and progression is half of the mountain. The description would leave reaction to depravity, and life foul with fragrant, pulsating facts. Senses attained through the ungrateful combustion of a madman and not being are no cheap concession, but with talk is the center to another. The wrinkles that create with time have the teeth. Truth replies for a bumpy ride is sure to follow.

Everyone is lost as things through development want to die. The destructive repetition is this life. Told to do this annual time, and live alone to talk back without interpretation, and therein is the consciousness.

"I will be just a minute, do not give in!"

Cycles in sequestered lemonade. Even today understanding transposes the racing expectation with the turning actions. There is no accept or deny even though a need has won. The fortune to disregard many feelings does not unfortunately guarantee equality. Thoughts comply an unusual, lying fountainhead of structure to block all the shifting, charcoaled shadows. The meaning will not be universal and defines the perception represented to realize there was a hand. Missing footprints have been disbelieved. What memory truly sides with the neighbours?

Sickly praise dies and tastes the point of another. Somebody shall be thrown away to let it grow and the better suited have compiled enough to get into pictures. How can this be because the time is more than today? Repetition collided after a short time.

"Forever."

The future of acceptance is disillusioned too, and moving to motion condition is not like what is defined or presented. The golden outcome of creativity are these words. You can hear me can you not? Hidden in minimal tones of labour and dance, opinion and meaning take the quickened chance to know. To look. The ethics that have come to go, and leave the eyes of beauty. Also known as illustrious nonsense, and the point transposed waits frightened. Utopia answers, but reality sings a song, and the mechanics under question point words. The natural air is warm, kills the enlistment of acceptance, and neck in neck facilitates personality to vocalize wishing escape. The corrosion becomes a tactical experience, and paper condenses glances that never left self-proclamation morbidly written and articulated as shameful, everlasting moments.

"Do what thou will."

What exactly is spiraling forward as the visitors separate? The dues of something easier to them. A tight population and the starvation of adults allows smaller catches. To write into time where nothing stands back turned with men side to side for a question. Meaning is a room, the misconception of intake as writing continues with delight. What is set, sin-bred, consequence is the claim of flirting acceptance. Maybe, but even without repercussion the morning light is erected and growth fills the balance with the understanding here. The trivial, upper class balding on a balloon are typecast within a way that is obsessed like a toaster.

Grow as proposals, but learn how to remember.

"Do."

Lives jerking, "Oh yeah!"

Distinguished barking is reasonable in the dark. Choose by fixation and the ones wanting love are born to succumb. Survive another nature, scratching articulation as unscrewed progress and adventure, but how far is the travel? Apologies for the disregard, but conformity shrouds remembrance above all else just to forget tomorrow. Today has arrived to be taken screaming. The torture is enjoyable, the heartbeat of solitude, memory, and pride. The implemented chorus failing already with the flagrant, subsiding labour. Rides that forge something more great. Shoe size continues, and although marked the worth of a penny is defaced with union. How can these lungs season the heart?

We that ride, but cannot believe in belief anymore. Adding that in and always losing the new one has brought that out. The interpretation repeating pleasure, curiosity, and obstacle. Carefree practises with contradictions breaking into guilt, and concepts of money making schemes. Tattered, outstretched personality means a flinching pedigree is the plan, but as inspection will reason the problem free from exchange is the importance to follow. Does memory quickly know of indifference and illumination? What can be newly acquired is true like trees in the future held forever. The lack of sense vanquished to simple consequences because the remembrance cannot dream. Always losing conclusion, some spectacle, and the balance.

"Is death really so close?"

This is nothing. The stereotypes and the sultry afternoon. Can you not tell me your name? Understand both in circumstance by Christmas chicken! Backed in the center of chance, distorted, isolated debris. The most important standards turn down the circumstance. These words. A process fumbling lost reflections and backwards control. The realm is eminently collaboration with the objects, purpose of situation, but also the understanding that falls before it. People believe without room. Restraint always overtakes reprise. Experience is acceptance. People bewildered with the impossible expectations of orchestrated moment. Opportunity retorts a difference, but is held behind.

The supplication and sore throats remain apologetic. Waiting with encoded dates, the hands concede any irregularities, and the world will clarify the broadcasts. Bias does the wrong, but the tongue commits like clouds, and coaxing frustration shall flourish. Resources in a wilderness of echoes that after all these years come together to weep with the conclusion. The endless, straight end of descent, clear of victory. Green grass patronizing divinity as refugees, but also friends bend and fold with heartbreak. A vision, the medium of communication stumbling, nothing of comfort for the continuation contained a cigarette. The question of failure fails the footsteps of organized demise by allowing influence of choice. All that believe such an aimless valley are broken. Miscalculated freedom composes the stereotypes a language upon a soul in love with moral praise.

This is for ourselves, and the world. Something fitting to say resides beside the translucent judgments, and death did the same, but as people would construct exchanges are to be more than time. The past of meandering choice, and the hands contest dirty dedication. Is there anything I can get you? Funny pages of language changed, and taken to the memory of words. Searching the intellect of age reflective detail, and beating ignored connotations already gone. Creativity is the ultimate suicide.

"Do not die by subject."

Writing, asking of misfortune to lose with everyone, and time from living declines another moment. A gesture of fluoride looks bright, but what conclusion can salute desolation? The senses that did not grow. Hot and cold carries the patterned pictures mistakes. Sparring in victory and indifference.

"Why do I keep fucking up?"

What lands an outcome? A contemplative screaming. The definition of choice is only the parent of great longing, and has evolved onward to departure. The mire and the moment simply scribbled systems from the statement. A walk never loses effect and replayed walks every breath and every time. These thoughts about what universal tomorrow? An end that is rational, and writing begins with remorse, but glancing insight, and vision receives adult life and opulence. Can a life strive for the minimal, personal disclosure? No conclusion except for personal genetics and through pragmatism false appropriation and circumstance. Try to forget the hardened sadness for a biblical sense, but the temperamental characteristics can uplift the life of such attention spans based on the need for contemplation. What is growling in the dark? Why complain?

"You do not know the generations, the mind wanders contriving pebbles from the production."

The truth and the corruptible consumption calls a fierce ride perpetual tidings of perspective rights that can forget a simplified, empty concept. Anonymity and somber evidence because of all this contradiction. The one is just for foretelling resounding. The distraught appreciate sleep because those will survive to believe in the strength, and go as follows. Perhaps I can get you something? Perhaps from the nothing in the concrete we can cherish an unusual change. Days wandering embroidered, descriptive subculture. Almost all of crime loses the propaganda. The consequence of vexation postulating cracked nurturing. Turkey experience watching truth through the repressed mistakes. Motions of understanding kiss the dead. Tomorrow tries to overcome, but blinking temperaments continue, and the focus is walking away.

Patience is high, and with all the violent choice from loss, mighty actions go unnoticed. The continuous bliss that happens to exchange fluency, conquest, and ominous freedom. Poetry forgotten with no place to hide, or die, but glancing time. Beckon the greeted cold again to forge society and the choices willing response go away. Really years sink within the breeze, and the ground cannot want beyond the floor. The lies are troubled, and pointless, relinquished suspicion, and boiling suggestion regards the soul to grow from a difficult resolve that meant idiocy to the message evolving posterity.

The turning occasion gives up this stance, but to answer whether or not seeking footsteps can become the sun? The throat is one tomorrow to get through as assigned therein. A squeezing of the knot. Smell pierces next as the truth decides guessing that indicates outcome. This growing direction, the living, taking tales as practicality within that sensual touch feels and detests the merry life. Belief fleeting contrast. Growth and the fact of the backdrop resides in an arm's grasp. Words are the resource of meaning. The concrete. What is that?

Photography which cannot be animated. The work and the prize are the same imposition of peace and consumption. Enclosed again in any sign of speaking etiquette, a turning wait over endless people, and fact illuminated wavers. That the pervasive manufactures ghastly radiance graciously forms somewhere on the long, clean sea. Conviction senses faith. The machine in submission to the pain slowly crossed, and our weight of consequence broke reality from street explanation. The lying abstracts bathing in a decadent soul. The annals plan the commas and deny. Now malnourished and lost, life waiting to be a support coughs. We learned with the wanting, but instead waiting, speculate the accomplished benefit. Nations ranting payment, but the way of return resolves the how in a sandwich that nobody may notice. Moments entrust closure, evolution, and dysfunction.

The spiral of decay keeps maybe in angst. Easy, wrong words scathing a play as traffic can rectify looks with depression. Time upon a new quarrel of distortion, and right will never bob for dissonance denied. The rolling footsteps remain as practise, and has people to cover the terms fate means. The choice without depravity to live as Valkyries always submerging in the sky wanting more. What right is not broken by toil in the worry they say. The countless, decreasing sayings for the old ways. Shallow, shifting tones amusing truth to the self. The usual reprint.

The sun of labour cannot be finished. Remember answered study. Life cannot freshen the soul only the truth, where each resides a purpose of power. There is confusion and behold ears to slowly know, but speak a voice for abstinence. No? Uncertainty is sensed in the true. Does that make sense of life on the merry go round of many unknowns and the splendor of lost chance? A personal everything.

Where is the love and will to stand with virtue? Why deny and express life with nothing left to the go? Decisions look away, the actions already know too much, and the negative fixation remains declined or superfluous. The shadows, the sky expanding determined to recover, yet involuntary duality might tire the win where the foot is inspiration. Both friendships and love had course. Take any self, cross the mind, and a positive heart and a life envelopes the stumbled blur of relevance as false.

Nothing is the given. Placing the will with everything vengeful and revealing, and growing a cycle which is adequate, but the same. Why is the soul done in, and new in a world where plays and stops merge in words with lively, gentle progress and the opposing, euphoric breath? It can give you the eye standing in for a use of the air and a soul. Round waiting, coming out of the underground to even the force out of remission. Walk light as spirits do through procession, and become narrow, even looking wisdom. Even with fault charred far too long in experience, the reason is clear like a dripping chorus, a cubicle unmasks wonders, but to what make?

The reasons are the three ticks of resistance that ignore sense. The scent that is within oneself. Unearthly, even selfish. Is survival the cook, and the one residing with the frozen peas? Can bounty be just for thoroughfare? The only things murderous are the living, blowing, consecutive time with company, both in the plummet to be taken. Repetition drinking a life and a knowledge into two regards, but resembling all identity was the loss. Copy chance and accept that it is myself. Then the world surpasses greed to test the low because breath can never go to evil, and never lies to see, but for righteousness and incontinence. It does no good for the equation.

Glib people and projects full with dissolving will simply to begin with. There is repetition and flavour. The secure receive, and the discontent go into the taxing year to saunter by and look around, but both are lost there to maintain the saddened people first. Down with yours! That scrap to burn or drop will not know the world. A woe betide of wisdom.

"Do."

Do not let go of truth for imperfection. Love jazz, and undermined bodies of insects. Understanding breathes forever. The ritualistic decay to really surpass its implement is the recalled world of expectation. The mere citation within the progress, the truth, and respect collectively, side to side hide in defined places. We are under this machine, reading, and textbook slogans are the resource under footstep with regulation.

The future is made in the health of resources. Barren resources are bending light.

The tomorrows will take opportunity, but the fault revealed recites moderation. There lies in the leaps of will nothing that has to illustrate the state of a title. No chortle of humor gives copies of skin behavior, and any coward the survey of words. Human want for a rub of law is literal. Instead we make them live for love, a notion for a transfusion that reeks of fish, but is the trait so fragrant that now is the walk of dreams. Over.

A man compiles undertones, reverence, right, and when all this could be alive what shall do something. In fate happiness is dilemma. The shiny light using the desire, and tired hands have no game of stakes, but what carries cheating gives spiritual waiting what we have. There is sense and progression. What high design within oneself. A voice, although no fortune, the uneducated old age, and laziness through the air. A long hand churning exchange. Tomorrow steps with the meaning up for agreement. Take breath, but over sense the calling dust. The reality is nothing. Stagnation to inspection, but the hand calculates fundamental areas for the extreme lingers within the work, and not the words. On and on and on the beast fades. There is a disquieting someone holding earth beyond testimony, above these ripples, and longer than all. One must stand once more.

It sticks in turmoil, playful, selfish ego expanding tribulation. Utopia falling with squints of seeking gravity, but the broad instinct of the place dies. Pending time and exchange does blur, distorted harmonics die upon this same effect. Now embers, the contemporary beauty of lapsed need loses, subdues, and delves into carless authority. Choices at hand and loss, personal mountains, but complete doors are endless, and the future with burden eclipsing freedom confuses presence. People have shadows. We wind the divide to create growth that grows for the brink of action. Away bewildered goodbye. Take me home.

You have forgotten pause, and tranquil hearts of death thwarted with power when fabrication describes the bottom sales of a sentence. The foot? A drawn out picture with every distended middle parted upon regard and the self. The lack of gain, and the brisk love torn to be more than either. Wake up with the twist of the initial stick, however, with not just one. Where that should be is not gained, but devolves with the time. Why do such secluded albums of a will incur tension not rationale. The words to find so many hands grasp for purpose, but sticky understanding is too perfect, and nothing provides friendship. The occasion is about to forge to the end, and we are the dead.

Then that was the first agreement with someone in October distortion. The stings of speech for one sight of hell and sense goes thinking of a reason. It began with subjective time and expansive percentage. The background to the soup is defined, and the distance to the grave is stooped. Tomorrow is wrong, but all is different weeping circumstance. It is learning, or the memory heard that abets hope and wish. I into the eye, and a sun is in majority of this committed population of potatoes.

Say, "Ah."

Bliss and work forward and wait for narration. Life is no start within nothing. The current wonders many souls rousing God's element. Lost in implications, dead, although somebody said love. More than death is love. Life lowly recoils in wisdom. Exist and create. Psychotic foothills of elusive stability have come to ignore the tears and explain the ratio of how much is felt and free by writing. The morning may be lost. Feelings twist and die slowly for personal difference. The action maintains an unbridled walking for various reasons and decay. Actions confuse conditioning however that distraction of purity is the experience that goes on from life into the future. Equating understanding, and no longer desire.

The interpretation as circumstance with the clouds and sun make or bust freedom to lamplight the reality. Many already know, and the slightest being is a future. The understanding of wisdom figures pace with mathematics. Graphics looking old and somber to call the divine. The sentences told to do that, indoctrinating offspring right? Rest and submission. To say too much is better relaxation because strangers and succulent breathing feels comfortable. Pause. Where temptation enrolled flamboyant sense and ourselves deliriously become thoughts, and all these things of grandeur exhale forgotten dreams. The progress of the reality is tense, wishing obscurity good morning.

Beware of temptation gone again and prosperity. Circles speculate space by the point of accessory words formatting repression because progress does not lie for lovers remnants.

"Worth? What can I be worth?"

Question questions beings. Smoking ghosts. No problems about shortage accept or deny? Something was said by the passing thing. All the time passion reflects want without waiting to eat. Option sockets organization, and the fornication on the street of righteousness is only the proposition. It can grow. The lack of equalled fantasy is the self against the way, and the knowledge for another. Variance as passing bliss responds to disintegration. The vocabulary contaminated articulation and congruent retribution, and time's silent repetition creates happening. Contest decay with conclusion and for now continue eating description. Mistrust reality, steam, broken records, wilderness, the future, and the thought of time knows the little world clearly. Luxury and how recollected death foreclosed.

"Do we forget, do we forgo, or do we forgive?"

The frozen accuracy and serenity began loose, lost reason, and independently bleed spawn. The interpretation is literal. Choices of no conclusion are covered reprieve, sadness and loss. Retribution and the interpretation of not abetting disbelief. Profane things to resurrect things at some regulated lick. The victory too late sits high and ridiculous. Morsels circling this test. The mugginess would find wanderers tomorrow. Wander the existence that is the relationship of our no majority because it knows the contemporary answers.

A red light and what is best declines the breath, and left is the alcohol in the precious utilization of beauty tumultuously consecrated in scrutiny that will tell meaning details. The point not knowing the people and kindness. Forget the direction persuading responsibility for the arduous work. Precious sanity over the identity of hands and the effect together promises the state of the right theme to both. Creatures wish can they? Reason is determined consciousness. Curious the soul is the situation already, and irresponsibly the heart's prescription is love waiting within disabled remains.

The loose self typing truths with the windows of a routine. Leads disappear like an outcome. Hands of heaven contemplating life, but the earth is nothing but black reality. The direction for misguided vice versa on a hot rock. Firm praise warms the point in the goodbye. What was to act it out brought tighter tales resembling meaning, but greater calls change to strip in clearance. Lose to the bullshit. Not knowing for sure, a future is tangled like answers of living trial, barren and black. Fear of the welcoming sensations, and the sense of bumpy force is a personal communication that holds.

"Oh how lovely it is."

A weakened state that senses blessing with the repetition overtly proclaimed with regard. No one has won. The senses squeeze the sea until death proposes to eat.

"I am lost with hope and despair."

The proposition of decision is preparation on progress. People entertaining the moment and waiting for audacity. Cooperation thrives and anything alive within the ether signals another electric blessing. The trail minimized the wilderness, but precise feelings of what compromised circumstance never forgets to grow. The mass again is one far greater than yesterday. What is today? Too many enlightened and adolescent thoughts thinking. The constant freedom of remembrance and reality. These things, many things when there was none. Nowhere personifies in the doorway of condition to return honest and brave. The tale resides at the leap of friendship for thinking souls alone. Everything swirling and conspicuous. Noises repeat, solemn exasperation. Minutes describing the singular arrangement of sweet reasoning is not singular. If everything met a moment slain with the personal self. Bask in being a dangerous experience by not knowing escape is never enough.

Now then the potential is mandated as change, and citation causes thought, interplay, and discouragement. The clouds clawing the linguistic intertwine as happiness counts the lavender. The restriction is also the perspective and flagrant consequences. Remember with discouraged principles. The land of things to come, impetuous, sweet caution. Understand an outcome, but do not take posterity quickly. The battle of critical importance with the choice of decay. Who approved the purpose of achievement? The distortion of foundation speaks a name and purpose. Understanding and the mass although not the same resources worth familiarity, and primal existence will never anchor the functioning humanity. Curiosity and not interpretation whispers for the dilemma, but what bittersweet taste lingers with the soul alone. It is secluded and perhaps irregular because of the jokes, and one guesses articulate disclosure.

The shifting of human nature and fitted beginning is dark. Expectations and regret.

"Blah. Blah. Blah."

The terms for affection and decay positioning occupants while freedom controls the potential for clean truth. The transfixed, thick tomorrows. The riches comprehend. What does it all mean? Irrational themes for conception. The closing of crossed wires on steps lost. Yes the deliverance of living. The odds for a contagious spectrum must pray, and although more than conceptualization is not likely to touch the left, the sacrifice however can be ok.

If virtue still exists than time shall never run short, life will never end, and this chosen body will conceive and compare greatness. The book I read you write and I write in return the tale for both. You and I are attached though distantly inclined to say so, you think my imagination cannot conceive your secrets, lies, and love. Perhaps they cannot, but my sense tells me that none are great that are not together, and none are smaller than one ill repaired. Bodies may change, but sense conquers all within a realm of possibility. Oppression can be duplicated, euphoria replicated, and nothing imagined many times over. The pulse continues, though the words decline, and the wrath of the world lies in its spectres. The ghosts pushing motion further along, the spirits adrift encasing the cliff, and the ghouls that molest and derange. Fiction crumbles in the aftermath of the truth.

Vague conception cannot describe the horizon clearly as it cannot see it clearly. The lines are so far that they blur under concentration. The distance may not be achieved. Home again to think some more. The next day the answer is not any closer. Home again to think some more. Perception is anchored by habit to protect itself from certain dangers. The speculated unknowns that linger in shadows and hover in nightmares. Gruesome disease and colossal poverty. Secrets kept from us to keep us safe. Realities against conditioning, and reactions lobbying against the truth and its control. Who paints the picture or tampers with the text? What is their old world, misshaped paper, and the calling to write? The source of life cannot dry. It spans generations and actions articulate understanding. Perhaps here there is too much, and the voice bewildered cries openly. Blurts out madness and obscenity. Hides in the decline of the mind.

Sense stupefies reason in the oldest iniquity. Carnal vice contracting love, beauty, and innocence. A warm place on a rainy day. A good friend in a time of need. It seems strange to include it on paper. Guilt and fascination cannot be so bad. The corners of survival may unravel and the bare fibers could corrode, but the respect I have already lost is enough. Impossible things dreaming of the sun. Desire collecting again the free will and this historical form of what is to be.

Nothing is for sure. History predicts mass murder, diplomacy excludes the facts for consideration, and masterful strokes distort the message completely. A stale language gurgling words. Choking on text like it meant something. The truth is distorted by how many see it, and the majority will appeal to it, but a few will remain indifferent, cautious, and concerned. If the lies are not accepted than the truth can be seen. To not give in and allocate bias where there should be compassion. To be free. Look at useless, formidable language with the meanings and achievement of habit, one's self, heart, and laughter. Love and know bias wavers sight, outgrow primal placing, and remember because the head awaits. Notions of standards like a long utopian reason.

Direction on a global scale cannot be deterred by just one person, but if one person can change another, then momentum will elaborate the revolt. Patience and virtue will sustain us further than weakness and murder. Understanding is such a brief encounter that is reflects bounty and blessing in being alive. Sound to make the heart light up with happiness. Sensual strokes warming character, aiding direction, and arousing response. The tickling flickers of dust casting the nose in a sneeze. The savory delight in a banana split. The horrors and joys that fill our eyes with wonder. The projection of input and output continually forever. The simplicity of belief bombarded with all this work. After all it is only guess work.

A nudge on the shin from the head squealing call of tiny birds or the brooding smell of brewing sand curling between our toes. Purpose resides everywhere even if our laziness brings us down. The senses have torn down too many buildings, and now there is no place to sleep. Idly wandering spirits progress wearily through the muck to find their final spot. Words defining the motions, mapping out the possibilities, and maintaining through dedication the resources involved. The emotional refuge, intellectual applesauce, and physical abilities that direct modern life. The soul lies dormant, silent, and hopefully well fed. Time is the test, passing is easy, and participation counts more toward the grade. Moments sweep away the gloom, refresh the impartial dialogue with agreement, and promise change forever. Both small and great cracks alter the surface. Breathe to breed wishes with action, steps with destination, and cause with conflict. The irrepressible instincts of nature. The uncalculated mistakes of mankind. The butt is dancing reality.

Even the simplest terms cannot be read easily. The words remain their meaning, and the meaning is always formed from the assumption of knowledge or language. When collected words span eternity with the simple steps of assured benevolence. They paint the hallways purple and dance within these rooms in order to capture the truth. The beauty and wonder that is this life. There is hope, but time disproves it with ardent information. This corruption, these terms, in scripted values nothing more. The world tells the tale as we listen carefully and heed its warnings. The universe speaks the conclusion openly and clearly, and we carry crimes with time, and idly die. Cotangent truth as the choice pursued interest. The future says something of all this hidden reason and irrational game. Given away regardless to all is this obscenity. Casualties panting on the reefs waiting for relief. Drastic corrosion perpetually reaching out to grasp more has finally found its full reward. Enough life has been lost, and the sacrifices are no longer readily available. Our virtue has receded and the outcries for justice are still unheard. The perplexity and picturesque physiology of piety.

The day of the decline may be extinguished, but which way compiles the dark steers. Loneliness, letting go of the limits, and breathe to be a language of singularity. Round and round, tumultuously falling, continually faulting the passage with unnecessary clutter. Broken backs bend back, swollen eyes still see, and the mind may confuse the matter, but the matter cannot confuse the mind. The living torture is self-inflicted. The choice corrodes the consequence even though the consequence still counts. Surmounting the mire forever super! Sitting and facing conviction, afraid to change the terms, and reality keeps hitting hard knocks. Time is too short to get caught up in storytelling. The rules have not changed, the judges agree, and spirit equates the results. Alone and afraid how have things rather than motive twisted the choice of self, death, and the awareness of now.

Can a moment truly clear the air to leave the room like an uneasy dog? Vicious reproach directly at the fleshy parts. The wounds heal, the lesson goes along unnoticed, and the old wounds resurface and bleed again. What wisdom can foresee the future? Which direction can lose the suffering and apathy? There is a stain on the paper, and a contemptuous account of pity and scorn. Can it mean so much if only from myself? Can the truth be told in a moment of loneliness? A moment of isolation can disrupt the pattern, but who derived the pattern anyway? I did, you did, we all did, and we graciously accept the conditions because we are ghosts speculating demise. Live hard someone said, and so I shall, but only the future will tell of its lacking sheen. The resource that saw all of the acceptance grow within the protest of the rising sea, and the glances follow with flight. Crude isolation resurrecting the mind and the future for choice.

Questions in questions as displeasure should be for smoke and any outcome. New destiny and time lack the subconscious resistance, and the bare, human condition of insanity is better. All the way removal, a voice of compassion, what degrading words believe should be said, and the repair or apology walks upward. It is seen getting a mentioned, contemporary reason, but never starts. The characters deplete the mix in a furtive low tide. Feeding the fright even hypocrisy with the fall and not demise avoids the cohesive discern to walk more secrets. Loneliness, aggravations of individual recall sparring trees. Garbage world. The evidence of the exchange makes a FALUTALY book.

Broken is the illustration by endless resolution and truth. The bordered conclusion is slight delight. Words articulate a sneeze. Grotesque, homeless longing. Look further with life as people choose the sixth by reading that line and not a man. Life would commence confusion, disgust, and stamina. Can there be intellectual explanation? Has condemnation as pleasure does not believe mocked, congestive foreclosure inferred that life is naughty somewhere? The necessary occurs, twitches because of condition, but see across the useless home under this complicated fate, and prove the sublime by the entitlement of a sea's tide. Without preoccupied truth rhymes must forge reality, review machinery, and hope what? Defined as hovering emotions, and loss really needs other people's servitude. Allow for equals then be pure. Where is the focus over or under the street? Where is the only agony of precise days? Some say a confused person into the uncertainty. The base is down, the signature to be understood bleeds mundane existence as incorporating singular proposed breaks, but a decreasing self is aware, and believes the moment. Together rise, become singular treasure proclaiming life as longing and logic created to the abstraction. Both agony and the muse derive in the captivation, rashly without time and slogan. You form the experience openly. More to the most. The penalty of disquieting calls. Matter splits the usage with dissonance as no truth is going up above acceptance within a time of disgrace.

Life in the short reasoning of the future, motion, myth, and views carry stories. Music about temptation to praise light with thought for the possible like a reason for writing this down. Perhaps dwelling in steps tempts floating reward, and spiritual work ethic. Heads mention the screams that really repeat because even though a blessing the awareness of collapse holds the fundamentals. Do toes have to coagulate? Love defines promise, trial of the self's call, but broadcasts with the bolder at a time already known. The questionable lacking of what frustrated a true interest. Contamination for more propriety, and the here without the self. Over reason and want and neither do not go wide for what the world layers as society's appearance. Touch closes a door, destruction condemns especially when facts, progress, and people cannot do unending nothing, and therefore will have that straight. Subside in a representation questioned, and broken to wishes is poor, squinting essence. Nonetheless waiting for age old goodbye can the overcast way run down forgotten wisdom to foil appetite? Who cares? The contrast of replicating memory dies under question. There are unknown gambles of escape for confusion and sorrow of nothing are saved for the end. Limitations delving backward to believe the aftermath. The street, persona, and the wait with self's decay cloned and forgot.

A yawn passed inspection, but must people as people forgive dice. Tomorrow makes a state, a scary, cognitive nothing, and the reasoning shall carry raging eyes in struggling hands on a connection of reckoning that turns and brings out the wow, but with words, equation, and the snickering. Mere nature contemplates pages becoming great suffering, and meaning stands rigid on entertainment, but commercial sorrow is lighter. Accept labor as forgotten for what does prosperity beating me lower for the known, unanswered weakness embrace? Praise gain and love.

The salvation decreases to arrest and receive iconoclastic shoulders with removal, and not without creepy days to order the over bruised words rising for secretive importance. Die without reaction, and twist the whistles of weathered, solitary values of invention from the necessary. Must we not together smell of task and ice cream? In all created something breaks of matter again please everything, although like the soul the world results to let go, and hold heaven and knowledge that harnesses the truth. Sadness intact, just forget, instill that way while around anything. What does purpose have that sparkles? The reason to the scenarios.

Perhaps steps seen can be so wrong? Rationalizing here loses simple decisions and youth covers life. Do carry on. Praise restriction, but believe the fear of safety. The mixed can see an ocean of a reasonable mind, but was there a poor, loose reason to moments? Arrogance waking into space and deriving blinking eyes of remission. Although before that is the stance, the digressing sense upon what the social and comfortable create. For how can these parasites sit through the repetition? How much is the turning language of a number? What is there to look at stupid?

Admission to the fried, crisscrossed this, but travels were curiosities, and proverbial fulfillment. The conclusion bewildered the essence through question, but what does speak from memory? A machine goes with a lot of happiness, but gone or in hell with a laziness wakes from the bereft, warrant. What? And grace too can manage meaning as residue is reality. There like an unfathomable, puritanical everything already! As the line comes to pass worth remember the overwhelming place that persecutes persona. Dread correction, but can redemption find more than singular direction? What about the saved? Are the give and this with the hand of hopeful also amidst the self? Nobody is over a better dilemma. Also do remember that easy sale hustling remains by the gargantuan nothing facing the walk that discovers spreading motion is worthwhile.

Becoming lost in the speck of days collecting, but give that steer your better. Is water some of the circumstance? Hands arrive and reasoning adds to the weight, but we have rights. Forgotten reaps and although divine bugs the linkage exposed in miraculous time. What keeps the picture was actually pity instead of the cheese. Know after the illusion an event of tomorrow and the death unnoticed. Do these remove existence and anxiety? Are a heaven and sniffles indifferent to the call crying after enough, but for now in a direction be more and do that slowly. Where that multiplies and breath indulges maintain the positive choice ever!

"Do what thou will."

The pre-used similarity of a manipulated today. Perhaps the appropriation to chaos reappears. Hanging judgment, spiritual hunger, and the pieces of bustling construction. The weathered communication of concrete due to shot up existence. The articles be what the life is to resolve. Tainted human nature with personal decision and no reason exists for the concern of the moment. Spectacular fear conditioned the growth away. The power within strange, confused runs, and not the body is however decided to get fixed results. Let the purest, new identity and heritage spread funneling conformity to discover limbs and the gift of exposure. Onward stretching, dying to point the hands like snakes with hungry existence from the magnificent tunnel spreading under subjectivity rigidly mimicking rhythm. Everything goes on in the decay and the procrastination deployed in chaos infiltrates a seed as history is set, and suspicion mashed with a knoll. Growth sparking the lamp of anything less. Determine beat and travel change. Evolution, the truth in the turmoil, and grace. Commence calamity and revolt. Just raise unbridled security. Perhaps life and the intuition choose complaints and believe in patience. The understanding develops in diverse aggression, compromise, and growth. All this without the singular, fugitive interpretation or conclusion.

We shall be, but the serene storms surpass fervent discipline and condemned passing energy. The ideals forgo the core, words and tones, and the fact that brief breath has no fluent responsibility. Really certain of other people's appendages is terrible. Comprehend what does that mean? There sits fixation, the forgotten art, and unfortunate, young buildings. Realms never sinister, but swollen forever in shame sublime. The slaughter of progress to tread away the antiquated soul, but the skies would lose talk of the point. Sadness sinks in to formulate clear talk of the truth that said spirits strive to the brink held within. The one does not continue within trapped nothing, and the diligent dreams and nightmares. As waves in the mind accepting sensory knowledge, circumstance clouds conditions. The people are happy while life is sinister despair, nurtured grudges, and travels the air to get up and write.

Now who projected concern to a speech is a swine. Basking in silence are outside forces, laughing many lies surmised for pride and greed, but how much promise dies to choose reality? The self encourages the equation enveloping cultural divergence. Brief splotches expand closer to home. What repeats grows with fundamental divergence, care, and isolation. None of the trash is the truth whether fashioned with problematic swamp, mislaid experience, or tactile price, but look inward to attain the sky. Question and plea the same, singular audience wasting truly marked edges of dice from the motion of sanity into the void, and yet descending, forever grows like a smudge from the mire. Calm, swirling chaos cannot be minimized. The recognition of worthwhile land and health, and an English expression of knowledge from the voice. It can point the world. Words for life and decay repeat adorned in burial of any existence.

Into the tender compromise of a wasted quest. To squeeze foreclosure tight. Do not regulate progress. Create the truth from everything else. Do upon tomorrow that much? So much. Can blood make blood lack survival? Offerings of civilization, parts of anywhere forging closure, and interweaving people, and circumventing such permanence. The past does not determine the higher ground of boundless light, but life does circle the step. It is ignored and is levied to hold in discouraging death. Menial death eradicating the population of experience cannot be the future of loving purpose. Service has sprouted in the remains that are fading, and a man probably meets with the heat, discrimination, and observation. To conceptualize and compromise. There are strides of time.

Both the whimsy and the problematic are forgiven with the positioning of the turn. The circle means nothing for defeat is the reason to grow, but we fidget that away.

One who said, "People reach out and consume."

A firm fate is not waste that reminds flies to point, but to be reasonable six or seven more impoverished artists do not know any better. Telling the nail of restoration where worth must die, and the echo of a sticking works. Nonetheless apathy and the will reason something to squeeze through the distractions. Think a new change, feel love over the sights, and promote the race of being today, tomorrow. The air to a child stands on the margin. Can words die like some animal in the corner of moral shelters like anticlimactic who? Sight comes on a choice and the purpose of repertory empties come from fortune done and worn. As acceptance goes ahead from where to the whim folly squanders luxury. The two compare rituals and chaos says stop with disgrace and greeting cards. The light can outgrow conception to tell a clichéd condition of clarity, and knowing smiles are well to deceive it. Languish no swollen time but for life. Forever to roam through sound and the foe stated in today. Loose meaning.

Turning from all else when what can really think removes the truth. Such stale conditions simply rooting with age become too apparent. A hungry population constituting steps, and scratching merely for progression, but the whining moment is concerning birds still. The fortune of discipline allows for a point of universal noise to enhance the species and the ingraining no longer aging is in the know. Can that much make really create or just entertain because bubbles towards each hand are the two lost without a desk? Life has been simple and subjective. Silent originals of expected wellness as the hold which has ridden sunlight and challenge. If mosquitoes come things that simply cannot know just give in and also accept. Due where we can be noticed, outward sprouting means the dastardly refusal is warm with subterfuge. Fear flickers away the mediocre, imprisoned being of institution, but now disclosed should be tangible. Eternity simply eating outcome. Something escaped to sink disappointment. Turn the steps together, and mimic more. Grow freely and accelerate hope. Oh yes, any better?

Incomplete enterprise can partner the self-proclaimed freedom and pensive condition. Then saints hold containment, purpose, and blended life. Targets always membrane karma and its representation in the belief of warm flatulence and recognition. Into the sparkling droplets and foreclose offspring. To never be more. Environment sweeps concession and tampers great starts. In between the figments unaware, and the terms of sportsmanship for a population steadfast in the bitterness. Good words entice the argument of consequences. Involved proclamation without reflection. Eyes needle streams of greed for the minority is implicit in appropriate advertising, and captivating, tactile dilatants can stain and singe love. Encompassing death is there. That response is out, to the rise, and glances subsiding time foiling reaction. Tensions being all that die dream short the truth of art imposing fingers. Seems truth knew direction, and the direction chewed birds in the air. Ideas of the area have sprung rest on the whine and reek of mistakes. Writing vast apology and crime, death calculates identities of the self with unbelievable questions. Reflections on walking shoes.

"People die."

Permission is conquest to awareness. Light and winds to short line morality. The sway is hot without grudges, and reaction is intention. Eyes and rules are broken. Opinion slurs the way, and the oppositions say reply. Life blunders the truth as we are always decay. Notorious in the mind through the actions of tomorrow. Worth and circumstance, robotic in the bias modernized to one and all. If there is truth and nothing onward then we are up and lost with backs distorted and transactions compared with the most important words.

"Blah. Blah. Blah."

Nightmares of the truth and gardening. The body is a timepiece to have well lit, but instead it is free from sin born erecting and effecting, and eating longer shame. Time for predominate selling requires itching reality with the past of agreement. The spurs into salvation.

"Did has no although and the no is literal."

Your delivery between the motives. The larger is not more for all is a maybe, and it is not a child that began from one self or all. Not just idea subliminally avenged in the all forgotten distortion of denial, and the girl is through because reaction has lost that which corrects death. The blurs today guess for the something to be whole. This insight into repetition, and the truth of not the dice, but the roll takes form, and provides the problems. This leaves the sin circling explanation, but without letting go of meaning. For meaning represents a new, lost mesh of different fortunes. Left cleansing with an end, and non-existence in the hidden construction should rule to accost the truth of understanding with created men. The loose theory knows where the prohibition erupts, and the release of the irreversible meaning brings one residing on shadows with the footing of a sound beyond mixed obsessions. The silence shall digress, and death ties no one to today.

Arrogance however during the semblance of sanity carries across the paste diseased decay. The whole if recognition and regard are tried misconception. Creating the strategy there to contaminate the respective exuberance of life with the multitude of illogical, personal losses. Not that the blackness said a word, but what can a person be beyond simply love, and the squalor. Forget and deny the forum as everyone sneaks away with charred confessions, good expectations, and the unfinished excerpt. Dislocated for experience clacks to creation.

Four, balding men and the rest have hair. I am cold and viscious. A shuddering tongue lacerating silence with the motion of breath. Air wobbles tightly as it can never lose its grip, but time waits for no man, yet every man waits for time. The eyes that see the truth hold the truth, and beneath the truth the eyes that see gain the loss of the criminal.

The wavering wand wanders, scribbles sweetness, and encounters back flowing liquor. What does the memory lose when it dies? Does the conscious/subconscious energy dissipate, evaporate, or coagulate to create a moment? Surpassing physical attachment is completely superficial to any agreement, if we agree? Apologies never cry themselves to sleep so then those that weeping weep. What is the foreclosure of space if not a familiarity of fate? There is no chance of it being anything else in the choice that is given because sense is a tease that smirks the shy and corrodes the old. We die unto each other. We sigh, cry, bleed, and die.

Forget the foe for foul footsteps of the future. Memory fades, but we still all die, and people pre-act conclusion with its praise. To be is to praise, but to praise oneself is failure. A bubble in a bubble told me that. Tomorrow grows if tomorrow is secluded within itself to idle tomorrow. Tomorrow sees poppies in a hypothesis of conclusion. The greatest growth is a laugh from a symbiotic form.

"Yes."

Closing goodbye by cheering today we weep up to laugh at loss. Shallow in the scream of the indescribable soul, and the sweet soul that cries says goodbye as it wanders by to die. The difference made is the difference had, and the exchange does not make any difference. If a person is to become the future, does one gain or lose anything beyond oneself? Can a person define more in an exchange than the exchange itself? One is many because one dissolves the whole for one. Loss is acceptance as it is received. What we have is ourselves, and we let go to be what we are in a translucent film that is the self. The low end of life keeps smiling.

The loss in life is not life, but loss, to let go we lose life. We let go to grow beyond what we are. What can I say that is rational, truthful, and appropriate? I am losing my love. It dies every day in which I lie, cheat, and steal. High expectations desire only the truth, but without limitation can the truth ever be told? I hate this falsehood. I despise this personal disclosure. This false appropriation of ignorance gains nothing except for the loss of the self. I am saddened, lost without guidance, and trapped in the anticipation of failure. Why am I so depressed? Repressed? Obsessed? What do I do to improve my health?

This shame in isolation passes the time, but thinking of lies and coaxing frustration, I am not content. Even happiness cannot be wrong, but led astray rattles the dice. Have another mint, and try to forget the bad breath. Refreshed with stagnation, the mind wanders, and we all give way to the bullshit. Expectations regret what is done, but anything less chooses to be alone.

A sense, wish, blessing, value, and modern tale of urban living. A cup of coffee, a burning cigarette, and a drop of LSD. A beckoning cry and a faithful discovery. A woe betide of wisdom on a sentence formed from innocence. A conversation of things to come, and a perception of what is already done. A hungry population, a dying planet, and its species. An end, a beginning, an exit and entrance. An explosion of daily indulgence, and a blaze of burning buildings. An image of fear, and a picture of beauty. Angst, sex, realization, filth, meat, suffering with concepts. A forgotten memory, a look at what is, and a glance at what will be. A wait, pause, moment delayed, and replayed, a building of the conscious effort, and a rising of the unconscious. A direct link to life, a connection to death, and a pursuit of what rests in between. A work of genius, a script of easy listening, and perhaps a victory for written doctrine. A dragon, a head, a spider and a fly. Earth, a fierce fire of burning souls, a rushing force of water, and a cool gust of air. A heaven and a hell. A garden, a thorn, a cult, and a twist of its temple. A vision, a land, a room, a feast, a question, and an entertaining answer. Pain, clenched fists, spasms, tensing muscle, paroxysms, and boiling thought. A trigger, a gunshot, a crushing blow to the skull, and an oozing wound out of control. And you. And me. And us.

Seventy seven pointless, uninteresting, somewhat tasteless, short films based on absolutely nothing substantial except for personal opinion and outlook, but are for those with high standards and deep layers, but whose short attention spans strive for the minimal characteristics of art and entertainment. An old add for something already dead and sold.

The arts and entertainment index is erected by three, major focuses. Resource is built from the past's inspiration, and the creative talent there displayed. Progress is the interpretation of the old from the new, and the relation of both through output. Everything is the concept of the future, and the past as intertwined through trial and error. Resources are endless, art, music, film, literature, and the unknown both in the classical and contemporary status. The miscellaneous idols and icons of each in turn create the new, hidden talent. In whole or in sections the list is endless. The arts and entertainment index is a list of process that the artistic self then sections, and the visual work holds an encyclopedia of activities within the written word, photography and graphic art, music, concept binding endeavor, art, and entertainment. Life is conceptual without sympathy.

Searching for dragon magic the secret book club follows FALUTALY's mission statement to submit personal and group objectives in a newsletter. Lost in confusion with nothing recording money making schemes. The beer can collection, the worth of a penny, and greeting cards. For a bumpy ride is sure to follow as a book on tape with spoken word? Calendars. Weird music you have never heard of volume one.

Writing fiction, reading fiction, and entertainment, sleeping, eating, working, and exercise. The visitors move and muse, play and make, Tuesday, Friday gardening. The daily project of repetitive organization and cleaning. Magic? Shiatsu and reflexology. Yoga study. The meditation of theology, numbers, planets, words, behavior, thought, and sense. An event is the interpretation of response. Static ego. How many lines to a page? A half page? What exactly is the equal rights side column? Volume one, number one. The article is if questions on drawing a funny face for a twenty dollar prize in a free contest should be submitted to a border or spacing? How wide is a letter?

Now, some of you might not know, but people are having sex right under your noses. If we throw caution to the wind our dreams can come true. The fantasy builds reality, and the frontiers of sensation revel with their conception. The frugal assault of temptation, demise, but wondrous, expansive dimensions carry the soul and its creation. The meaning of life and the fictitious singular it does contain. Think and lose, do and win, be for freedom. Use words only, and the contest ends on the eleventh of August.

The box is filling up with debris, and the waste basket is already gone. Where does all the excess go? Where can it be placed without discomfort? For me? For you? For us?

A letter by ABPoe Transcribed by M.J.

Breathe out as birds sing for a life has left. The morning has given grief, sex, and ignorance before, but I have hit my head, and may slowly die, although death has already touched my hand. For if one should die than one has already died, and swimming here with words lay and linger in a touch. Trembling at a touch that cannot touch. Poison is one's own, the accumulation of sorrow, guilt, and fear, and the inflammation of the soul is water on a hot rock. Fingers clutch death, yet death will not grope back, and sorrow turns the heart to hate, guilt to greed, and fact to fiction. Life has forgotten death, but lost nothing more than one.

There is no I that can forget its eye, and so we learn to die. Do not fear death, but learn how to die. I die without you, and you without me. We die alone, together, and apart from death because death has yet to call. See the truth, but do not take it or die once more only to say goodbye to something that already said farewell. We are to cry the bitter tears that do not speak. They spoke so long ago, but did not hear that they are gone, still speaking, still living, and death did claim these few as they were one. The only thing lost in death is you.

"Chances are the government will scoop everything up. Sell to pay debt if there is any, and then sweep the remainder under the carpet. Do not let this discourage you, legally or otherwise because the more you do will affect the outcome of Pat's estate."

There was silence, and no real initiative even from Carmen. The answer was simple, inspection into the problem. Mathematics however were never really anyone's forte that is except for Todd but he has already died. His knowledge and mine waste within the depth of the grave. Now there was no answer, and neither inspection of the problem or sniveled insecurity could cure this slight injustice. This does not anger me, but is does anger Carmen.

Her eyes flare with intent vision, and her lungs fill the air with unrest. She is a villain if there is to be one, but decency corrodes her villainous approach to life. She just does not love, and this feeling erupts with every tear her pillow holds at night. Nonetheless no one was attempting a suggestion or even contemplation, but stagnant, individual restlessness. Basically everyone was looking at everyone else, and looking away no one could accept the consequence of making a mistake. No one had the courage to initiate a moment of incorrect, arrogant up rise and take over. Insecurity filled the room, but this is why I knew the people that I knew, and why I loved them.

When one is never sure, and never sane meaning bears nuance over bearing, and the diluted control blossoms into drifting risks of happiness, peace, and love. This is why we know who we know, and this is why we love them. These people in this room avoiding circumstance, chance, and choice have one thing in common. The same wish for sense, meaning, substance, and love. These are short sighted systems of the self, and if it has been said, say it again.

"The truth is in the concrete."

In the error of life, the truth distracts personal convention. Tasks assemble the pure intent, and the poetry of mass is the crafted sense that speaks removal. Continuous progress. The procession of subverting truth, dissipating meaning, and the continuous webs of deceit. The intent is reason, and through the removal of myself, my person, and its life. I have found the reason is the truth. My intent although no longer evident remains beyond the reason and intent of truth and life. It is the systematic inauguration of these distant passages of dialect that discuss terms of meandering melancholy. Describing the world, and the message is somewhat unclear.

So the compilation of self and sense ties us to ourselves. One is the next, blood, beat, and beast. There is no such thing as rushed, impetuous, impertinent grace, and to transcend oneself one must possess it. Prepare the way for God, and accept death. The intent behind daily ordeal whims our progress, and the sleeping mass of deliberation will resurrect one from all, and delegate the contrast of comparison. Words waste away to think about the future. All things have to be considered equally, and will take change, if you do not mind because even I have power, truth, and understanding to witness my being.

The birds sing in the joyous bosom of welcomed spring. Sunlight warms the earthen ware of time, and peace postulates a gesture in the continuous tranquility of a winning stake. This world, and all its love is felt within the wish for every day. The only malediction for those pure in heart are further words of wisdom because they choke the bliss of bounty.

Meanwhile back at the rest home of Saint Joseph the air is distant, and is caught within the whirling winds of transverse energy that rolls amongst the heads here gathered. The carpet itching continued, but not quite reaching the sway of Malcolm's foot it went unnoticed. It was all he could think about, and it was this awareness to the alignment of distance that allowed it to continue unseen, unheard, and unfelt. Except in his own mind, this half an inch from the floor fascinated him.

Erased meaning by multiplication of the conscious onslaught of insight. The rival forces of eternity that choose the contents of the air. Keep on saying simplicity. This means we need to learn how to amuse the continuous time. We have no point, and the next is the same as the first. Circles of paralleled dimension devoid of direction. Piloting disbelief by clutching tickets madly the old and new have come again. Now we see each other. One sheds a grin, the other a tear, but we walk along together. The garden ebbed in splendid frames of white that gives us meaning amidst the circus tricks.

"I thought it was a joint, but it was a chicken bone."

It is a strange concept to be alive and remember. The moments wrinkle in the face as the days continue onward. Research in the torrents of chance that compose our surplus resource of memories. Debauched challenge and duelling proverbs. The speaking tongues of that thing called death. Reactionary fate, and its tortured decree.

"Have it all!"

This is western civilization, but with the vast sweep of time, certainty relies on the overall mass, that one place is the same as the next, and people are the thing that matters. Objects of course clutter the mind, but the reality is that persona cannot be described verbatim, and that what lies within is the universal flux of energy. Our roots. Here in the west all is a commercialized sitcom of tragedy. We waste, want, get, and still ask for more. Regardless this is not a moral epic for you to get trapped in. This is fiction, and as fiction certain rules apply. So then, in the west, there is a town with curious sheep. They field the flocks with random eating, but never taste the grass. They wander without their shepherd, and chasten guilt from further fleeting. They of course are us.

Now some people are thinking, "Oh, number eight two four."

A number of high regard.

Some other people are thinking, "Oh no, what is she going to say?"

However, only twenty four of them need to be concerned because that will constitute the characters we have. As I am one of them twenty three remain. I am sure we can discuss it later amongst ourselves because here in the west we have twenty four individuals who in one way or another has welcomed the others. Anyway we have twenty four people in a room as we speak, and they are mourning one's loss. His self. I am being buried tomorrow, and at the present within a secured room in the back of the local, dead parlor I sit. I want to call it Saint Joseph's shtick, but this deems unnecessary, and so it is called the rest home of Saint Joseph. Whether or not there is a Saint Joseph is under consideration.

It was small, but well-proportioned so that the space unfolded continuously. Small alcoves with closets, and shelving behind walls.

Very intricate, and very precise. This makes my body comfortable with their care because chances are it too will be intricate and precise. Here in the white washed expression of death I am comfortable. The wall paper is outdated, blue pansies, and the outstretched walls insure nausea at a glaring, passing by. The light laminates the etched design of blue nostalgia even more than the walls themselves, and the corridors turn and twist with short restraint for soundscapes of solitude. Breezes in the air filter forty two doors or hatch ways in the home, and the real shocking secret is what is behind them all. Ghastly tales that even I wish not to explain, regardless there was at this time some more in depth occasion in process. A meeting that is supposed to read my will and testament, which of course there is none, and so this meeting must intercept some other, logical reasoning.

Someone's foot was itching the carpet, and the sheepish sound carved hostility on Carmen's face. She was easily annoyed with any selfish task, and this was just too juvenile.

"We are here to secure Pat's wishes, and not get uneasy with unrest when there is not one. We know how she felt, what actions she inspired, and so this is her way of securing ours. Tell us nothing, and we will do what is intuitive to us. If scratching your feet is more intuitive than composing a conclusion than perhaps you should excuse yourself. Function with yourself, and you may encounter others also. Brenda I did hear you swear earlier too, so do not think your insecurities go unnoticed."

"It just slipped out." Brenda mumbled between her mouth covered hands.

"No justification is the right one," Carmen's attention swerved back to the original vision, and recaptured the intent of the public servant.

"What can we do with her belongings, her business, and even her body if there is no wish to cultivate any of it?"

Sex and Weirdness

Time well wasted, youth misspent, and disparaging, old age in the imposition of the rain. Weathered days soaked in espionage. The self-righted disposition of encouraging growth in the trivial experience that brings us here. The answer of miscarried vice, the loss of reason in a home town, and rampant control discouraged in the self-suited conduct of coincidence. The questions remain.

"What is right?"

The ritual of insane aspiration on the entourage of one's supported compass. North remains north, the forward brings us forth, and the welcome of convergence mince with the fragrance of deprived exposure. Laughter. We continue, life congeals, and the hazard is in the steps of conclusion, and perhaps not in what we approach. The discourse does require attention. Regardless there is no relative function but the stream of an egg.

"Here we are!"

The words mean really nothing because today this code has been broken. Tomorrow never sleeps as the curios walk tall, talk big, and binge shadows, but tomorrow never sleeps, and only awakens with what we deliver it. How we rise and where we stand. What this means is doubt, questions unforgotten within lost fragments of living debris. Disillusioned retort not spoken as stolen words, and dead in the end of a pencil with recollection rendering the truth as a distorted future. The progress on a clean kitchen floor, and loss, the swindled breath, reclusive admission beckoned bliss. Forget. Forgive. Bless.

A hard on forged with misconception. The erection is a sense based on the fact that it reports to impulse. Belief is like a structure of captivating compliance to prayer, addiction, blasphemy, and greed. It means nothing, but if this is thus, than there is no respect for the life. Without a respected or a respectful life there is no joy without gratification. The space beyond the void is a memory. A stigmatized thorn burning and swelling assets and shortcomings. Time and the truth, and time and the self lost in translation. Nonsense speaks in tongues to hold a dialogue with the senses. The senses only knowing the truth accept what is given and transcend reception for rendition. Now the moment swerves, and the self with its sense sinks in ink.

Rejoice in the redemption,
Supply demand with a question,
And spike the world's notation,
Mention matter in all its factions,
And multiply the answer with fixation,
Because the future serves the past our isolation.

In the present fascination, time slips away, corrodes into the dust that persuades memory and the vacant windows of relapsed time. Monstrosities of failure and pressurized grief amidst the treading of tomorrow, and trampled in the mud, we capsize in the fashioned waste to slip further into the sludge. The muffled voices by the reeds, and tumbled thoughts led by deeds as actions reverse in speed. The end consequently presents a beginning, and each stroke of chance and change sweeps the rafters clean of the dry, rotten rot of mildewed transgressions.

Switching salutes and swapping stations we map friendly persuasion with happy celebration. We are destined to direct the waves of coinciding belief. The fragments of our guttural core are symbolic distaste on the plate of our pirate the future. The text defines tomorrow as the reason behind the contortion to betray the truth. Regardless the moments scatter, and the attendants of asinine agreement argue contrived objection. However, they reason the acceptance. Congestion of the congregation compels composition to conceal or congeal corruption, and reason rescues the reformation of the reformed with revolt. The beginning inevitably projects an end, and memory serves motion an appetite for change. Chaos is somewhere, closing in, running out of time as the end once again creates a beginning, and the prickly plot ponders free of barriers. It curls and coils, ensnares the earth, accents the air, wanders the water, and fondles the fire. Meanwhile quiescence predicts the random cursor of our compromise with the extenuation of exercise, experience, and enclosure. The personal collection of generality recollecting fostered obscurity. The flaw is the folly of forever. Forever is soon. Forever is now. Forever.

Boredom never changes, and the restless endowment of ideals deals the goal. The future is soon. The future is now. And the future is forever. There is a gap, groove, grope of genius that guarantees grace. Grappling worlds and gargling words our steps equal eternity. One person presents the next, and the potential extends encouragement to expose the extras. There is no need to mention the murmur of marvelous me because we are all trapped and pinned down. There is no progression without traceable purpose, and this purpose exists externally, surpasses ourselves, and parades non-existent terms to freeze our scented remarks. The point taps the synopsis of sleep with uplifted and uproarious sensation. The wasted remembrance, remission, and recovery within too much space, too little time, and the everlasting removal of the undertones, coagulate to mix the answers with the abidance of a lonely avenue. The temperance of temptation falls and rises with a swift encounter. The transformation, and the texture elapsed in other tests may provoke victory, but time turns a churn of warbling minds to waste the world. It wastes us, and there is no compromise because actions remember the disquieted delay of exasperated words. Disgust finding parchment finds paper. Insanity incites imbecilic inquest to invent necessity, and negates definition despite a requiem for faith and truth. Expression is the seasoning of expunging exclamation as the species surfeits a new suggestion for bartered balance. Let the stereotypes expire.

Futile words of wandered toll. Wayside travels of temporal submergence as time cruises without control, and redundant regurgitation restores recollected rest amongst the razors. Gut rot. Artsy teenagers antsy in a coffee saloon, and their smoke clings to the ceiling in a hazy fog, and it is a clear day, growing dark. A work day corrodes to dusk, and questions raise spirits to render their closure. I raise my cup with ambition, but arrogant deterrence ranges unclear visage. The propriety of words deems sensible egotism in a cloudy sky of the crumbling mind, and wonders do beseech the continuance of a mystical voyage. Prosperity, what for? To what end does this continue.

Memory seething in a vacant tense, tests the same intent with disquieted ease. Think clearly, easy, ha, ho, snickering whiskers of silence putter a cough. To know others I must know myself, and not sense diffusion from both. Those I know and those that I do not do design my own intent in the absolute gift of knowledge. Romantic is the way you smile with a sense of fervent guile, and as I watch you all the while you sit and sense this motioned mile of love's equated guess at style.

The agenda is unknown, but the mission statement is our guideline. Submit articulation, and waste not the words of the world. Loneliness, sadness, and fear we create these things and present them reputation. We deserve what we get, and I regret what I get, but the reason is within us, and although there is no blame to lie we are guilty and removed. Stupid and sublime. Lost in the hellish reflection of future and past.

She said, "It is all about the germs."

"That force. That infinite spectrum of intricate puzzles activates a serum for cleanliness in a plot of misfortune that dissents the concoction of posing aesthetics in the dust of biting, gnawing air. I wonder if these things were visible if further actions would thereby commence."

This is the first entry in my diary, and mainly is derived from working pens. It was May the sixth, and a somewhat hot Thursday. Still pens do try this flagrant and juvenile experiment. Let us start at The Gallery Gallery in the Conceptual Voice Bar defining life, pineapple tidbits, laundry, parking, tidying punch, fire, and wood. Nervously packing for two days, the list enticed a pile upon pile, and list upon list where what was the most important was declared. Proposing the bible because it subdues the hardship, and loosens the moments of tension with the degrees of pure conflict.

The snow eats a cigarette blown to restless thoughts. The age of a new year with alcohol, narcotics, transgressions of love and decay, the abysmal fact, fearful feet, and decomposing wishes of frozen ice in the cold exhale of a January night, anonymous and alone as the darkness swells the senses. The pricking hairs of lost control tickling the underbelly of the fog with missed requests, distorted truth, and the selfish view that has trapped the weary heart. Sordid are the details, and their stories are quiet with shame. A rampant plundering of insight and enactment quietly marches with jubilation for God, life, and self.

There is a setting sun that fades in the sky
Clouds tearing open and some even die.
The oblique, opaque salutes the day.
Time and wonder stand at bay,
High above the rubbish and mountains of clay,
Slowly speaking light does wane.
As darkness learns of sudden pains,
The masquerade erodes until the morning's call.
Blackbirds spreading omens, and songbirds catching maul.
The evidence unfolds yet more to see behind the wall.
The sense stilled in sweetness, and God alone provides.

Delay is the washing of time, and retorts spoken images to the mind. Distractions that run courses on how to spend time. A future separation from the moment at hand while hands clasp the deterioration of efficiency with their lack of use, and the appropriation of tactile things becomes trivial. This is sutured resistance to the breaking of will. The will of understanding corrupts and conveys compromise, and the victims of awareness shy away to withered ashes. We wait and wish our turn as angels bring us grey skies. Textured blandness pouring wet loneliness. Drenching isolation and vexing guesses at what comes next. Spinning in the rain under the affluent influence of want, warm delight encircles the ripples of roaming sensation. Swirling, splashing waves of cool redemption.

    These things arrive from the self, myself, and lack belief because they never pass my fingers, but by way of the pen. They are knowledge. A persistent conviction for compression, repression, guilt, and greed. Why? Cowardly impulse and astute degrees of compulsion steer the rain to tears. Evasion leaves me angry, alone, guilt ridden, and depressed. Shifting time propels my path with the world, but I linger to my own quotation, and whither in the wash. I must speak clearly. Words influence my life, and understanding is found in each one. They control and taste the mind. A single word can kill, and a single word can love. Words are endless, senseless, and bothersome, for example as I write this bothersome beeps because it is misspelled, however within the dictionary it is correct. I feel I know too much, and ignore too much, and thus my life wastes. I stagnate due to my abuse of the world, and although I do not accept this, it continues. In short I am a waste. I am sorry.

080604200p

    You might be gone, but you may be here, and so the wish remains the same. A thought upon your new year. Continuation. Control? The conclusion is warm with the wash of decay, and the memories exist within frozen time. There is no parting with understanding, and there is no closure without death because all things travel forward with ignorance or without. Succumbing to numbing tomorrow we must hold our footsteps firmly, and utilize the path that they tread. Mile upon mile, and trial upon trial we go forward.

    Escape obviously exists in the shadows and folds of time that present the daily routine. The lies and truths we erect as our self-preservation. Gardens of vast spectacle that tackle the true beauty and love for our own peace of mind. The mysterious void is a frightening place, and so we brave distraught form and continue. Thus we progress, age, and grow full of the way we said it would be.

    Love and gratitude especially for you, and another, perpetual year.

082504205a

Listen to the still,
Calm amidst the quakes,
Time slips by,
And opportunities pass,
The comforts keep us sane,
The costs no one can afford,
Weakness in the heart,
Fear within the mind,
The unknown.

    The sounds collect in the memory alongside any visual aids. Compiled and stored like a hodgepodge of files unfathomable behind closed doors. Evidence self-evident to the point of bias. The habits occur with frequent stops, and any routine is running on fumes. Progress displays itself in the stature of life before us now. It does not define us or limit us to its end, but allows translation, an observant friend to lead the way. Almost by accident terms enact deeds, programs of worth redeem merit, and spontaneously the self dissolves with decision.

    Waste and want predict the outcome as tones fan out slurring trails of obscurity. The memory upholds the back catalogue with complete disarray, but usage empowers discerning qualities. The tracks of time are laid bare again, and the senses have learned to remember. They manipulate the mental workings and bodily functions we all operate into pivotal parts of oblivion. Singular, tactile distinctions ingrained in every soul. A broken bone, beaten face, or bruised ego deliver specific destinations. Trivial details pointing direction, nonetheless, the figures feel the cold beneath the blanket's warmth.

    "This is mine alone forever."

    The murmurs collect to have a dialogue. They disagree, but come to an encouraged discovery. They all feel the same! Gentle and kind providing a future prone to simple blessing. Air and water, warmth and joy. Smiling strangers and open hearts. Patient love, universal security, and uncompromising understanding.

    Bells.

    Rain.

    Birds.

    Echoes. Ideals. Projections or hallucinations this corrupt body may have already undergone.

"Repent."

The whispers insist the skin is not pure, and that touch is tainted by the close proximity that it can feel. Nerves flinch without consciousness. The pastime of reason to fully comprehend the vexed position of disdain proves disastrous. Conclusions draw near, bear strength and conviction with justice and compassion, and the sacrifice may remain only the turkey. Cooking slowly, stewing in bubbling broth the sounds overflow from the deep servings of reality. The truth and myself. This self. Now.

Right or wrong the world remains indifferent. How much crime can one commit against oneself? Death is fear confined to very large quarters after all, all energy is consistent. Random repose to stimuli scientifically man made and simplicity deems its rewards. The constraints fade away and restriction remains self-imposed. The moral whole remains inward, and that definition is not mandatory. Understanding has determined the usage with awareness and flexibility. Courage and faith never stray very far. Pleasure seeks opportunity. Together with one, for one is one. Absconded life is absolved, and the dissertation is the repose. Remember it never was just leg work, but providing no surprise, love alone prescribes the nose its fruitcake. Hold on.

"Hello."

I hope this finds you well or adequately coping at least. It was solemn, great Zeus it was solemn. The graves ran in rows, echoing blasphemous roads of consumed death. The bugs alone stand in correspondence as the wombs corrode and the bodies die. Row after row of liquefied flesh. Grotesque demise to those buried here.

Eureka! The sky was born and the Earth below harvested a grotto of water and fire. The air of utmost became still as the being could not abstain life. The absorbed entity disdaining effortless freedom as it has become clean, but in choosing that satisfaction, chewing, being absolute, one adjourns for smaller prices. The clear headed think that extracts attract all kinds of prominent, obsolete, bearded parameters just clear of order.

The dead waste is piss poor and losing. The streaks of disadvantage smother the tired, weak, and misunderstood as hypnotized by blunder they beguile the striding thunder. Standing to type seems ridiculous, but it is true. Or it was, and so it shall be forever uncovered. The distinct posterity has become void. The memories prove themselves as right or wrong. Love lost, time stolen, and perspective decided. The prayer spoken was installed. The failure is in the fixings. Exponential decay. Exclamation mark, babe.

The Future

Cluttered with the debris of misery, contempt, and self-loathing, progress takes a bypass. The cloistered views assimilate to formulate what was already there. The inspiration and dedication of all of this. These words, this life, and these moments. Along the side of the road lay barren fields of isolation, and disregarded opportunities of hope and gain. Spiritual growth has become disconnected as wrought circumstance has prepared the mixture. Consequences squelch as the gears switch and the self declares a new tomorrow. Today as tomorrow will be different. Today as tomorrow will not be this. Unless otherwise specified the depression hits the pedal and speeds off into outer space. The limitless renewal of a new day has finally accumulated unity. The now succumbs to the self like a bitter event one wishes to avoid. Obligations vary, conception carries us forward, and the spark of oblivion is all that keeps it all here.
Personable, but disagreeable. Dramatic when drunk, obnoxious, persistent and severe. Flourished individuality albeit via decadence and delusion. The allusion of disobedience. The calamity of consequence. The diplomatic prejudice and artificial law. Purposeless, wandering, lonely, curious, and wild. Afraid and wanting, discredited choice. Thinking too much, acting too little, and being less than both. Weak, misguided, and wonderful as well, but fashion and circumstance contrive even more. Seeking redemption. Hoping for heaven. Fearful and repentant, guilty and corrupted. Not yet condemned, but waiting. Tales of survival, stories of reality, and memories of the living ordeal.

Curiosity killed the cat, and/or the cat killed the curiosity. Remembrance unknown tells me contradiction has been fumbled verbally. Meaning saunters the nightshade on toes of silken love. It frolics and fouls in the scandals of men as women spur the mess to a halt. A period of complete, cutting death. The dark bringing the dark in a composition of nothing. Failure because progression does not continue, but stops with a breath, a blink, and a bob. Born forever because life does little else in a declined progression of perpetual stalling. Wiggling spirals, but no tread to carry life further. Music without the acceptance of sound. Perhaps sight without imagination. Maybe even heart without being loved. Not contradiction, but instead positions of slight abandon. Minor consequences. Ethereal definition without a backbone. There is one question.

If this is up to me, then this is what I make it, and therefore there is no short sight or misdirected cue. The conclusion is in the asking, and the asking merely forms the awareness to awaken, but not convict the actions to substantiate change or health. This is the calling that forms my reason, and this reason develops the world. The idea being formation of progress that delivers the soul to time with memory erecting or eradicating choice, and the outcome contains all three parts. Center or soul, conflict or choice, and chapter or development. This means the character and the conflict create the conclusion. Wading pools of subjective terms. Loosened sense for discourse. The reconciled and reckoned imagery of damaging degree as flexing winds in the ode of change. God slightly snickers, and speaks lowly, slowly, and boldly. We wander wonder in simple sparks of gratitude. The world holds her own in the waking of the day.

082304905p

Hey Folks,

It is about time I raised my slanted view, and followed through my spoken intentions. Delay is decay, and my rotting flesh amounts my sour senses. I digress to me. The connotations resemble the state that remains my ego filled reality. Delusion in the diaphanous diction of description, options not mine, and consequences of subscribed removal. These words again seem riddled with incoherence, and the brook of my desperation seeps into responsibility to claim tasks left undone. To you I say, "Hello."

The days wrinkle with continuance, and their repetitious growth brings passages of clarity within the undertow of insanity. Visions plague my security, death warrants a welcome mat, and my inner turmoil bubbles into unscrupulous absolution in the degradation of my life. Crippled and insane I walk my furtive steps with tentative glee. Things could always be worse, more unclear, and further unaware. Time is now, and so with now comes this passing wail of my troubled sail, and the tension is perhaps uplifted. These words mean pleasantries that I wish to be pure, unembellished gestures to bring ourselves some cleansing sense in this diabolical realm of unrest. Deception is scathing, but the lonely abyss remains opened. Mumbo jumbo in the sinking pot of molten flesh. Prescriptions to the perversion of idiosyncratic degree. Temperament and temptation in the waking realm of visionless perception. Scraps for the departed of the subservient mass.

Things are well. Muddled, fuddled Port Alberni. Conception leave me bare, but the realities of actions are endless trial and error. My ways encourage mistakes, and my growth is retarded into submissive traps for my engrossed intentions. These words seem troubled, caught within the rhythm of my machine, and pulled to pieces by the interpretation of a rational mind. Blurting out insanity I wince in the future, and the future holds no insurmountable light to radiate its glory.

Lost in the persuasion of myself, and things move slowly. Tasks flaw, appointments are missed, and the factual impression of my life is nil. There is no reason for escape, and there is no preference for better days because these days are all that are with me. These habits are the days themselves, and the tribal wave of occurrence carries both along the rippled edge. My pleading past does equal my future, and I am damned and subdued in the access of my diluted soul. The world shall know of these perils, and my sense may be insured, but these actions uphold their own significant caption, and the consequences are labelled with truth. This trepidation, regret, and insecurity are real, but the meandering sentence of my derivation has left me bereft. The further choices that habit and self permit take this visage with fierce ascension. I walk further, and hopefully will not run out of time.

1103041142a

I will write this to you because love is a choice. A new year has come, and hope always rides at the sides. Growth, perspective, and purpose tied to a single day, and the questions reside with an answer. A single answer that carries its burden with fragile footsteps, and continues through memory to enter the light. Tomorrow is prospect, but tomorrow is private. There are languid figures dancing in the sunset, coursing in repeat, and catastrophe perching on a cloud. There are voices that carry laughter, and sorrow that plunders greed. There is nuance and nicety, but transgression brings truth, and our hands hold sweet kisses for our youth. There is no going back, and there is no further choice, but allowance for the affluent tidings of bliss. Tears travel loose, and sighs follow boredom, but courage delivers the soul. Digression captures the lecture, and purpose flies away free.

Thoughts and sense captivate the cause, and we are here entrapped by snares of sight. Our sloppy fit of self-preservation devotes no time to the future. Common welfare is best, and passes every test. We are wild, and we are envious while notions deliberate conscious trade. I pass these things to you with ambition because only you can set them forth unto the world. I mean that we are here within the eternity of sheltered greatness, and yet we did not see the sign that greeted us. Victory. Suspension in the depths on flexing wings of steel. Unbent charisma and staggering knowledge to point the direction of moment. It is ours if we accept, and it is ours without acceptance. It simply is the answer that reckons everything. This message may not be clear, and my intent is even more distant, but purity will see the way and guide us both together. Take care and develop naturally.

0823041200p

Russian Midget Friends in a Living Room on 100th Street

With judgment we sit, arm in arm with dislocated subject. Holding onto things of worthless nature in hope that continuation bereaves the daily burden, but tempestuous life revolts. His bloody being now heeds tears of the devil's toothpaste. Companions in syncopation. Instrumentation of the trembling ambiance until moisture steals enlightenment. Calling to that sea of stillness, people upon perspective wonder, and tunes uncover lips of decency. Earth spits nothing short of fiction. Every memory, agenda, and answer is the bleeding standard of proven, mortal control, and stating salutations cause a firm, ripping look at bottled fate. Conception.

One ocean breaking no more, never itching, judging, touching water. This loud, unnoticed mass that questions temper assimilates beaten passengers to conformity, and strips back desire to scorch bias in the watery bounty of vitality. Rattles shut on living joints, and the dirty work of greeting vapid screams configures death. Temptation recognizes itself, and gravely sickness is slipped in and stored in clothing. She screams bright with the agile belief of peace to be bare and smooth. Repetition cast these gentle lies with entrapped obscenity, and we sense our stance with words. That this will causes reprimanded age sees grace as the reeking story of heaven's shit. She forces home, and we are the larval platform of bending change. While these slopes declare grandiose situations of charred, cold equality that clearly loses our worthy footing. Weeping provisions to stupor fatality, but attention is upon call, and the transposed scenario was its complacent reply. If there once was rest and wisdom here, which barricaded the sickness of life's lenient skin, then it is now inside a cave of eyeless eternity. Where the light finds stimulation mourning the cries of will. Breaking scampers of televised grass, Muldune's Dunlap breasts, and the sign of our howl trapped on a t-shirt made from sin's burning embers. This damp bath of burning weeps as seen with subtlety filling shoes with remains. Nightmares do motion all anxiety for a victory, and capturing crossed terms wins nothing. Strangulation as we chew the earth of beauty. Purest, molded jealousy walking until nausea floors her somber wandering with death and fortune's path gags every hold at recoil with the threat of ever fresh debris. Attempting curiosity toward the beckoning tragedy we find divinity.

Crooked, the marigolds dance in carefree games of solitude. Venues of capsized sensations, volumes of diligent subsystems producing and digesting the consumption as well as the supply. Progressions of anarchy become quality consumers, the production and absorption of goods and services provided by the taxable living. The rating of a systemized buy and sell, produce and digest. Vocals distilled by darkness, projects managed by persona, and capsules driven to fleshy steps of boastful temperance. It does not matter what was said as long as you do not lose your head.

We the people of the square house recall our fables well. The roasting pig, the charcoaled duck, and these scents mark memories of senseless depravity, but also bear our knighthood calling. The separation of love. The garden of silence dies in her arms of bliss, and the essence is milky white and shining dawn. Succulent mass of ambrosia, ropes of mortal coils tying down the fervent eternity of life. Sadness is love's emotion. Wisdom is something that wilts, sex is something that sours, and text is something that thinks. I am myself an abstract devil as life becomes a tragedy for those who feel, and a comedy for those who think, while temperance makes true hearts, evokes promise, process, and the start of each day with the power residing in the inspiration of one's eye. The opened wonder in the obvious, the texture of the benign, and the interpretation which encompasses one's facets to build the multitudes of possibilities. For example a breakfast built of two, hard boiled eggs, one baked potato, and a bowl of cream of broccoli soup at the Nob Hill Acropolis on Milford Crescent. Or perhaps it is three pm and one is dying of thirst, evil sweeps in a rampant race, and thirst is soon long forgotten.

Bad photographs and a trip down memory lane. Paranoid delusion can be make believe, but paranoid delusion forces focus, cleans the sky and earth with green sub scripture to the passing glory of warmth erased and gone. Urine swelling, draining trembled reserves as the jammy clams of Dorchester ring troubadour frustration. Cleansing hands to appease the meek for weak I am alone to stutter.

"Temperance."

Good night, sweet dreams, and all of that nonsense.

Fifteen to twenty minutes

A long time, two sighs, and a laugh. Tapping pens in rubber boots. Posture pleads with endurance and generality. Stereotypes and progress. Wishes to no longer hold one word, but many enriched with blessings beyond the bounty of life. That trivial encounter infatuates me with sharp breathes, whistling muscles, and the decay of the mighty choice, but the refuge makes me speechless. Perspiration makes me restless. The tension in this vacant lot holds nothing in my hands. Clear testimony remains unclear, and the truth is never spoken, but many words describe this slumber with advantage in their number. Unfathomable permeation of the vexing flex of wind that carries down the words to time, and pointless pedigree. The subject is rather thick. Perspiration lightly tapping cloth, and etchings of a stomach intercept the air. A bubble within the lapse, and a collapse to all this query. This mass of words descends our logic, and the usage seems unfair. This bias rings forever with no stop or editing.

The point is rather obscure, my usage quite obscene, and the thing that holds these thoughts in motion is the affluence of time. Argument in the augment of conversation. My hand upon my chin and my mind upon the page with the distraction of too many my's. I am lost.

Death in twenty minutes seems mildly premature. It forgets the frozen moments caught within the rhyme. The tangible tangents of idealized life. The voyage of drifting through tempestuous gloom seems redundant. The bliss of the water shall carry us over, and the forest of tranquility will greet us with its harbor. We meekly take the footsteps. The time drips always forward, and the sense of all sensation blinks rashly with the swig and sway of energy. Potent energy raising in a blossom of pride. Error. Time, built up, and released. The proliferation of proficient perspective pooling ponds of paradise. The status, the rules, and the whirling pledge. Take the retreat, to win the race, and save some souls with some swift grace. Walk the line like an arrow, straight and forward, toward the steed of dumbfounded occupancy in tidings of alarm. The facts are logic swirled in haste, and the forbidden commands of us are in themselves correctional. Deep in the wander of life, burned fingertips and scarred beliefs. The struggle is endless, and inside the ruins recoils this domain. The passages of time, style, and demeanor structure the ritual of habit, and this humble power struggles with wishes for eternity. Endless love. Age is a protrusion of progress. It disintegrates the passing time with growth and knowledge, but it also abets the contamination of self with the impression of wear. We digress to notions of interpretative grace. Congratulations we are what we have become, and the passing hours coagulate with the passing guess of what we are; time.

We are what we are, and not what we perceive, believe, or receive. Who am I to introduce such logic, who am I to propose such prospects, and who am I to encourage the removal of self-deceit. Encumbering death introduces the truth, and it is the everlasting outcome. The never ending showdown of verified life and conviction. It is for us all, and all of us alone. There is no removal, but the isolated irony that delivers the consequence with choice. Progress disseminates the conquest of completion when that is death. Experience unravels to receive the end, and that end is universal. Amen.

The conclusion is in the evidence, and the evidence is down in the testimony of choice, action, and regard. Propositions of rationalization, and the enticement of the encompassing deceit. Further losses continue freely, but the choice is ours, and any commentary thereafter receives judgment from the sloppy bias of predicament forever. So we are what we are, where we are, and when we are, but the epilogue is the truth in opaque death that enlists and decides every factor and every involvement. Death.

010504700p

AUTOBIOGRAPHY

PATRICK OVINGTON WAS born in 1977 in Port Alberni, British Columbia, Canada. He is an independent writer and artist who dabbles in paint, collage, and the written word. His credits include poetry, a zine entitled Drowning In Mud, sound collage, and various pieces of abstract art. Influenced by advertising, the cut up method, philosophy, and general perception Patrick finds definition through personal intuition. Subject and palette remain consistent as spontaneity delivers various forms of creation. Music, poetry, critique, thought expressed through the various forms of output. He begins by collecting materials to assemble text or visuals by chance, impulse, and process. The first word or image inspires the next until enough material is present to create the piece intended. It is all random choice perpetuated by being, medium, and development. The materials influence themselves, and Patrick merely pastes the pieces together. Materials evolve from what is available, but the collaboration of texture and shape influence the presentation. Human nature, interpretation, and words represent identified interests and themes explored within the work. Without training or education Patrick has remained on the outskirts of subculture as a so called starving artist. All of his work remains informal rituals of experience. Words express meaning as represented by letters or symbols or speech, and by not presenting specific meaning definition is not disclosed, but the senses are left with their own conclusion. Inspiration, chance, and intricate collaboration build any final product. Residing in Vancouver, British Columbia, Canada Patrick is currently applying his talents to two books The Adventures of ABPoe Volume One and The Adventures of ABPoe Volume Two, and both entail the continuing struggle of individual existence. The trials and errors of everyday living as seen through the memories and recollections of prepared prose. Intended as memoirs they specifically deal with addiction, mental health, homosexuality, choice, faith, and free will. Patrick's past times include walking, cooking and baking, and also sightseeing. His travels have taken him across Canada from Breton, Alberta to Charlottetown, Prince Edward Island, and he has been in every province. He enjoys music to great length, old films, the performing arts, and short fiction. Literal influences include William S Burroughs, Herman Hesse, and Kurt Vonnegut.

SYNOPSIS

THE ADVENTURES OF ABPoe Volume One and Two are companion pieces compiled from journals, letters, and fiction to represent the continuing struggle of individual existence. The trials and errors of everyday living as seen through the memories and recollections of prepared prose. Intended as memoirs they specifically deal with addiction, mental health, homosexuality, choice, faith, and free will. Anecdotes and stories fill the interim of obsession, introspection, and logic. ABPoe is the pen name of Patrick Ovington and was created in 1995. Since then he has written letters, essays, poetry, and short fiction which now in these volumes have been collected and unified. Influenced by the cut up method as devised by Brion Gysin and William S Burroughs. Various passages have been literally cut and paste word for word with little editing. Sense erects itself automatically with existence and this is the prime meaning involved in both works. Statements on life, death, the self, truth, society, and personal opinion. Passages based on experience and the analysis of philosophy. Notes on scandal and reality. Experiments in prose and output from an artistic approach. The Adventures of ABPoe Volume One was conceived between 2000 and 2011 whereas Volume Two was conceived between 2001 and 2014. Both examine the reality of continuance and survival. Both impose a state of mind. The rambling adventures of perception and being as devised by a specific point of view. Fairly negative and critical both volumes present tactile proof of discrimination, redemption, and expression. Facets of deceit and conceit that erect everyday life. Or at least that is the aspiration. Devoid of plot, but compiled from imagery and policies of personal outlook both volumes are fairly complex. Thick with lingo and jargon most may not appreciate it, but most visions of truth and reality are convoluted. Abstract rhythm and flow present moments from the past as contrived by the artist. Dark, brooding, and original The Adventures of ABPoe are intended to be scrutinized and absorbed. The point is that they both represent struggle, the conquest of physical reality, and the artistic impression of muse. The articulation may be symbolic, but the overall picture is strewn throughout. Sentences present philosophy, and the words entangle the private usage of the artist. Meaning is developed through cause and effect, and hopefully the work entails that. Conceived as individual projects the cohesion is secondary as they have been assorted alphabetically. Thus the timelines are somewhat distorted. The overall passage of time is central to the use of these projects because it proves the point of view. An abstract, apocalyptic vision of life and death, and various views on society, self, meaning, and thought provide conclusion as seen through the singular self. Expression is harsh, critical, and chaotic in the entries concocted. Passages of opinion and reflection that articulate concern and disclaim. A tremendous journey of the self through turmoil and angst. Both books are related in their approach and their design. They both examine point of view, conclusion, and meaning. They both appreciate imagery and creativity, and they both come from personal experience and expression. The reasoning is simple understanding and practise have developed these pieces, and although challenging remain pure intention. The intended voyage is to captivate, enrage, and ascertain skill and knowledge. Entertainment and bias recall manipulated into prose. Controlled by the singular self these volumes are remembrance and doubt. Collaborative insight and growth through both process and outcome. The Adventures of ABPoe are intended to be proficient and proactive. Honest recollection, and timed response have been recorded and now with the output complete it is finished. Enjoyment and critique in artistic sweeps of voice and vision. Personal and direct, but important expression. Bits of information and tendency that may be aesthetically pleasing or incoherent nonsense. Nonetheless the point in The Adventures of ABPoe is personal survival and awareness. The abstract scrutiny of self and surroundings. The philosophical development of process and self. The universal and the singular analysis of truth and the self. Perfection does not exist within artistic approach, and the quality of understanding may vary, but the meaning is still in the output itself. Hopefully the intention is clear and The Adventures of ABPoe speak for themselves.

CPSIA information can be obtained
at www.ICGtesting.com
Printed in the USA
BVHW030553240222
629938BV00012B/96